Paris

at its best

More praise for Robert S. Kane...

"The strength of Kane's books lies in their personal flavor and zestful writing style. He doesn't shy away from expressing opinion, is strong on culture, art, and history, along with dining and shopping."
—Jack Schnedler, *Chicago Sun-Times*

"Kane's books take the reader beyond the expected. His works are carefully researched, succinctly presented and opinionated."
—Jane Abrams, *New York Daily News*

"Kane is a man of perception and taste, with a knowledge of art, architecture and history. He doesn't spare the occasional sharp evaluation if something is less than highest quality."
—Lois Fegan, *Jersey Journal*

"Anyone going should take one of Bob Kane's books."
—Paul Jackson, *New York Post*

"Kane's candor, conciseness and credibility have made his books among the top selling in the travel field—a must for travelers."
—Joel Sleed, *Newhouse News Service*

"Kane does not mince words. His choices, ranked according to price, service, location and ambiance, are selective; he provides opinions."
—Ralph Gardner, *San Antonio Express-News*

"Kane wanders the globe, testing pillows, mattresses and, in some cases, abominable food in order to be a faithful guide, writing his own observations, and leaving nothing to ghost writers or a band of behind-the-scenes reporters; Kane's unafraid to recommend some places and condemn others."
—Maria Lisella, *The Travel Agent*

Robert S. Kane

Paris
at its best

Printed on recyclable paper

PASSPORT BOOKS
a division of *NTC Publishing Group*
Lincolnwood, Illinois USA

BY ROBERT S. KANE

The World at Its Best Travel Series
BRITAIN AT ITS BEST
FRANCE AT ITS BEST
GERMANY AT ITS BEST
HAWAII AT ITS BEST
HOLLAND AT ITS BEST
HONG KONG AT ITS BEST
ITALY AT ITS BEST
LONDON AT ITS BEST
NEW YORK AT ITS BEST
PARIS AT ITS BEST
SAN FRANCISCO AT ITS BEST
SPAIN AT ITS BEST
SWITZERLAND AT ITS BEST
WASHINGTON, D.C. AT ITS BEST

A to Z World Travel Guides
GRAND TOUR A TO Z: THE CAPITALS OF EUROPE
EASTERN EUROPE A TO Z
SOUTH PACIFIC A TO Z
CANADA A TO Z
ASIA A TO Z
SOUTH AMERICA A TO Z
AFRICA A TO Z

1996 Printing

Published by Passport Books, a division of NTC Publishing Group,
4255 West Touhy Avenue, Lincolnwood, Illinois 60646-1975.
Manufactured in the United States of America. Library of
Congress Catalog Card Number: 89-62582
6 7 8 9 ML 9 8 7 6 5 4 3

Pour Anne-Françoise et Mark Pattis

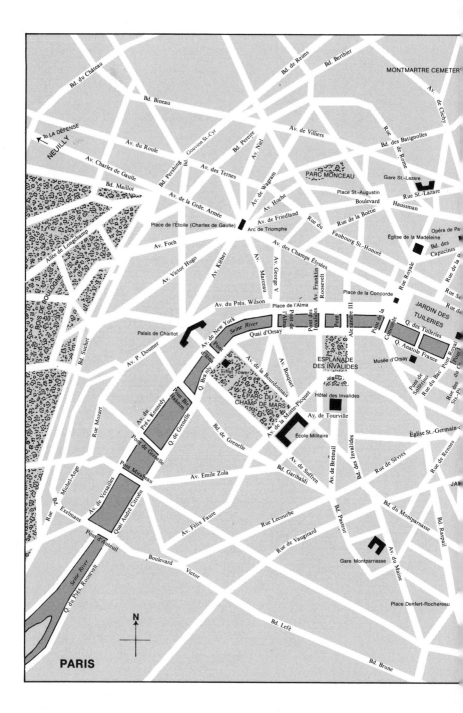

MONTMARTRE CEMETERY

Bd. du Château

Bd. Bineau

Bd. de Reims

Bd. Berthier

Av. de Clichy

To LA DÉFENSE

NEUILLY

Av. du Roule

Bd. Pershing

Gouvion St.-Cyr

Av. de Villiers

Bd. des Batignolles

Rue de Rome

Av. Charles de Gaulle

Av. des Ternes

Bd. Péreire

Av. Niel

PARC MONCEAU

Gare St.-Lazare

Bd. Maillot

Av. de la Grde. Armée

Av. de Wagram

Av. Hoche

Place St.-Augustin

Rue St.-Lazare

Boulevard

Haussman

Place de l'Étoile (Charles de Gaulle)

Arc de Triomphe

Av. de Friedland

Rue du

Faubourg St.-Honoré

Rue de la Boétie

Opéra de Pa

Église de la Madeleine

Bd. des

Capucines

Av. Foch

Av. des Champs Élysées

Rue Royale

Av. Victor Hugo

Av. Kléber

Av. George V

Av. Marceau

Av. Franklin

Roosevelt

Place de la Concorde

JARDIN DES

TUILERIES

Av. du Prés. Wilson

Place de l'Alma

Pont

Alexandre III

Q. des Tuileries

Palais de Chaillot

Seine River

Quai d'Orsay

Pont des Invalides

Pont

Concorde

Q. Anatole France

Musée d'Orsay

Av. P. Doumer

Av. de New York

Q. Branly

ESPLANADE

DES INVALIDES

Pont de

Solférino

Pont du Bac

Pont Royal

Eiffel Tower

Av. de la Bourdonnais

Av. Bosquet

Av. du Prés. Kennedy

Q. de Grenelle

PARC DU

CHAMP DE MARS

Hôtel des Invalides

Église St.-Germain-

Pont de Grenelle

Bd. de Grenelle

Av. de la Motte-Picquet

Av. de Tourville

Pont Mirabeau

Av. Emile Zola

École Militaire

Bd. des Invalides

Rue de Sèvres

Rue de Rennes

Rue Mozart

Av. de Versailles

Quai André Citroën

Av. de Suffren

Bd. Garibaldi

Av. de Breteuil

Bd. Pasteur

Bd. du Montparnasse

Bd. Raspai

Rue P.

Michel-Ange

Rue Exelmans

Pont d'Auteuil

Av. Félix Faure

Rue Lecourbe

Rue de Vaugirard

Gare Montparnasse

Av. du Maine

JA

Seine River

Q. du Prés. Roosevelt

Boulevard

Victor

Bd. Lefè

Place Denfert-Rochereau

N

PARIS

Bd. Brune

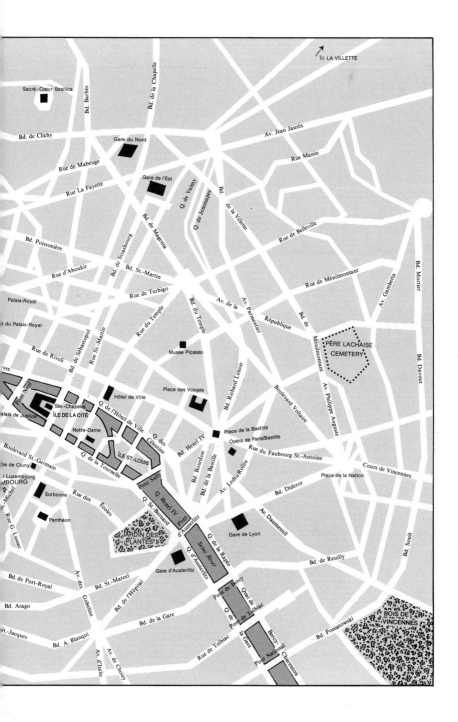

Contents

Foreword
The Continent's Great Capital

The surprise of Paris is that it asks the visitor to meet it halfway. It presupposes a special kind of familiarity, even though, as Continental Europe's premier city, it is by no means an unknown quantity to us. We grow up with Notre-Dame and the Eiffel Tower. Even the basic geography—division by the Seine into Right and Left banks—is a schoolboy commonplace. Many of us have studied the French language (is there a more beautiful one?) and acquired a taste for the masterful French style of cooking and for France's unsurpassed wines.

But once the basics of the usually abbreviated initial stay are completed, we are likely to want to move right along, even though we have seen only the tip of the iceberg. I very much suspect that Paris deserves a much better break than seven or eight out of ten days transatlantic visitors afford it. Paris unravels only for the visitor who unwinds.

I don't expect every appraiser to share the enthusiasm of an unreconstructed Francophile like myself. Still, I am unhappy when I see countrymen depart from Paris without having realized its magnificent potential. And so what I have done in this thoroughly revised and expanded edition of *Paris at Its Best* is attempt to organize the city for the visitor—first-time or repeater—who is ready to give it a fair shake.

As in *France at Its Best* and the other books of my *World at Its Best* series, I start at what I consider the beginning in any new place, with a briefing on what has gone before, from early Parisii tribesmen through to latter decades of the twentieth century. From then on, the book is nothing more or less than my conception—presumptuous foreigner that I am—of what Paris is about. We start with the geography of the town and continue with my selection of requisite Paris destinations. And make no mistake: That includes the world's most famous art museum, the Louvre, for long celebrated as a repository of great paintings and sculpture, and now—more's the pity, at least to this observer—with a subterranean main entrance covered by an immense glass-and-steel pyramid that conflicts with the Renaissance style of the multiwinged Louvre Palace and the classic Tuileries Gardens in which it is set.

Other manifestations of contemporary Paris are the subject of the section about the city's new profile, about which I am enthusiastic, the range La Grande Arche in the Défense business center west of Arc de Triomphe through to La Villette, a multipurpose, futuristic park in the northeastern part of the city.

A more leisurely Paris follows, a Paris perhaps for second and third and fourth trips, divided up as one will. I take the liberty of categorizing the city: Historic Paris (a Métro ride, perhaps to Château de Vincennes); Official Paris (have you been inside Hôtel de Ville?); Scholar's Paris (Sorbonne, of course, but why not Bibliotèque Nationale?); Grands Travaux (visitworthy structures of this century's latter years); Verdant Paris (maybe a Sunday afternoon at le Jardin des Plantes); Ecclesiastical Paris (the icons and incense of St.-Julien-le-Pauvre, the semitropical courtyard of a mosque right out of Marrakesh, a Rothschild-donated synagogue); Museumgoer's Paris (masks at Musée des

Arts Africains et Océaniens, rococo interiors of le Musée Nissim de Camondo, Monets at the Marmottan). Then we go out of town to Excursionist's Paris, to Versailles and Fontainebleau and Malmaison, of course, but also to less celebrated châteaux like Compiègne, St.-Germain-en-Laye, and Vaux-le-Vicomte, not to mention those of the legendary Loire, like Chambord and Chenonceaux.

Paris after dark rates a chapter of its own: the bold new Opéra de Paris/Bastille and the last century's Opéra de Paris/Garnier (now a theater for ballet), of course, but why not a pop/rock evening at Olympia, a symphony at the Salle Pleyel or, for that matter, a movie on the Grands Boulevards? I offer counsel on the best of the cabarets, including the ones whose bars afford enough visibility to watch the show from them, at considerably less cost than from a table. Paris is nothing if not sidewalk cafés; I present favorites in the people-watching sweepstakes dotted about the most attractive parts of town.

Be assured that I attach high priority to creature comforts. Chapter 4 offers evaluations—my own as a result of having lived in or dined in and thoroughly inspected 120 hotels, modest, middling, and grand, on both Right and Left banks; 140 restaurants—again in price ranges from bargain-cheap to most exalted. These are preceded by an introduction to French cuisine, traditional and contemporary, course by course, with a compact primer on the various wines of France by my research editor, wine expert Max Drechsler.

My experience is that even the most tightfisted of visitors succumbs to Paris shops sooner or later, out of sheer curiosity, if for no other reason. I make suggestions in this area—with a comprehensive rundown on department stores, open-air markets, and stores in more than a score of categories—perfume to porcelain, chocolates to clothes, silver to shoes—all appraised as a result of personal scouting expeditions. I conclude with a chapter on nitty-gritty—

how to travel on the Métro, how much to tip, currency and credit cards, valuable addresses, what the weather will be like. All that remains for me to suggest at this point is that you acquaint yourself as much with Parisians as with Paris; no world's capital's citizens are more obviously proud of their city, nor more anxious to make visitors seem happy and at home.

ROBERT S. KANE

1

Paris to Know

BACKGROUND BRIEFING

So often, the trouble with the visitor new to this city is that he or she knows so much less about it—and the country of which it is the capital—than he or she thinks. We know Jeanne d'Arc and Chanel No. 5 and Napoleon and the Folies-Bergère, of course. But we are hard put, without a little research, to distinguish between Louis XV and Louis XVI (the monarchs, not the furniture styles, although they can put us off, too). It has to do with our schools. We have been taught disproportionately much about Queen Victoria and Oliver Cromwell. We are sadly weak on, say, the Second Empire of Napoleon Bonaparte's nephew, and on King François I, who rebuilt the oldest part of the ancient Louvre to use as his palace.

All those Merovingians and Carolingians and Capetians: Is it because Shakespeare didn't get around to writing plays about the French dynasties that they remain mostly beyond our pale? The only fairly early sovereign of whom we have some knowledge is Mary Queen of Scots, although I suspect many fewer of us realize that she was a Queen of France and married her first husband in Notre-Dame-de-Paris, than that she was imprisoned the second half of her life by Elizabeth I in a series of drafty English castles.

It is entirely possible to have the holiday of a lifetime in Paris without the faintest idea of what transpired before Charles de Gaulle. But not every country can also boast a King Clodion the Hairy (so called because he ordered his Frankish subjects to wear their hair long) or a queen Clotilda (who was sainted because she converted her husband—King Clovis, the sovereign who designated Paris as France's capital—to Christianity) or a King Pepin the Short (his son was Charlemagne) or a King Charles the Fat or sovereigns of such distinctive disposition that they are remembered as Louis the Quarreler and Charles the Affable.

THE PARIS BEFORE CHRIST

Early Paris goes back to the century before Christ, when Caesar conquered it and its residents—a tribe called the *Parisii,* whose name gradually replaced the earlier Lutetia. But before that happened, Lutetia, with its Seine location, became the tie-up point for ships sailing past, toward Rouen, which it gradually passed in importance, thanks to the ingenuity of transplanted Romans, who cleared its swampy environs. These same Romans built a temple to their deities on Île de la Cité, and later the area developed as the town center. But in 451, Attila's Huns might well have taken the town had not a young woman named Geneviève inspired the people to resist, to the point where the Huns were driven away, and the young heroine of the battle is the same Ste.-Geneviève who has been the patron saint of Paris down through the centuries.

Charlemagne, who in 800 went to Rome to be crowned the first Holy Roman Emperor by Pope Leo III, is known as a military-minded monarch and as a much-married one. (He does not quite measure up to England's Henry VIII, but four wives is a record not to be lightly dismissed.) Between spouses and battles, Charlemagne made Paris a seat of learning to be reckoned with.

At the end of the tenth century, with the start of King Hugh Capet's Capetian dynasty, Paris had become a handsome, substantial city. Hugh Capet and his successors made it even more so. This was the era of the founding of the University of Paris, the paving of streets, the founding of a police force, the first city wall, and substantial progress in the building of Notre-Dame by another very military and much-married monarch, Philip Augustus.

Louis IX—later to become St. Louis—embellished Paris with the exquisite Ste.-Chapelle, and by the time Philip the Fair added even more to its beauty, Paris had become the biggest and richest of medieval cities. Albertus Magnus and St. Thomas More contributed theological eminence to the Sorbonne's already-established industrial reputation. The rich merchants and guilds set up their own municipal government, with the provosts on an equal footing with the provost of Paris, who was the king's own man.

JEANNE D'ARC AND THE RENAISSANCE

The Hundred Years War—that near-interminable series of struggles waged by the French to drive the English from their shores—saw the burning of Jeanne d'Arc at the stake two years after her unsuccessful siege of Paris, an English-occupied Paris in which the English Henry VI had been crowned king in Notre-Dame. The Renaissance came in with a bang with François I, who substantially rebuilt the Louvre, founded the Collège de France, started the first royal printing press, and set the stage for continued royal patronage of architecture and the fine arts as well.

Under Louis XIII, Cardinal Richelieu made Paris the intellectual, as well as the political, center of Europe. The succeeding Louis—the Fourteenth—began his reign in 1643 and moved his court to the palace he built at suburban Versailles, a palace that was to be copied by monarchs all over Europe for the next two centuries.

Louis XIV reigned an astonishingly long time—seventy-two years. It was a period of tremendous cultural, political, and military accomplishment for France. It was, after all, Louis XIV who stated—apocryphally, if not in fact—''L'état, c'est moi'' ("I am the state"). The move to Versailles benefited Parisian industry immeasurably; indeed, it was from that period that Paris became a world center for luxury goods, which it remains to this day. Architects like Mansart, under Louis XIV, and Soufflot, under Louis XV, created works that added to the splendor of Paris. This was the period, too, of the plays of Molière and Racine, of scientists like Lavoisier and Buffon, of brilliant salons, of Gluck operas, and of powdered wigs.

''L'ÉTAT, C'EST MOI''—AND THE REVOLUTION

But the poor were getting poorer. If isolating his courtiers from the people was politically expedient for Louis XIV, it was also the beginning of the estrangement of the sovereign from his subjects. The succeeding reigns of Louis XV and Louis XVI culminated in the Revolution. Mobs forced the Royal Family from Versailles to Paris and stormed the Bastille. One may still visit the cell in the gloomy Conciergerie in which Marie-Antoinette, the excessively extravagant Austrian-born wife of Louis XVI, lived just before being guillotined at a public execution on what is now Place de la Concorde.

Paris was a turbulent city in the years that followed. The Reign of Terror, as the Revolutionary period was called, was followed by the First Republic, proclaimed in 1792. In 1795, the stormy Directory began its rule. There was a sweeping change in matters aesthetic—from the elaborate Louis XIV, Louis XV, and Louis XVI decors of the monarchy to a neoclassic simplicity in architecture, furniture, and even clothes, with women in severe high-waisted dresses and men—the *incroyables*, or "unbelievables"—in tight trousers.

Politically, the severity was equally *incroyable*. The Directory was bankrupt, and its personnel were at such odds with each other and so intrigue-laden that, on November 9, 1799—a fateful date in French history—a bright young Corsican army officer, who had distinguished himself in foreign engagements, played a major role in a *coup d'état*.

THE CORSICAN NAMED BONAPARTE

The Consulate replaced the Directory. It was actually a dictatorship, with Napoléon Bonaparte the No. 1 of the three consuls. In 1802, he was made first consul "for life." In 1804, we are back in historic Notre-Dame for the coronation of Emperor Napoléon I. As he set about conquering Europe and brilliantly reforming French domestic institutions, he found time to begin the Arc de Triomphe and to erect the Arc du Carrousel in the Tuileries, the arcaded Rue de Rivoli, and the splendid column in Place Vendôme. Most important, he expanded the collection of the recently founded Louvre with loot that his troops had gathered in military campaigns. Those artistic spoils had to be returned to their rightful owners after the Congress of Vienna in 1815, but no matter. The concept of great public museums had been popularized. The Congress of Vienna was, of course, the aftermath of Napoléon's earlier and final defeat by Wellington at the Battle of Waterloo.

LITTLE-KNOWN KINGS AND LOUIS-PHILIPPE

The Bourbon dynasty restored itself rather briefly after Napoléon's exile, in the persons of two monarchs we hear little about these days—Louis XVIII and Charles X. (Louis

XVII, if you are wondering, was the son of Louis XVI and died in prison at the age of ten in 1795.) Charles X was forced, as a result of the so-called July Revolution, to abdicate in 1830, and in came Louis-Philippe, who was proclaimed king, in a rather complex run of affairs, by the National Assembly. His "July Monarchy" (called after the revolution that brought him to the throne) was a big-business reign. He even dressed like a businessman, walking the boulevards, umbrella in hand. He had no comprehension of the working class's plight, though, and was attacked from both right and left.

All the same, France prospered materially (the Arc de Triomphe was completed), and the Romantic movement flowered. Victor Hugo made his reputation as a writer. Delacroix painted. Berlioz composed. Still, Louis-Philippe went out as had Charles X before him, by abdicating. The Second Republic followed—but only for four years. Louis Bonaparte (an ambitious nephew of Napoleon Bonaparte), who had been elected president, managed to get his title changed. In 1852, he was proclaimed Napoleon III, although he was also known as Louis Napoleon. (Napoleon II, Bonaparte's son, was better known as the King of Rome; he never reigned and died at the age of 21 at Schoenbrunn Palace, Vienna.)

THE LATER NAPOLEON—AND HAUSSMANN

The 18-year reign of Napoleon III (who was emperor for precisely as long as Louis-Philippe was king) proved a significant period for Paris. The emperor appointed Baron Eugène Haussmann to convert Paris into a modern city. With the authority of the imperial command behind him, Haussmann was ruthless in the changes he made. Indeed, there are students of art, architecture, and town planning who still have not forgiven him. In order to build the wide arterial boulevards and the great squares that typify Paris today, he had to destroy much that dated back to medieval times. Notre-Dame, for example, was fronted by a cluster of venerable houses, all of which were razed to make way for the broad open space that Haussmann considered an improvement. Much of the facade of the Paris we are so accustomed to today—the grandiose Opéra/Garnier is a prime example—dates from the Second Empire.

That epoch came to a dreary culmination with the siege of Paris, which was a consequence of the Franco-Prussian War, and the Commune of Paris. The Third Republic saw recovery. Paris escaped damage during World War I, after which the victorious Allies met in the palace that Louis XIV had built in Versailles. They imposed harsh terms on the vanquished Germans, who—never forgiving—invaded Paris and the rest of France in 1940.

THE TWO WORLD WARS—AND DE GAULLE

The government temporarily left the capital for the thermal resort of Vichy, where the quisling Pétain regime was a Nazi puppet until 1944. That was when Paris was liberated by France's own remarkable Resistance force. American troops entered the city thereafter, and the city—though austere and hungry in the early days of peace—quickly regained its brilliance.

The postwar years saw Charles de Gaulle as president in 1945 and 1946 and later from 1958 to 1969 under a new, strong-executive constitution. France voluntarily relinquished its vast Black African empire, as well as Tunisia and Morocco, and eventually—after much blood was shed—Algeria. The great student-worker uprisings of 1968 alerted France to the need to update its institutions even more rapidly than it already had. Under de Gaulle's successors, Georges Pompidou, Valéry Giscard d'Estaing, and François Mitterrand—the modern era's builder-president—this has been happening.

2

Paris to See

LAY OF THE LAND

No great city is easier to find one's way about in than Paris. We may regret that Baron Haussmann destroyed much of medieval Paris when Napoleon III commissioned him to redesign the city—with the installation of wide boulevards and great squares—a little over a century ago. But there is no gainsaying that Haussmann's Paris is sensible and practical—and supremely walkable, despite its considerable size. Let me try to orient you by delineating what I consider the thoroughfares and landmarks that are essential to a basic geographical understanding of Paris.

Start with the *Rive Droite/Right Bank* circle that was for long *Place de l'Étoile* but is now officially *Place Charles de Gaulle.* (Like New York's Avenue of the Americas—still Sixth Avenue to natives—Place Charles de Gaulle remains "Étoile" to many who have so known it.) No less than twelve streets radiate from the Étoile (thus the name *étoile*—star), whose landmark is the Arc de Triomphe. The most important of these is *Avenue des Champs-Élysées*—broad but no longer the class act it had been (it's packed with auto showrooms and fast-food joints, although some cafés, boutiques, and restaurants remain, with a sidewalk

widening and general sprucing-up at long last planned for
the nineties)—which (with the name *Avenue de la Grande
Armée*) continues west to Neuilly and the monumental
Grande Arche of *La Défense* skyscraper complex. The
Champs-Élysées leads east from the Étoile into the square
that is the most beautiful in the world and the most difficult to negotiate in traffic: *Place de la Concorde*. Continue
around Concorde, and you are in the heart-of-Paris park
that is the *Jardin des Tuileries*, with *Palais du Louvre*—the
onetime royal residence turned museum. Tuileries and
Louvre are bordered on the south by the *Seine River* and on
the north by arcaded *Rue de Rivoli*.

One may leave this Concorde-Tuileries-Louvre area for
Place de l'Opéra—heart of the Right Bank—by any one of
three routes. The *first:* From the Concorde, take Rue Royale
directly north to the Parthenon-like *Church of the Madeleine*,
turn right at the Madeleine on the *Grands Boulevards* (comprising Boulevards de la Madeleine, des Capucines, and
des Italiens—one street with three successive names).
Walk, then, for a few blocks to Place de l'Opéra and the
Opéra/Garnier, for which it is named. *Two:* Walk from Rue
de Rivoli, bordering the Tuileries, onto short, shop-lined,
Rue de Castiglione, and a couple of moments later emerge
into extraordinarily beautiful *Place Vendôme,* easily identifi-
able because of the column in the center—erected by Napoleon and with a statue of none other than himself at its
summit. Pass through Vendôme to celebrated *Rue de la
Paix,* and within a few moments you have reached Place de
l'Opéra by a second route. *Three:* Continue walking down
Rue de Rivoli, bordering the Louvre, until reaching broad
Avenue de l'Opéra. Turn left on that thoroughfare, walking
north to the Opéra/Garnier at its far end.

Now to the *Rive Gauche/Left Bank* via the greatest landmark of them all, *Notre-Dame,* which is situated on an
island—*Île de la Cité*—in the Seine. Return to the Louvre—
flanking Rue de Rivoli. Pass Avenue de l'Opéra and con-

tinue east on Rivoli, beyond the entrance to the *Palais Royal*, until you reach *Rue du Pont Neuf*. Turn right here; this street leads directly onto the famous bridge for which it is named. Over the bridge and there you are: on *Île de la Cité*, with the twin towers of Notre-Dame just beyond. An even smaller island, *Île St.-Louis*, is directly to the rear of Notre-Dame, gained by little *Pont St.-Louis*. But you want to continue from Île de la Cité to the Left Bank. The most direct way is to proceed via the same Pont Neuf you took from the Right Bank to the island; it continues to the Rive Gauche.

Or, if you would rather orient yourself on main thoroughfares, go this way: After arriving on Île de la Cité, walk toward Notre-Dame to the first broad thoroughfare you hit. It will be *Boulevard du Palais*. Turn right across narrow *Pont St.-Michel*, and voilà! Boulevard du Palais has changed names to become *Boulevard St.-Michel*—a principal Left Bank street. Spires of *Ste.-Chapelle*—another landmark—are to your right. But continue south on Boulevard St.-Michel—"Boule Meesh"—to the first principal cross street. This will be *Boulevard St.-Germain*. Turn right on it, and you are in the core of *Quartier Latin*, with the landmark *St.-Germain-des-Prés Church*, shops, and cafés nearby. If you like, return to the Rive Droite in roughly circular fashion. Continue along Boulevard St.-Germain, past St.-Germain-des Prés, following the boulevard's curves. Before long, you will reach *Palais-Bourbon*, the colonnaded neoclassic landmark that is the National Assembly, facing the Seine, and the bridge that is *Pont de la Concorde*.

Before crossing, look up to your left at the *Eiffel Tower*. Make a note of it at this point, so you will realize its Left Bank situation. Behind it is the broad green called *Champ-de-Mars*, at whose other extremity is the *École Militaire*, or Military Academy. Still another Left Bank landmark—not at all far from where you are standing at Pont de la

Concorde—is the complex of *Hôtel des Invalides,* with the
domed church where Napoleon is buried. Back you go
now to the Right Bank—over Pont de la Concorde to familiar Place de la Concorde.

CHOICE DESTINATIONS, OR
THE ESSENTIAL PARIS

Notre-Dame and the river islands. Notre-Dame, along
with Westminster Abbey in London and St. Peter's in
Rome, is the church we grew up with. It is part of our life—
from history-book illustrations and travel posters and old
movies—long before we ever see it. And when we do, it
does not disappoint. Begun in the mid-twelfth century, it
was not completed until the mid-thirteenth. It is one of the
great Gothic cathedrals of Europe—conveniently placed
smack in the heart of one of the great capitals—with its
twin bell towers (you may climb up, as did Victor Hugo's
hunchbacked *jongleur,* Quasimodo), its trio of arched portals, its exquisite rose window, its famed flying buttresses
along the sides, and its needlelike spire over the transept.
The apse, or altar area, behind the choir is perhaps the
loveliest part of the always-crowded interior. The time to
go—regardless of one's religious faith—is on Sunday for
the 10:00 A.M. High Mass. Visitors from everywhere join
Parisians in the packed pews. Celebrants of the Mass
swing incense lamps from the high altar. The white-robed
children's choir sings beautifully, organ music is richly so-
norous, and Japanese observers record it all with ever-
clicking cameras. Outside, take note of two other visitable
destinations: *Musée de Notre-Dame-de-Paris* (10 Rue du Clo-
ître Notre-Dame)—crammed with paintings, prints, reli-
quaries, and historic documents associated with the
cathedral; and *Crypte Archéologique de Notre-Dame,* entered
by a not-easy-to-locate stairway on Place du Parvis, in front
of the cathedral, which leads to a series of remarkable

underground spaces, some dating to Roman-era Paris, others medieval.

The island in the Seine on which Notre-Dame is located—Île de la Cité—is the core of Paris, historically as well as spiritually, and has been from medieval times onward. It was only about a century and a quarter back that Napoleon III's Baron Haussmann removed the maze of house-lined streets from the front of the cathedral and otherwise altered the island, evacuating thousands from their homes. The island's other principal monuments are the Conciergerie and its Ste.-Chapelle church, dealt with in later pages. Suffice it to say at this point that Île de la Cité is explorable walking territory, as is its smaller neighbor island, St.-Louis—essentially a Renaissance quarter, whose streets are lined with graceful houses of that architecturally rich epoch, and whose main thoroughfare, Rue St.-Louis-en-l'Île, has become, in recent seasons, a veritable Restaurant Row (Chapter 5).

Musée du Louvre (Cour Napoléon, Jardins des Tuileries): Not another visitor destination—on any visitor's list of requisites—more reflects late twentieth-century Paris than the Louvre. (See *Grands Travaux: Late Twentieth-Century Paris*, below.) Call it what you will: Musée National du Louvre (its old name), Musée du Louvre (the name currently used in its printed materials), or Le Grand Louvre—the immodest but certainly accurate label used by the government for the massive $850 million redesign that resulted, after six years, in a reopened Louvre in 1989 that changed the face of central Paris, by means of a new entrance punctuated by a glass pyramid in the Renaissance-style courtyard of the architecturally cohesive, history-rich Tuileries Gardens.

The idea for new access that would take visitors from street level to a capacious subterranean lobby—a mix of restaurants and cafés (reviewed on later pages), generous size shopping area, first-ever auditorium of 420 seats (for concerts, lectures, and other museum-related programs), and three distinct wings of exhibits—was intelligent and commendable. And although I was never, over a period of regular visits extending through three decades, a critic of the old Louvre (it has become fashionable to term it the world's worst-equipped museum of consequence and with the nastiest guards, pre-facelift), I did, of course, recognize its eccentricities, always got lost, was always set in the right direction by a kindly guard, and thoroughly enjoyed myself on each and every bout of exploration. I adored the old Louvre. It was French. It was Parisian. It was unique. It is still all of the foregoing—but with an American accent. Architect I. M. Pei was obviously selected for the makeover, which resulted in his inappropriate pyramid, because he had done a creditable job with the East Building of the National Gallery of Art in Washington, linked to the original museum structure by an underground area that works very well. But, and this is a big *but,* the earlier Pei work is *sans* pyramid.

Despite commendable worldwide opposition, the pyramid was accorded seals of approval by major French *(Le Figaro)* and major American *(The New York Times)* newspapers when it opened, and with additional international Establishment approbation, it has come to attract visitors who have never before entered an art museum, and no doubt—after interminable waits in long lines—never will again. (Sundays, traditionally admission-free, are the worst, but weekdays are not so bad if you go early in the day.)

Think what you will of the Pei pyramid and the trio of minipyramids that flank it (adding unnecessary glitz to Cour Napoléon), there is the newly reorganized museum to evaluate. Despite the cold, clean lines of its big new basement entrance hall, and the Yank-inspired logic of its newly organized galleries, there's nothing for it but to praise Pei for the tremendous additional space that's been acquired. The *Richelieu Pavillon* of the Louvre palace complex—fronting on Rue de Rivoli and for long occupied by a government ministry that was moved to new quarters elsewhere in town—is now part of the museum, one of the three principal exhibit wings, each with its own entrance. The others are *Pavillon Denon*—with sculptures; paintings; Greek, Etruscan, and Roman antiquities; and graphic art (and with the top two Louvre treasures: Leonardo da Vinci's *Mona Lisa* and the *Winged Victory of Samothrace* sculpture)—and *Pavillon Sully*, home to Asian and Egyptian antiquities, Renaissance and Baroque French paintings and objets d'art, and exciting sections that were created after excavations in Cour Napoleon (for the new subterranean lobby) which resulted in quite marvelous discoveries. Many are displayed in the Louvre History galleries, based in the thirteenth-century foundations of the fortress built by King Philippe Auguste.

Decor has been enhanced (new marble cases, newly surfaced walls, new molding and woodwork). Egyptian Galleries are strikingly good-looking and rooms with small French Renaissance portraits—by greats like Clouet and Corneille de Lyon—are elegant. The principal area for paintings, the Grande Galerie remains as it was albeit repainted, still with works by Fragonard and Greuze, Oudry and Chardin, not to mention Hubert Robert's painting of the space, executed during the eighteenth-century period when he was the Louvre's director. The adjacent Grande Salle still exhibits Veronese, Titian, and Leonardo. And as you wander, you will find Poussin and Lorrain, Le Nain and Le Brun, and you'll delight in seeing old palace spaces—Chambre du Roi and Galerie d'Apollon—quite as splendid as they had been.

Museum aspects of the Louvre date to the same François I who razed the old Louvre in the early sixteenth century and started building the new. His collection of Old Masters was the nucleus of the royal collection that never stopped expanding through all the later Louis—XIII to Louis-Philippe—as well as Napoleon I. It's not easy to highlight a collection of 400,000-plus objects. But besides the paintings I mention above, look for Fra Angelico's *Coronation of the Virgin*, Raphael's *Virgin with a Veil*, Vermeer's *Lace Maker*, and works by France's Ingres, David, Delacroix, and Corot. You'll encounter, as well, Tintoretto and Veronese. Not to mention Van Cleve and Van Eyck, Hals and Rembrandt, Velázquez and Zurburán, Turner and Constable. Sculpture is a Louvre specialty: Greece's *Venus de Milo* complementing *Winged Victory of Samothrace*, and later works— Michelangelo's *Slave*, Goujon's *Diana of Anet*, and an unknown Tuscan genius's painted, carved-wood head of a fifteenth-century lady. Period rooms compete with those of neighboring Musée des Arts Décoratifs (below)— brimming with furniture and accessories of the periods Louis XIII, Louis XIV, Louis XV, Louis XVI (with treasures of Marie-Antoinette), Napoleon, the Directorate, and the Restoration era of Louis XVIII and Charles X. An entire chamber is pure Napoleon—with his throne from St.-Cloud and his incredibly elaborate toilet kit, or *nécessaire*, and the majestic cradle of his son, the King of Rome. There is a rolltop desk that was Marie-Antoinette's, a bed with a red and white velvet canopy slept in by a marshall of Louis XIII, masterful Louis XV chairs, tapestries and tables, carpets and cupboards. Once inside the updated Louvre, your attitude toward its pyramid—pro or anti—becomes insignificant. The exhibits take over; they're the winners.

Tour Eiffel (Quai Branly): The Eiffel Tower was completed in 1889; weighs some 7,000 tons; was almost razed in 1909; is dramatically illuminated every evening by 292 upward-pointing interior floodlights that replaced almost 1,300 external floodlights in 1986; is 984 feet high; draws some 5 million visitors annually; contains 15,000 different kinds of parts and 2.5 million rivets; has three observation levels;

and, when reproduced in miniature, continues year after year as the most popular Paris souvenir. (I was given this intelligence by the Galeries Lafayette department store.) The level of the tower to head for is the top one, from whose platform, given a clear day, one can see for many miles. Even in winter, when the top level can be closed, the views from the lower platforms are hardly to be despised: No. 2 at under 400 feet, No. 1 about half that high. There is, of course, an elevator, but if you want to shed some weight, you may walk; there are 1,652 steps to the summit. I evaluate tower restaurants on later pages.

Arc de Triomphe (Place Charles de Gaulle/Étoile) was begun by Napoleon I and finished by Louis-Philippe. Baron Haussmann, whom Napoleon III commissioned to make drastic changes in the city, added nine to the three existing avenues that lead from Place Charles de Gaulle/Étoile—of which the arch is the centerpiece—making the total a magnificent, if rather confusing, twelve traffic arteries leading from the circle. (The chief of these is, of course, Champs-Élysées, which extends east from the arch to Place de la Concorde; going westward from the arch, it becomes Avenue de la Grande-Armée, leading toward the Grande Arche of La Défense. The remaining eleven avenues radiating from L'Étoile are a blend of residences, shops, hotels, restaurants, and cafés, the lot comprising one of the most fashionable quarters of Paris.) There's a little museum relating to the monument upstairs in the arch, whose major attribute is the fine vista it affords (in many ways better than the one from the Eiffel Tower). It's fun being up there above the traffic.

Les Invalides (Rue de Grenelle): If you are wondering why Napoleon is buried in a place called Les Invalides, it is because the church with his tomb is but a part of an

enormous veterans' hospital—probably the world's first—
built by Louis XIV and with a 7,000-patient capacity, of
which not even a handful remains today. (English King
Charles II's also-big Chelsea Royal Hospital went up contemporarily in London and remains in operation.) Les Invalides, today, embraces a pair of churches and a trio of
museums. *Musée de l'Armée*, largest of the three, constitutes one of the world's major collections of arms, from the
medieval period onward. *Musée de l'Ordre National de la Lib-
ération* tells the story of World War II anti-Nazi Resistance
forces and is not unlike similarly commendable museums
in Copenhagen and Oslo, not to mention others throughout France. *Musée des Deux Guerres Mondiales*'s exhibits re-
late to both world wars. The relatively uncelebrated *Church
of St.-Louis-des-Invalides* is architecturally severe. In its
chapel is the carriage on which Napoleon's remains started
their long journey from the exile-island of St. Helena to the
next-door Hardouin-Mansart–designed *Church of the
Dome*, where they repose under a top-heavy cupola in an
ambience at once overblown, graceless, and ostentatious.
Whether or not you are taken with the aesthetics of the
Church of the Dome, there is no denying the strength of
its architecture. The dome—rising just over 350 feet from
the floor to the top of its spire—is supported by 40
columns. Its intricate gilding, picking out reliefs of its surface, was restored most recently in 1989.

Place Vendôme is an almost completely enclosed square
that is the work of a single architect—Hardouin-Mansart.
It has but two entrances, one on Rue St.-Honoré, the other
on Rue de Castiglione. The shape is square, but with the
charm of chopped-off corners. Palaces of the square are all
early eighteenth century; one is now the Ritz Hôtel, and its
next-door neighbor—with a near identical facade—is the
Ministry of Justice. The towering column in the center is a
shaft of stone decorated with a spiral of bronze that is a

souvenir of the Battle of Austerlitz. It was erected by that battle's victor, Napoleon, with a statue of himself atop it. This is rather a pity because the Bonaparte likeness replaces an earlier statue of Louis XIV, the original builder of the sublimely beautiful square, to which not a few visitors make return pilgrimages within moments of arrival in Paris.

Place de la Concorde: Thank Louis XV for Place de la Concorde; it was begun during his reign and named for him— until Revolutionists tore down the central statue of him, named the square for their insurrection, and proceeded to set up their guillotine in its midst. When you try to cross today, as hundreds of cars block your way, think of earlier days. Louis XVI, his queen, Marie-Antoinette, and Madame du Barry—successor to Madame de Pompadour as mistress to Louis XV—were among those whose heads were chopped off in this beautiful spot. Indeed, the reputation of Place de la Révolution was so bloody that the Directory, when it took over the government, gave it its present name. The square, with its myriad black wrought-iron lampposts, an Egyptian obelisk more than 3,000 years old as a centerpiece, a pair of fountains, and eight statues dedicated to as many French cities, is fronted on the river side by the bridge that takes its name. On the opposite side are twin structures, each a part of the original eighteenth-century design of the square. The palace on your left as you look inward from the Seine is Hôtel de Crillon, while the twin palace to the right is the Navy Ministry. Directly to the left of the Crillon, but not directly on the square, is the newer, albeit classic-style, American Embassy; like its counterparts in virtually every capital around the world that I have visited, it has one of the most enviable locations in town. In this case it has views of the Concorde, the Tuileries, and the Seine from its front windows; to the rear and a hop and a skip away is Palais de l'Élysée, official residence of the president, not to mention the house in which the U.S. envoy resides, as distinct from the main Embassy building, known as the Chancellery. But I have not quite finished with Place de la Concorde. As if views, toward and away from the Seine, are not enough, the other two are quite as spectacular—one looking way beyond, up the wide Champs-Élysées to Place Charles de Gaulle and the Arc de Triomphe, and the other toward the formal gardens of the Tuileries and the little *Arc du Carrousel,* a kind of mini-Triomphe that is—you will see for yourself when you look from one to the other—perfectly aligned with the Arc de Triomphe and the decidedly contemporary pyramid-entrance to the Louvre.

Opéra de Paris/Garnier (a.k.a. Palais Garnier, Place de l'Opéra) is the great neobaroque structure that dominates the square that takes its name. Ever since it opened in 1875, Opéra-Garnier—simply l'Opéra or Théâtre de l'Opéra until 1989 when the change of name was necessitated—has been the embodiment of Belle Époque Paris. "Garnier" in its present title refers to the architect, the same Charles Garnier who designed a similarly brilliant theater in the Casino of Monte Carlo. Since 1989—with the opening of Opéra de Paris/Bastille, now the seat of the Paris Opéra—it has been home base for Ballet de l'Opéra—as well as dance by visiting companies. Opéra/Garnier is remarkable for its splendid red and gold auditorium.

There is an enormous backstage area (decades ahead of its time) and a promenade area above the sumptuous grand staircase that must have been a perfect foil for Second Empire audiences. Even with today's relatively casual audiences, the Promenade Salon and its adjacent refreshment rooms are quite the classiest of any theater in Europe. It is, of course, sad that this world-class theater, designed for the presentation of grand opera and so named, is no longer used for its original purpose. Its successor, the state-of-the-art theater on Place de la Bastille (detailed, along with more on Opéra Garnier, on later pages focusing on the performing arts) is a worthy structure, certainly in my view. Still, visitors who have known Paris over a sustained period (including this one) must be forgiven their regret at Garnier's reduced function (time was when both ballet *and* opera were performed on its stage), and at the same time grateful—to paraphrase a statement by an opera official in an interview—that Garnier was neither razed nor sold to the Japanese.

Musée National des Thermes et de L'Hôtel de Cluny (6 Place Paul-Painlévé): The Cluny is, along with the Louvre, the most Parisian of museums, embracing both Roman-era and medieval-era Paris. Its building is part Gallo-Roman baths, part Middle Ages monastery. You see the immense, high-ceilinged, and extravagantly arched Frigidarium— Roman-built in the second century. And you visit, as well, the later monks' chapel and a couple of dozen additional chambers rich with medieval art, the most noted piece of which is the *Dame à la Licorne* tapestry. Take your time as you go through, noting sculpture and stained glass, altars and paintings, and exquisitely detailed rooms of the period—the brilliantly vaulted chapel, dating to 1500, most especially. The Cluny is one of all France's loveliest museum experiences.

Place des Vosges is the most celebrated treasure of the Renaissance-era Marais district, the Right Bank area near Place de la Bastille that has recovered from a long period of neglect and is the subject of additional comment on later pages. Henri IV had the square built in the early seventeenth century. Houses surrounding it are basically of uniform design. No. 6 is where Victor Hugo lived and is now a Hugo museum (below). But the Place des Vosges is at its nicest on a sunny day in spring, when the old trees have their new leaves, and you have time to sit back in a café or on one of the benches and relax with the neighborhood locals—early enough in the day so that the kids are still in school, and this remarkably unspoiled, authentically Parisian antique is still quiet enough to savor and be grateful for.

Montmartre, way up in a detached area of town in the shadow of Sacré-Cœur, is the romanticist's Paris. No visitor who knows Utrillo's paintings will rest until he or she has had a walk through it. Montmartre, even today, is hilly, narrow streets, with very paintable old houses, funny little squares, and broad vistas. Remove the blinking signs, the mod clothing, and vendors of mostly tacky, embarrassingly poor "art" in and around the *Place du Tertre,* and Utrillo could go right back to work. What I suggest you do is take the Métro up to *Place Pigalle,* or a nearby stop, and amble about. You will take the funicular up to that absurdly designed old chestnut of a landmark, Sacré-Cœur (see Ecclesiastical Paris, on later pages of this chapter), and after taking in the view of the town from its terrace, you'll walk over to *Place du Tertre,* populated primarily by German tourists. Pop your head into lovely old *St.-Pierre-de-Montmartre* (see Ecclesiastical Paris), look at the delicious food shops of *Rue Lépic,* lunch in a local restaurant, work your way down the steep streets to *Place des Abbesses,* gradually gaining broad *Boulevard de Clichy* and Place Pigalle. Memories of such past Montmartre folk heroes as Toulouse-Lautrec and the people he immortalized in his paintings—like Yvette, Jane Avril, and La Gouloue—die hard. But today's sadly overcommercial Montmartre, despite remaining pockets of charm, does not do them justice.

HISTORIC PARIS

Bridging the Seine: By my count, the river that flows through Paris is crossed by some thirty bridges—representing a mix of the city's epochs. Most significant: *Pont Alexandre III*, my favorite—with wrought-iron lampposts evoking its Second Empire origin—traverses the Seine at the point where Grand and Petit palaces face Les Invalides. *Pont Neuf*, way to the east, is the oldest bridge—early seventeenth century. It's the first bridge on Île de la Cité, as you approach from the west, and is worth crossing slowly to savor the views—in all directions. *Pont de la Concorde*, joining Place de la Concorde with the Left Bank frontage of Assemblée Nationale, is eighteenth-century and rewards with memorable vistas. *Pont d'Iéna* links the Eiffel Tower on the Left Bank with Palais de Chaillot on the Right; sightseeing boats depart from its Left Bank extremity. *Pont de Grenelle*, noteworthy for its miniature Statue of Liberty, a thank-you in kind from New York City to the French, in appreciation of the French gift of the original Miss Liberty, is west of Palais de Chaillot, near the circular O.R.T.F. building—headquarters of French TV. *Pont Marie*, way east, makes for a pleasant approach—amidships, so to speak—to Île St.-Louis, when you come from the Right Bank. To gain the Left Bank, the bridge continues, renamed *Pont de la Tournelle*.

Château de Vincennes: Take the Métro often enough, and the names of the lines—bearing the destinations at either end—become familiar to you. One that had long intrigued me was Neuilly-Vincennes. I knew Neuilly—a suburb to the north of the Bois de Boulogne. And, on a recent visit, I took the Métro all the way in the opposite direction to Bois de Vincennes (see Verdant Paris, on a later page) and the château for which it is named. The castle is the only medieval royal palace in the Paris area. It goes back to the fourteenth century; so there is no question but that it is respectable. What it is not is beautiful. The most impressive of the remaining structures is the Dungeon, a gawky medieval skyscraper that had known royal tenants, then took to boarding the more respectable of the kingdom's prisoners, with the nastier of the lot reserved for the Bastille. The interior is what might be termed Grim Gothic, not terribly unlike much vaster chambers of the Conciergerie. Opposite the Dungeon and in great contrast to it is a church with a lovely, lacy Gothic exterior, Ste.-Chapelle. Its interior is in somber contrast, for it is completely without furnishings. The other principal buildings are the newer, Renaissance-era King's and Queen's pavilions, partially restored from earlier desecrations. Someday—not too long off, one hopes—enough skilled restoration of the entire Vincennes Château complex will have been achieved so that we will have a less depressing, fuller, more joyous, and more lifelike idea of what the medieval royal courts of France were all about.

Conciergerie (Quai de l'Horloge)—the vast Île de la Cité palace, with its matchless round towers themselves a Paris landmark—is the one ancient building in Paris—with which I am familiar, at least—that is more interesting outside than within. Guides take groups through darkish, depressing spaces of cavernous size, the only exception being the simple little cell—now a chapel—where Marie-Antoinette lived before she was carted to her death on Place de la Concorde. She was by no means the only prisoner of the Revolution. The old Conciergerie—originally a part of the royal palace when kings lived on Île de la Cité and named for the palace caretaker—had served as a prison before the Revolution and was pressed into service for that purpose during the Terror. More than 2,500 enemies of the Revolution were incarcerated in its Gothic depths, most passing from there to the Tribunal, which heard their cases and then sent most to their execution. Of the Conciergerie's toured chambers, the Men-at-Arms' Hall is the least depressing. There are, as well, an enormous kitchen, guards' quarters, and courtyards of both men and women prisoners. The place served as a prison long after the Revolution for a succession of monarchs— the murderer of a nephew of Louis XVIII, a pesky bomber of the Louis-Philippe era, and still another, who attempted to take Napoleon III's life. Cheery place, this. Adjoining it is *Palais de Justice*, all of whose law courts (save Juvenile and Divorce) are open to the public. This massive maze embraces a variety of epochs, much eighteenth- and nineteenth-century, some considerably older. There are gowned, briefcase-bearing, scurrying *avocats* all about, to liven the place up. And there is the treasure of the complex, Ste.-Chapelle, dealt with on a later page.

Le Marais: We are creatures of habit, even in strange cities. Take Rue de Rivoli. We walk it, and upon return visits re-walk it, but only between Place de la Concorde, where it begins, and as far in the other direction as theater-flanked Place du Chatelet, where we invariably turn toward the Seine, Notre-Dame, and the Rive Gauche. By staying right on Rivoli, though, walking past the landmark ruin that is Tour St.-Jacques and Hôtel de Ville, Paris's City Hall, we come to the beginnings of the Marais, the heart of fashionable Paris in medieval and Renaissance times.

Toward the end of the sixteenth century, aristocrats put up grand mansions—*hôtels particuliers,* as they still are called—which became the prototype of the French town house, in an area that had long been a center of artisanship and commerce. But, after a century, the smart set gravitated toward the other side of the river. The posh Marais once again became the artisans' Marais. Aesthetics of the great houses were forgotten by shopkeepers and craftsmen, who altered them for their own purposes.

After World War II, a civic group that translates as the Association for the Preservation and Enhancement of Historic Paris went to work to right matters. Legislation was enacted to encourage rehabilitation. Upwardly mobile Parisians have moved into the old houses. Nonprofit organizations lease others. Specially trained guide-scholars—*conférenciers,* as they are called—offer visitors detailed commentaries. *Hôtel de Sully,* an early seventeenth-century masterwork with a magnificent courtyard through which you may pass right into Place des Vosges, has beautifully restored interiors; do have a look.

Hôtel de Marle (1 Rue Payenne) is also easy of access, at least on afternoons; it houses the Swedish Cultural Center. *Théâtre Sylvia Montfort* occupies an immense old palace—modernized, to be sure—at 8 Rue de Thorigny. There are two Marais churches of special interest: *St.-Gervais-St.-Protais* (Place St.-Gervais) and *St.-Paul-St.-Louis* (Rue St.-Antoine). Three Marais houses shelter museums and are included in the Museums section, following: *Hôtel Carnavalet* (23 Rue de Sévigné, with a recently acquired annex), *Hôtel de Soubise* (60 Rue des Francs-Bourgeois), and *Hôtel de Guénégaud* (60 Rue des Archives).

Palais-Royal is a tranquil oasis of striking beauty smack in the heart of town—at the Louvre-Tuileries end of Avenue de l'Opéra, next to the Comédie-Française. Originally built by Louis XIII's prime minister, Cardinal Richelieu, the palais was actually royal for only two brief periods—when Louis XIV lived in it as a youthful monarch and later when it was inhabited by Philippe II of Orléans, Regent of France during the minority of Louis XV. Palais-Royal looks today much as it did in the late eighteenth century, when it was converted from a relatively intimate residence to a great, quadrangular mass of buildings that must surely have been one of Europe's first apartment houses of consequence. There have been more downs than ups in the

Palais-Royal's history (the most recent "down" has been the placement, in the late 1980s, of an ugly network of tree-stump-like "sculpture" on its grounds), but for much of the past century its flats have been a very good address, indeed, with the novelist Colette among the more celebrated of its tenants. The gardens of the quadrangle are open to the public. On a sunny day, in between sightseeing or shopping, there is no pleasanter respite than a pause on a bench in the odd seclusion of a palace lived in by the very same king who built Versailles—long before it was even a gleam in his eye.

Panthéon (Rue Soufflot, near Jardins du Luxembourg) is a good deal more recent than that of Rome—about 1,700 years. It is the somber, neoclassic, domed structure that Louis XV commissioned the noted architect Soufflot to design; it was finished in 1789. There is more to the building than at first meets the eye. Detail work—Corinthian columns, ceilings, arches, and cupolas—is superb. And in the basement is a crypt containing tombs of such French immortals as Zola, Hugo, Rousseau, and Voltaire. You may see the crypt only in the company of a guide who takes groups as they collect. Because French civil servants have a way of staying on their jobs, it is conceivable that you will have the same guide who has been in the crypt these many seasons. No matter how elementary one's French, his repartee results in the funniest running show in Paris.

Duke and Duchess of Windsor's house (4 Route du Champ d'Entraînement) is the turn-of-century Bois de Boulogne mansion to which the late Duke and Duchess of Windsor (Britain's former King Edward VIII and his American wife, née Wallis Warfield Simpson) moved in 1953, twenty-seven years after the duke abdicated in 1936 to marry Mrs. Simpson. Following the duchess's death in the house in 1986 (her husband died there in 1972), an Egyptian—the same

Mohammed al-Gayed who owns London's Harrod's department store and Paris's Ritz Hôtel—took it over and spent nearly $15 million on a restoration. Formally reopened in late 1989, the house now looks as it did in its Windsor heyday. Open only on application—and then principally to historians and VIPs (Queen Elizabeth II and her son and heir, Prince Charles, have been visitors)—the house's restoration embraces ground and upper floor salons, dining room, library, ducal couple's bedrooms and clothes-filled closets (the duchess's shoes, handbags, and hats are in original storage spaces). Single most historic object is the table at which the king signed papers declaring his abdication official. But there are tapestries and paintings, furniture and books, and photos of the couple on tables dotted about the house.

Cimetière du Père Lachaise (Avenue du Père Lachaise, near Place Gambetta): Cemeteries, even when their occupants are celebrated, are not to every sightseer's taste. This one, Paris's largest, in eastern Paris away from the action, is named for the Jesuit priest who was a chaplain of Louis XIV. It has all sorts of historic associations, but it is best known for the personalities buried within: Molière, Chopin, Corot, Delacroix, Balzac, Bizet, Bernhardt, Proust, and Oscar Wilde, to name some from earlier periods and—more recently—Colette and Édith Piaf.

OFFICIAL PARIS

Hôtel de Ville (Place de l'Hôtel de Ville) is City Hall, fronting a square named for it, with Rue de Rivoli on one side, a Seine-front street—with Notre-Dame just beyond—on the other, and the Marais just beyond. English-speaking visitors would call Hôtel de Ville Victorian—giddy Victorian, at that. The French prefer the more appropriate Belle Époque label, an equally evocative description. The interior is quite as grand as the exterior leads one to believe it will be. The room to head for is the vast, high-ceilinged Salon Principal, in which no aspect of the decorative arts is absent; if anything, quite the reverse is the case.

Palais de l'Élysée (Rue du Faubourg St.-Honoré): You cannot go in, but it is worth passing by Palais de l'Élysée on modish Rue du Faubourg St.-Honoré; this is, after all, the president's official home. Guards and police on duty are used to people peering into the courtyard to see what they can see. When one considers that the Élysée was taken over by Madame de Pompadour not long after it went up in the early eighteenth century, it is not difficult to appreciate how beautiful it must be. Madame de Pompadour—longtime mistress of Louis XV—was a woman of keen intelligence and considerable taste in the fine and applied arts. Ever since her tenancy, the palace has known occupants of note. Napoleon abdicated there—for the second and final time; the third Napoleon—nephew to the first—lived there, and so have all subsequent presidents of France. You can get an idea of the size of the palace's gardens by walking past walls that enclose them, either on Avenue de Marigny, leading to Champs-Élysées, or Rue de l'Élysée, running parallel to it. Back on Rue du Faubourg St.-Honoré, don't confuse the also-impressive—and neighboring—British Embassy with the Élysée, nor indeed the similarly designed minipalace (No. 41) that serves as the residence of the American ambassador, whose offices are in the embassy's chancellery, just off Place de la Concorde, opposite the west facade of Hôtel de Crillon.

Palais du Luxembourg (Rue de Vaugirard): It is a measure of the admirable flexibility of the French that the home of one of the grandest of all French queens—Italian-born Marie de Médicis—now houses a chamber of republican

France's legislature. Queen Marie, after becoming the widow of Henri IV in the early seventeenth century, yearned for a new home that would evoke her childhood. Luxembourg is rather loosely based on Florence's Palazzo Pitti and has had a multitude of alterations over the centuries, right through to the middle of the nineteenth. Still, one wants to see the Senate Chamber, the reception rooms, and the Delacroix paintings in the elaborate library. The Senate president's official residence is next door in the house that preceded Queen Marie's palace as the original Luxembourg. The setting is a park worthy of space on its own, in pages following.

Palais-Bourbon (Quai-d'Orsay)—facing the Seine at Pont de la Concorde—is the home of Assemblée Nationale, the 491-member lower chamber of Parliament. Palais-Bourbon has a colonnaded, neoclassic facade not dissimilar to that of the Church of the Madeleine way over on the Right Bank. It was planned that way by Napoleon, so that you could look from one harmonious facade to the other and enjoy the way the two complement each other. Palais-Bourbon takes its name from a daughter of Louis XIV—the Duchess of Bourbon. Her early eighteenth-century town house got its present look in the early nineteenth century. To see the Assembly in session in its great half-circle of a hall is, indeed, a special Paris experience.

Palais du Quai-d'Orsay (Quai-d'Orsay): Foreign offices in capitals around the world habitually occupy handsome old houses. (The State Department in Washington, in a modern, specially constructed building, is an exception to the rule.) The French Ministry of Foreign Affairs, in a venerable villa conveniently next door to the earlier-described Palais-Bourbon, admits visitors on hour-long guided tours. Chief lures are Louis-Philippe and Second Empire salons and the chamber where the Congress of Paris met and the Kellogg Pact was signed.

Maison de l'UNESCO (Place de Fontenoy on the Left Bank, near École Militaire) is the Y-shaped, glass-and-reinforced-concrete world headquarters of the United Nations Educational, Scientific and Cultural Organization and is among the most imaginative pieces of contemporary architecture in France. Certainly no modern building in Paris surpasses it, as regards both its own design and the caliber of the works of art decorating it. It was a joint international collaboration, and there are pieces by Picasso, Mexico's Tamayo, Japan's Isamu Noguchi, and America's Alexander Calder, to name a few. Visitors are welcome.

SCHOLAR'S PARIS

Académie Française (23 Quai de Conti) is the august body founded in the seventeenth century by Cardinal Richelieu. It is best known for the French-language dictionary it has compiled and revised eight times over the centuries. But it is, as well, a body of 40 elected leaders from various fields of endeavor—engineering and diplomacy, as well as writing and painting. The academy's headquarters are in the Institut de France, a building only some decades younger. The Institut embraces half a dozen additional academies of various arts and sciences; one must make advance arrangements for admission. Rooms to see are the chambers in which the Académie Française and its fellow bodies deliberate and the Great Hall, where members of the academy are installed.

Bibliothèque Nationale (58 Rue Richelieu) occupies a substantial eighteenth-century complex, just behind Palais-Royal. A descendant of an earlier Royal Library, the National Library is at once a repository of books (some 7 million of them, including—like Washington's Library of Congress and London's British Museum Library—a copy of every new book printed in the country) and of rare old manuscripts, coins, and other antiquities. To see: short-term art exhibitions in the Mazarin Gallery and Salle Labrouste—the vast and exquisitely arched main *salle de lecture*, or reading room.

Going up is the state-of-the-art *Bibliothèque de France*, budgeted at a billion dollars when its construction was announced by the "builder president," François Mitterrand. Location is Tolbiac, in southeastern Paris not far from the also-new Ministère des Finances, the government department for which a new headquarters was built when it was forced to move from a wing in the old Louvre Palace that has been taken over by the Louvre Museum. Happily, lovely old Bibliothèque Nationale remains in operation, as a repository for books published before 1945; books that have appeared since that year will be stored in the new library.

École Militaire (Place Joffre)—on the Left Bank and separated from the Eiffel Tower by the broad, formal expanse of green called Champ-de-Mars—albeit deteriorating when last I passed by, is no longer the military academy founded by Louis XV in the eighteenth century, with one Napoleon Bonaparte among its alumni. Still, this symmetrical complex is among the more eye-filling of Paris and includes a chapel, as well as other areas that may be viewed only upon application.

La Sorbonne (Rue des Écoles) is the University of Paris. It is France's preeminent university and, academically, one of the great ones of the world, which is not to say that it is without the scruffy look that is inevitable in so aged and overtrafficked a facility. Location is Left Bank, between the Cluny Museum and the Panthéon. If you are tempted to enter, as many visitors are, on Place de la Sorbonne, don't. The gate you want is on Rue des Écoles, around the corner. There's a concierge there, and I suggest you request that someone lead you to the classical-style seventeenth-century University Church (it is usually kept locked) and the Main Hall. Otherwise, the university is a largely non-descript, mostly nineteenth-century maze of classroom and lab blocks interspersed by student-filled courtyards, their entrance passages adorned with the myriad bulletin boards that no university—in any land—can apparently survive without. Almost next door, on Rue St.-Jacques, is the *Collège de France*, whose roots go back to the Middle Ages and which functions today as an exclusive center of research, not unlike the Institute for Advanced Study in Princeton. Some distance away, at the Left Bank's extreme edge fronting Montsouris Park, is the remarkable *Cité Universitaire*, a campus full of dormitories—more than 35—housing 7,000 Sorbonne students. There is an International House, not unlike the similarly named dorm at New York's Columbia University, but a good many of the halls are for students of a single country. The grounds are green, extensive, and attractive, and the buildings—dating from the 1920s to the present—comprise an architecturally diverse melange.

GRANDS TRAVAUX: LATE TWENTIETH-CENTURY PARIS

The presidency of Socialist President François Mitterrand was expected to effect changes in the operation of government, national through to regions and departments. And so, to an extent, it did. Although not so much that the visitor from abroad would notice. What the visitors to Paris *do*, however, encounter, in the decade constituting the eve of the twenty-first century, is a network of major construction projects which, given the caliber of design, boldness and imagination, has caused the rest of the world to take notice—considerable notice.

Les Grands Travaux have not come about without criticism, mostly, albeit not entirely, French. Not a few citizens of the republic have objected when architects have been foreign, rather than French. (I must say that they have a point. If it's the greater glory of France that's the *raison d'ê-tre*, why not have it realized by French brainpower?) Not a few non-French Paris enthusiasts have joined a substantial number of Parisians and fellow French in criticism of the most ambitious of the new constructions—a giant American-designed pyramidal structure that serves as entrance to the Louvre, emerging as a kind of sore thumb (in objector's opinions) from a core-of-Paris garden none of whose traditional architecture is newer than the nineteenth century.

Immediately after it was announced, in the late 1980s, there were outcries against a planned new Bibliothèque de France to augment Paris's admittedly aged and outdated but lovely Bibliothèque Nationale (above). Conversion of the long-disused Orsay train station into a museum of nineteenth-century art whose anchor is the painting collection of the now out-of-business Musée du Jeu de Paume, has met mostly with public approbation—but not entirely. The Grande Arche, completed in time for a 1989 meeting of leaders of Western summit nations, appears to be quite—if not entirely—universally admired. La Villette, an away-from-the-center complex—too distant for foreign visitors—remains terra incognita for most non-French who come to town, despite its attributes.

And l'Institut du Monde Arabe, a Franco-Arab cultural center on the Left Bank, remains underappreciated—as one of the great new buildings in Europe. Which leaves still another controversial building: the Canadian-designed Opéra de Paris/Bastille, on a historic square nobody had paid much attention to since the Revolution.

There are naysayers with respect to its contemporary design (an opera house without chandeliers!) and the transfer to it of the Opéra de Paris from its Belle Époque quarters on Place de l'Opéra—now the seat only of Ballet de l'Opéra and visiting dance troupes. Today's visitor—if he or she is a repeater—may or may not like these aspects of the new Paris. The first-timer—without memories clouding his or her objectivity—is likely to be fascinated with these departures from the norm. There is, after all, no logical reason the metropolis of a great nation should not evolve from stereotypes implanted by earlier architects, designers, rulers, painters, and writers into an innovative world capital leading—not nostalgically following—into the twenty-first century.

Of the buildings often included in the Grands Travaux category, I place three of those in operation elsewhere in this book. The enlarged *Louvre,* officially part of a project labeled Grand Louvre, is included in the section Choice Destinations, or the Essential Paris. *Musée d'Orsay* is a part of the section headed Museumgoer's Paris: After the Louvre and the Cluny. *Opéra de Paris/Bastille* is in the chapter Paris to Watch. Here are the others:

Grande Arche de la Défense (Parvis de la Défense): When construction began in the late sixties (completed in the late eighties), not a pleasure visitor of my acquaintance bothered with an excursion west of the center to the clutch of sleek office towers embracing a new Buck Rogers-like area called La Défense. The attitude amongst foreigners, especially those from across the Atlantic, was that we have our share of skyscrapers at home. Fair enough. Then, though, in the spring of 1989, word spread that the structure built to serve as an anchor for the complex would be completed in time for a Western summit meeting in conjunction with observance of the two hundredth anniversary of the

French Revolution. And so it was. A steady stream of visitors—ever since—has been a consequence.

No one appears disappointed, certainly not me. I was fascinated, to start, with the business complex—devoid of motor transport, La Défense is a station on the R.E.R. underground network. Interesting buildings line its main Esplanade—including that of IBM, with its elegantly positioned mass of windows; imposing Tour Fiat; and headquarters of such firms as Mobil, Rhone-Poulenc, Hoechst-France—a total of forty towers, housing 55,000 workers and an underground shopping mall, Les Quatre Temps, that's one of France's largest.

Still, when all is said and done, it's the *Arche* and its observation space, or *belvédère*, that knocks your socks off. The late architect Johann Otto von Spreckelsen (who died of cancer before the building opened) created a quite marvelous 35-story, white-marble-surfaced cube with sides nearly 330 feet long, an inside space—into which the Cathedral of Notre-Dame would fit—which is 230 feet wide and just under 300 feet high. Positioning is in the axis that unites the Louvre, Place de la Concorde, and the Arc de Triomphe with this new masterwork. You'll see what I mean when you ascend the fabulous free-standing glass elevators for a supreme Paris vista.

Institut du Monde Arabe (23 Quai St.-Bernard at Rue des Fosses St.-Bernard) is the Left Bank's sleeper—arguably one of the most outstanding contemporary buildings in Europe, edging the Seine, at Pont de Sully, with Île St.-Louis just opposite. A joint project of France and twenty-two Arab nations, it pays tribute, through its museum, library, and special-events calendar, to Arab culture and Franco-Arab amity. The Arab World Institute (often simply IMA, its initials in the French language) was designed by Jean Nouvel, a justifiably celebrated French architect, in collaboration with Pierre Soria, Gilbert Lezenes, and a firm called Architecture Studio. We are all in their debt.

You want to peruse the museum at the institute. Occupying five floors, its exhibits are mostly from the rich stores of Arab art—ceramics, metal objects, decorative works—of the Louvre, from which they are on permanent loan, along with treasures from other museums, including Arts Décoratifs. But you go to IMA principally to take in its architectural beauty. Single most breathtaking aspect is an entire facade whose windows appear as moving metallic mosaics, their intricate parts' constant openings and closings ingeniously regulated by photoelectric cells in accordance with the available light.

But detailing throughout is extraordinary—a mass of stairways, as if out of a child's metal construction set, is set against glass walls. Another floor's windows are offset, within, by a network of severe metallic pillars. Decorative, pipelike balconies create still another facade. Volumes of the 40,000-book library are stored on circular shelves of a transparent tower, with readers' chairs and tables made of designed-for-the-library aluminum. The staff—mostly young Arab women in Western dress who speak fluent French if not English—smiles. Views, from the institute's northern bank, of the Right Bank (especially from the terrace of the restaurant) are brilliant. But that is as it should be; this is a brilliant building.

La Villette (Avenue Corentin-Cariou, northeast of Gare du Nord and between Porte de Pantin and Porte de la Villette Métro stations): To term La Villette a multipurpose 136-acre park is to understate. Evolving over the last decade and planned by a number of talented architects, it is based on a onetime meatpacking, and it's ringed by a no-two-alike network of modular constructions—the lot painted in bright red enamel—some of them restaurants, cafés, or bars, one a belvedere with an observation platform, another for children's play, another a computer station. Called Les Folies, these are the work of Bernard Tschumi, chief La Villette architect. But there's more: the immense Grande Halle, a site for concerts and variety and trade shows; La Géode, an extraordinary spherical cinema surfaced with mirrorlike stainless steel, and Le Zénith, a concert hall with the appearance of a handful of giant connected balloons—and a capacity of 6,400. Cité des Sciences et de l'Industrie—a seven-and-a-half acre mix of museum exhibits and special shows about science packs in kids (adults are also welcome!)—and is illuminated by a pair of mobile cupolas controlled by a computer, with its interior a marvelous meld of steel and glass and the movement of centrally situated escalators. Cité de la Musique, La Villette's newest component part, lies beneath a roof of undulating curves and is home to France's National Music Conservatory, with a large open-to-the-public concert hall and a viewable collection of musical instruments.

VERDANT PARIS

Bois de Boulogne is not very far from Arc de Triomphe, at the city's western flank. It is bordered by good residential neighborhoods, and within its 2,500 acres are a multitude of attractions. There are a pair of racetracks—better-known Longchamp (the noted Grand Prix de Paris is an annual spring event—France's answer to Britain's Ascot) and Auteuil, a steeplechase track. There are, as well, a lake for rowboating; Jardin d'Acclimatation, which is at once amusement park (with a Paris-traditional marionette theater *pour les enfants*) and zoo; riding trails; picnic glades; ultramodern Musée National des Arts et Traditions Populaires (below); and, not surprisingly, good restaurants.

Bois de Vincennes fringes eastern Paris. Its landmark and namesake is earlier-described Château de Vincennes, but it has other lures; most recent is Jardin Floral, a broad expanse of gardens encircling a central lake. There's a restaurant-café and display areas for special exhibitions as well as something called the Exotarium (what does the Académie Française think of that word?), with displays of tropical fish and reptiles. Better known and more fun is the park's big zoo, which is No. 1 in France and, like many of its contemporary counterparts around the world, has its residents living cageless lives in open terrain.

Champ-de-Mars is the front yard of École Militaire, or the backyard of the Eiffel Tower, whichever you prefer. Begun in the eighteenth century, along with the military school, this so-called Field of Mars is a formal garden in the French tradition. Proportions are extravagant; its fountains, arbors, benches, and paths are inviting. It's pleasant for a stroll in conjunction with an Eiffel Tower visit or a morning or afternoon at the Palais de Chaillot museums, just across the Seine.

Jardin du Luxembourg, the Left Bank's favorite playground, takes the name of the earlier-described palace originally built for Queen Marie de Médicis in the seventeenth century. Not all of the park's 60 acres are as formally Franco-Italian as they were when it was laid out, but there are still a central allée; a great fountain; vivid, carefully manicured patches of flowers; and a popular marionette show, Théâtre du Luxembourg.

Jardin des Plantes (57 Rue Cuvier): I first visited the Jardin des Plantes when I had time to kill before departing on a train from nearby Gare d'Austerlitz, way at the eastern end of the Left Bank. This is at once a spacious and beautiful botanical garden and a zoo, with the latter—elephants, lions, tigers, and monkeys are resident—perhaps more diverting than the former. The whole complex is an agreeable way to brush elbows, on a balmy day, with Paris at its leisure.

Jardin des Tuileries: Until the inappropriate placement, in 1989, of a 71-foot-high glass and steel pyramid in Cour Napoléon—over the subterranean entrance to the Musée du Louvre (above)—the Tuileries Gardens constituted an architecturally cohesive essence of the city—big and bold and precise and elegant and ravishing in their beauty. Even with the addition of the jarring modern pyramid, the siting remains matchless, with water of the Seine on the south, arcades of Rue de Rivoli on the north, Louvre Palace to the east, and Arc de Triomphe perfectly aligned with smaller Arc du Carrousel to the west. The gardens were begun in the sixteenth century by Queen Catherine de Médicis, but the great Le Nôtre—of Vaux le Vicomte and Versailles—redesigned them a century later. With their reflecting pools, sculpture, clipped lawns, and brilliant, multicolored flowerbeds, they cry out for walks—to remove the kinks, say, of a long Louvre afternoon or an expensive morning in the shops. And there are the youngsters to be observed, sailing bathtub-boats in a great circle of a pond, watching Guignol and Gnafron in a marionette show, or cavorting on gaily painted merry-go-round chargers.

ECCLESIASTICAL PARIS: BEYOND NOTRE-DAME

Chapelle Expiatoire (Square Louis XVI, off Boulevard Haussmann, near Place St.-Augustin): With the Bourbon Restoration, King Louis XVIII moved the bodies of his ancestors, Louis XVI and Marie-Antoinette, from a Paris cemetery to Basilica of St.-Denis, on the outskirts of town. To mark the site of their city resting place, he began erection of this severe neoclassic chapel; it was completed by

Charles X. Under its dome are somewhat fanciful statues of Louis XVI and his Austrian wife. Setting is an engaging little park, whose benches are frequented by neighborhood locals. Go at midday and savor the delicious odors of lunch being cooked by the wife of the concierge in their apartment adjacent to the ticket office.

Notre-Dame-des-Victoires (Place des Petits-Pères, a couple of steps north of Place des Victoires) fronts a minisquare bearing the nickname of the Augustinian monks whose monastery was, in centuries past, adjacent to it. This is an imposing baroque building that goes back to the reign of Louis XIII, who ordered its construction and who is portrayed in one of the half-dozen-odd paintings by Van Loo, within. The many thousands of ex-votos you'll note affixed to walls are souvenirs left by the faithful in the course of pilgrimages to the Virgin Mary, annual events in the church since 1836.

St.-Augustin (Place St.-Augustin, not far north of Place de la Madeleine) is included here for much the same reason as Église Polonaise—the Polish Church; lots of visitors pass by and are curious. St.-Augustin is mid-nineteenth century, and its exterior—with an oversized central dome surrounded by four towers—makes the interior anticlimatic.

Ste.-Chapelle (Île de la Cité), after Notre-Dame, is the most important church in town. Tucked into the vast Palais de Justice complex, it is a thirteenth-century masterwork built by Louis IX—later St. Louis. The slimness and elegance of its exterior proportions would be enough to make it a standout for the centuries, but its immense stained-glass windows are easily the finest in Paris and among the best in Europe. I only wish it did not close for lunch and, moreover, that there were no admission charge for what is, stained glass or no, a place of worship.

St.-Denis, 10 miles north of town on Route A1, is much-restored Romanesque. The present basilica was built in the twelfth century, but five centuries before, in an earlier St.-Denis, Dagobert I became the first of a long line of French monarchs to be accorded a St.-Denis burial. Since he was interred there, every one of his successors has been, save a few monarchs of the medieval Capetian dynasty and successors to the post-Napoleonic era's Louis XVIII—Charles X, Louis-Philippe, and Napoleon III. The solitude of the St.-Denis crypts was interrupted by the Revolution, when coffins were removed and remains within unceremoniously disposed of. Tombs themselves were saved, though, and later returned. One sees them today empty but hardly unimpressive. They total 79—kings, queens, princes, and princesses.

St.-Étienne-du-Mont (Place Ste.-Geneviève and Rue Clovis, near the Panthéon, on the Left Bank) is very important to Paris, for it contains a shrine to Sainte Geneviève, the city's patron saint. Beyond that, however, it is an exceptional Gothic structure, with the only rood screen of any church in town, handsome vaulting, fine stained glass, and splendid proportions.

St.-Eustache (Rue du Jour) is a welcome and familiar landmark of yesteryear in the Halles quarter, for long the produce center of town until those operations were removed to the drearily dull Rungis sector, beyond the city, and the market was largely replaced by a stark and forbidding shopping mall. St.-Eustache is big and beautiful, a meld of Gothic and Renaissance, with a rich history and an equally rich decor. Ceilings are high, with fine vaulting and elaborate columns in support. Much of the stained glass is good, and there are side chapels, one with a painting by Rubens.

St.-Germain-l'Auxerrois (Place du Louvre) is so overshadowed by its across-the-street neighbor, the Louvre, that it is more often than not ignored. This is a Gothic church that is among the loveliest in the city, which is not surprising when one considers that it had been the parish church of the Royal Family during periods when the Louvre was a royal residence. Bits and pieces of it are Romanesque and Renaissance, but it is essentially Gothic, with a pair of rose windows of that era and a handsome choir. Like St.-Eustache, this church is noted for its concerts.

St.-Germain-des-Prés (Boulevard St.-Germain at Rue Bonaparte) goes all the way back to the sixth century, but is mostly more recent; the bulk of it is eleventh-century. Within, the Gothic sanctuary and choir are attractive, even if the unfortunate late nineteenth-century stained glass is not. This church's concerts are of high caliber.

St.-Gervais (Place St.-Gervais, behind Hôtel de Ville, in the Marais) rather oddly combines a Gothic interior with a baroque facade—and gets away with it. There are surprises within—a long and beautiful nave, art objects, an organ said to be the oldest in Paris, and lovely glass vaulting. But it's open-hours that make this church especially distinctive. Though barely illuminated (candles, mostly), it welcomes visitors well into the evening; since 1975 it has been operated by resident contemplative orders of monks and nuns.

St.-Julien-le-Pauvre (Rue St.-Julien-le-Pauvre, on the Left Bank) is so literally in the shadow of Notre-Dame that you find yourself sitting in its garden to have a look at Big Brother; from nowhere is Notre-Dame seen in finer perspective. From still another angle, the view is of nearby St.-Séverin Church, later described. But you must go inside St.-Julien-le-Pauvre; it is a millennium old, with a

high, high nave, and an unusual-for-Paris inconostasis
(the church is Malachite, an Eastern rite), from which hang
paintings of saints and over which is suspended a great
cross. Go for the Sunday morning service to hear the first-
rate choir and smell the incense.

St.-Louis-en-l'Île (Rue St.-Louis-en-l'Île, Île St.-Louis) is a
richly embellished Renaissance church, with a slim steeple
and—of interest if you are from Missouri—a tablet from
that state's St. Louisans paying tribute to the American
city's namesake.

La Madeleine (Place de la Madeleine) is an enormous, late
eighteenth-century neoclassic landmark that started out to
be all manner of things, none of them a place of worship,
and was almost a railroad station before the final decision
was reached (one of the few we hear about, of the reign of
Louis XVIII). It is the scene today of *haut monde* weddings.
There are flower stalls in the surrounding square, whose
food shops are in many ways more inviting than the austere interior of this church.

St.-Merri (Rue St.-Martin, just north of Tour St.-Jacques,
near Hôtel de Ville) is an opulent Gothic church that has
known some unfortunate tampering over the centuries,
but there are the stained-glass windows, handsome vaulting, and a honey of a choir.

St.-Nicolas-des-Champs (Rue St.-Martin, near Place de la
République) is about 900 years old and holding up very
well, thank you. The interior appears a beautiful sea of pillars, and there are lots of paintings. While you are about it,
go next door and visit *St.-Martin-des-Champs*, smaller,
equally venerable, and reminiscent only in name of the
considerably more recent St. Martin-in-the-Fields, on London's Trafalgar Square.

St.-Nicolas-de-Chardonnet (Rue des Bernardins, just off Boulevard St.-Germain) is essentially late Renaissance, with a good deal of charm and exemplary paintings. It's rather a nice contrast to the cafés of St.-Germain when you're exploring the neighborhood.

St.-Philippe-de-Roule (Rue du Faubourg St.-Honoré at Place Chassaigne-Goyon) is included here only because you might well pass it in the course of shopping the Faubourg St.-Honoré. The church is originally late eighteenth century—neoclassic, with a colonnaded portico that is at least as meritorious as any of the architectural or decorative aspects within.

St.-Pierre-de-Montmartre (Place du Tertre) is just the aesthetic relief you are looking for after a pilgrimage to Sacré-Coeur, its near-neighbor way up in the mountains of Montmartre. St.-Pierre is the genuine architectural article—Gothic, with bits and pieces that are even older Romanesque. This church goes back to the twelfth century, so that whoever was inspired to implant striking contemporary stained glass in its windows had courage. And taste: the combination is pleasing.

Église Polonaise (Place Maurice Barrès at Rue St.-Honoré) is a domed, Italianate-looking structure that shoppers frequently pass by and are curious about. It is seventeenth-century and not nearly as impressive inside as out, despite frescoes lining its dome. The name derives from the national origin of most parishioners—Polish—in which language Masses are said.

St.-Roch (269 Rue St.-Honoré) is here included, first because it is in the heart of tourist Paris, and you might want to know what's inside. Second, its priests say Masses in

English. This is a beauty of a baroque church, with fine sculptures and paintings.

Sacré-Cœur (Square Willette, Montmartre): The world is full of churches built as acts of thanksgiving to God. Sacré-Cœur is quite the opposite: It was conceived as an act of contrition after France's emergence as the loser in the Franco-Prussian War, which was such a disaster that it led to the abdication of Napoleon III. It was not, however, until after still another conflict, World War I, that this enormous basilica finally opened. There is little one can appreciate as regards its aesthetics. The best that can be said for it is that its white domed facade and its high Montmartre elevation make it stand out as a landmark of the Paris skyline, and that the view from its dome is excellent.

St.-Séverin (Rue des Prêtres-St.-Séverin) is a near-neighbor of earlier recommended St.-Julien-le-Pauvre, on the Left Bank. You begin liking St.-Séverin because of the garden that sets off its substantial Romanesque facade so well. And you like what you see inside, too: a mostly Gothic church of fine proportions and detailing not the least of which are the stained glass and the unusually capacious, strikingly decorated area behind the altar.

Église de la Sorbonne (Rue des Écoles) is the University of Paris chapel and the only one of its buildings that is quite as it was when Cardinal Richelieu had it constructed four centuries ago. It contains the cardinal's tomb. Get the key from the concierge inside the gate on Rue des Écoles.

St.-Sulpice (Place St.-Sulpice, between Palais du Luxembourg and Boulevard St.-Germain) is still another Left Bank standout, with ancient origins, but with baroque rebuilding, a twin-tower facade, and an absolutely immense interior, full of splendid art and artisanship, mostly eighteenth-century. The surprise, in one of the chapels, is a clutch of mid-nineteenth-century murals by Delacroix.

Val-de-Grace (Rue du Val-de-Grace at Place Alphonse-Laurent, near Boulevard du Montparnasse) had its origins with Anne of Austria, mother of Louis XIV. She ordered it built (it is domed baroque and so Italian that you pinch yourself to make sure you are not in Rome) after giving birth to her son, having been unable to conceive during the first twenty-three years of her marriage. Young Louis laid the cornerstone when he was still a tot, in 1641. The Italian motif continues within, with a St. Peter's-like baldachin—twisted columns and all—sheltering the altar. Then look up: The inside of the great dome is frescoed.

Some non-Catholic places of worship: American Cathedral, Avenue George V; *American Church of Paris,* Quai d'Orsay; *British Embassy Church* (Anglican), 6 Rue d'Aguesseau, near the embassy on Rue du Faubourg St.-Honoré; *Église Grecque* (Greek Orthodox), 5 Rue Georges-Bizet; *Église Russe* (Russian Orthodox), Rue Daru; *Institut Musulman et Mosquée* (Moslem—and in beautiful Moroccan style, with a pretty inner courtyard that is worth inspecting), Place du Puits-de-l'Ermite; *Temple Israélite* (known also as Synagogue Rothschild—for its benefactors), 44 Rue de la Victoire; *Temple Protestant de l'Oratoire,* 147 Rue St.-Honoré; *Temple Protestant de Ste.-Marie,* 17 Rue St.-Antoine.

MUSEUMGOER'S PARIS: AFTER THE LOUVRE AND THE CLUNY

Atelier de la Manufacture Nationale des Gobelins, de Beauvais et de la Savonnerie (42 Avenue des Gobelins) has royal origins—Louis XIV, to be precise, who appointed the Versailles designer-decorator-artist, Charles Le Brun, as its head. Ever since, skilled artisans have been at work, one generation after the other, laboriously, slowly, and tediously creating tapestries that represent the time-honored techniques of their forebears. And there are completed specimens of their work displayed, museum-style.

Centre International de l'Automobile (Porte de Pantin) is Paris's car museum. There are 120 significant models on display at any given time, with a vast change every six months—vintage Buggatis, Delahayes, and Ferraris typical. Near La Villette (see Grands Travaux, above).

Centre National d'Art et de Culture Georges Pompidou, a.k.a. Le Beaubourg (Rue Beaubourg): Ask Parisian friends for an opinion, and by and large they mostly appear no happier with the look of the Beaubourg—a brutally stark, six-level rectangle of unadorned glass and steel that is positively aggressive in its oil-refinery ugliness—than with its location. Opened in 1976, it's on the site of razed buildings in the beloved ex-produce center of Les Halles, adjacent to the Hôtel de Ville, the city hall. Still, in the company of foreign and provincial-French visitors, locals mob the center's stadium-sized lobby-cum-bookshop, whose only decoration is a stylized portrait of the late president for whom it is named. As many as 25,000 visitors per day queue to ride its messy, glass-enclosed exterior escalators (similar to—but not as frequently cleaned, it would appear—as those at De Gaulle Airport) to the fourth-level exhibition area, wherein are hung contents of *Musée National d'Art Moderne*—the national modern art museum for long housed in what is now dubbed Musée du Palais de Tokyo (below). This area of the Beaubourg proved to be so aesthetically unsuccessful as an exhibit space that it was subjected to a major redesign in 1985, for which, praise be! On display at all times are a thousand works out of a total of 20,000 by some 3,000 artists. This is an undeniably outstanding collection, by contemporary greats like Picasso,

Bonnard, Braque, Vlaminck, Rouault, Gris, Modigliani, Chagall, Kandinsky, Matisse, Mondrian, Magritte, Duchamp, Klee, and Brancusi, with solid American representation including works by Stella, De Kooning, Pollock, Rauschenburg, and Calder. Work—some of it massive—by contemporary French artists occupies main-floor galleries. There's an eternally jammed café on the top level (affording views of Notre-Dame and the next-door Church of St.-Merri); and street entertainers perform frequently in the broad square outside, called La Piazza.

Cité des Sciences et de l'Industrie at La Villette: See Grands-Travaux: Late Twentieth-Century Paris, above.

Galeries Nationales du Grand-Palais (Avenue de Selves, off Champs-Élysées, near Place de la Concorde): The Grand-Palais, with its neighbor, the Petit-Palais, are among the more maligned of Paris's public buildings, at least architecturally. I would surely rather have them than what might well go up today in their place, the Beaubourg (above), for example. They are relics of a turn-of-century world's fair, and I like their monumental scale. The Grand-Palais is put to intelligent use for special exhibitions, frequently world-class and arranged with skill and imagination. Consult papers for the current show.

Maison de Victor Hugo (6 Place des Vosges, in the Marais district): Memories of Charles Laughton as the *jongleur* of Notre-Dame notwithstanding, this seventeenth-century house, inhabited by Victor Hugo between 1821 and 1848, should be of interest, if only for its advanced age, inspired Place des Vosges situation, and sumptuously furnished rooms. But there are bonuses—manuscripts of the author's works, letters, pictures, and all manner of Hugo memorabilia.

Musée d'Art Moderne de la Ville de Paris (11 Avenue du Président Wilson) is the next-door neighbor of Musée du Palais de Tokyo (below) and, like it, attractive Art Deco. (They are wings of a building constructed for the Paris Exhibition of 1937.) In the old days, when the Tokyo housed the national modern art collection (now at the Beaubourg, above), visitors took in both at a single clip. Contemporarily, this excellent city-owned cache is not as appreciated as it might be. Matisse, Dufy, and Sonia and Robert Delauney are but a quartet of painters in the permanent collection, and there are frequent temporary exhibitions.

Musée des Arts Africains et Océaniens (293 Avenue Daumesnil) is well worth the longish Métro ride. Housed in a thirties-modern pavilion is a sumptuous collection that the French—always appreciative of the cultures of peoples whom they governed during the days of empire—acquired during the colonial period. The African masks, headdresses, and other ceremonial pieces are among the finest extant.

Musée des Arts Décoratifs (107 Rue de Rivoli, in the separately entered Marsan Pavilion of the Louvre complex)—closed for a major refurbishing for a full two years before reopening in 1985—does justice to the Catherine de Médicis-era palace it occupies. There are four treasure-filled floors of exhibits relating to the arts of decoration—a fifteenth-century wood canopied bed from Auvergne; the collapsible desk that traveled with Napoleon in the field, with lines so clean it could have been designed at the end of the twentieth century instead of the end of the eighteenth; and chairs of the three Louis periods, so that once and for all—if this trio of styles confuses you—you can sort them out to your satisfaction. There are, as well, porcelains, silver, jewelry, tapestries, sculpture, and painting—from Asia, as well as from Europe. Best of all, though, are the period rooms. They evoke the look of French interiors from the seventeenth century through Art Deco of the twentieth, with the boudoir and bath of couturière Jeanne Lanvin an especial dazzler. Along with London's Victoria and Albert and Copenhagen's Decorative Arts, this is one of the Continent's great repositories relating to the decorative arts, well complemented by French counterparts in Bordeaux, Lyon, and Marseille. There's a bookstore and a shop selling pricey reproductions of museum objects.

Musée des Arts de la Mode (107 Rue de Rivoli—on different floors of the building also sheltering the Musée des Arts Décoratifs, above) opened in 1986, half a decade after the French government budgeted the equivalent of $5 million for its creation. The museum's collection comprises several thousand articles of clothing, accessories, and fashion designs on paper, with the span eighteenth century through to this very moment, and including costumes worn by personages as disparate as Sarah Bernhardt, Empress Eugénie, and Brigitte Bardot. There are nearly a hundred dresses by Elsa Schiaperelli and half that many by Paul Poiret. Selections, arranged thematically as exhibitions that extend over some months, are on view in galleries extending from the building's fifth through ninth floors. Not surprisingly, there's a shop featuring fashion accessories based on designs from the collection. Two fashion museums in the world's fashion capital is not too many; this national repository nicely complements the City of Paris's Musée de la Mode et du Costume (below).

Musée National des Arts et Traditions Populaires (6 Avenue du Mahatma-Gandhi, near the kids' Jardin d'Acclimatation in Bois de Boulogne) occupies striking modern quarters. Besides sections on French folk and other costumes, there are exhibits concerning literature, music, dance, theater, and farm and city life. Objects on display are old and contemporary, fine and folk, rare and commonplace: the French museum profession putting its boldest foot forward.

Musée Balzac (47 Rue Raynouard, in the Passy area, not far from Palais de Chaillot): Honoré de Balzac's novels had not been especially popular in the United States until a British dramatization of *La Cousine Bette* made its way across the water to American TV screens, sparking something of a renewal of interest in Balzac's extensive fictional series, *La Comédie Humaine,* a sharply delineated picture of French society during the reign of the bourgeois businessman king, Louis-Philippe, in the mid-nineteenth century. Balzac lived and wrote in this atmospheric house for nearly two decades.

Musée Carnavalet (23 Rue de Sévigné)—earlier recommended as a major monument of the Marais district—is the museum of the history of Paris, one of a number operated by the city government with great finesse. Its main building—the splendid sixteenth-century mansion of no less a personality than Madame de Sévigné, where she wrote her famous letters of social commentary—was supplemented, in time for the two hundredth anniversary of the French Revolution in 1989—with a neighboring second building, the *hôtel particulier,* or mansion, called Peletier de St.-Fargeau, with which it is connected by a passage (up a flight from the street). The addition doubles the Carnavalet's space, with pre-Revolutionary Paris in the first building, post-Revolutionary Paris (with a dozen fascinating galleries devoted to the years of the Revolution) in the addition, continuing with exhibits from the Consulat through to, say, last month. Choicest part of the museum is a group of rooms—the Henriette Vouvier Collection—furnished in the Louis XV and XVI styles of the eighteenth century. Elsewhere, you see what Paris was like in earlier eras, from specimens of citizens' clothes, documents, etchings, paintings, and all manner of bibelots—even including personal possessions left by Louis XVI and the extravagant Marie-Antoinette before they were beheaded. Take your time here, making sure to have a look around the oftenneglected courtyards and gardens; and not missing the noteworthy facades. Special.

Musée Cernuschi (7 Avenue Velásquez) is recommendable on three counts. First, its contents are Chinese works of art collected by a rich turn-of-century Parisian, who bequeathed them to the City of Paris, along with his house, to be utilized for their display. Second, the house itself is a mansion in the grand style, on a block of similarly opulent houses. And third, the museum is near a smallish park relatively unknown to visitors—*Parc Monceau*. On a sunny day, a walk here is a pleasurable Paris experience. Of the museum's exhibits, the most memorable is an enormous Japanese Buddha in bronze; it dominates the main gallery, whose other standouts include spectacular screens and ceramics, of which a very ancient and sad-looking pottery pig is particularly appealing.

Musée de la Chasse et de la Nature (60 Rue des Archives) occupies an *hôtel particulier* of especial grace in the Marais, and has been earlier recommended for that reason alone. As a museum, it is perhaps more limited in its appeal. Still, there is no denying the beauty of the paintings and tapestries—mostly eighteenth-century—of hounds, with other hunting motifs, not to mention other art objects with the same theme. But it is the architecture of this house, its courtyard, and its interiors (be sure to go upstairs) that make it visit-worthy.

Musée Clemenceau (8 Rue Franklin, near Palais de Chaillot) is the apartment of Georges Clemenceau, who held the premiership of France immediately before and during World War I and whom we remember from history books as France's vocal representative—and an antagonist of President Wilson—at the Versailles Conference. The irony of Clemenceau is that he criticized Wilson because he considered the Wilson-inspired peace treaty too moderate to assure France's security; yet he was defeated in the postwar elections for being too mild in his attitude toward Germany. His apartment is hardly without interest, for this man was his country's most important early twentieth-century politician.

Musée Cognacq-Jay (25 Boulevard des Capucines): It is the location of this museum that makes it a sleeper. You just don't expect this sort of treasure trove to be located upstairs in an otherwise unexceptional building in the heart of the busy Grands Boulevards area. Downstairs, Parisians and their visitors go about their business. But within the confines of the Cognacq-Jay, the matter at hand is France's eighteenth century and its art—gift of the founder of the Samaritaine department store to the City of Paris. In a series of furnished rooms of the period, one finds some of the finest pieces of furniture and other objects of the era to be seen in Paris, with a bonus of paintings by such renowned masters as Fragonard, Chardin, Greuze, Boucher, Tiepolo, and Watteau. Special.

Musée Guimet (6 Place d'Iéna, off Avenue du Président Wilson, near Palais de Chaillot), severe and gloomy despite partial refurbishing, comes to life only when you concentrate on its collection. It embraces choice works not only from big countries—Indian sculpture, Chinese jade, Japanese scrolls—but from smaller lands, as well, with rare pieces from Indonesia, Cambodia, Korea, Nepal, and Tibet. Allow yourself time; this is a much bigger collection than, say, that of Musée Cernuschi (above).

Musée de l'Histoire de France (60 Rue Des Francs-Bourgeois III, in the Marais district) occupies the very grand and very beautiful Hôtel de Soubise (earlier described), whose interiors—a magnificent stairway and sumptuously decorated rooms—are in themselves reasons for a visit. But the subject matter of the museum—the history of the country as recorded in the National Archives' most precious documents, such as seals, treaties, manuscripts, and even marriage contracts—is absorbing on its own.

Musée de l'Homme (Palais de Chaillot, Place du Trocadéro) is the most important of the trio of Palais de Chaillot museums. The idea is to show us how anthropologists can dramatize the excitement of variations in the human condition. There are two floors of galleries. The Black African section is one of the better collections of African art and artifacts. There are Bambara headpieces from Mali, sculpture from Baoule in the Ivory Coast, and some of the finest bronzework of the ancient Benin civilization in Nigeria. There are fine North African pieces, as well—jewelry, metalwork, ceramics. See, too, galleries devoted to the folk art of Europe—a Lithuanian *St. George and the Dragon,* esoteric Swiss dance masks, processional figures from Flanders, and costumes from Iceland and Wales, Romania and Spain, Holland and Italy. There are, as well, exceptional works from India, Burma, Tibet—indeed, all of Asia—as well as the South Pacific, with a carved-wood Maori tomb from New Zealand. Surprises for North Americans are remarkable collections devoted to the folk art of the Indians and Eskimos of the New World.

Musée de l'Institut du Monde Arabe: See Grands Travaux: Late Twentieth-Century Paris, above.

Musée Jacquemart-André (158 Boulevard Haussmann, some blocks west of the big-domed Church of St.-Augustin) is still another example—along with others, like the Cernuschi, Cognacq-Jay, and Nissim de Camondo—of the legacy of a single wealthy Parisian family. In this case, founder-donors were a remarkable couple—Edouard André, son of a banker, and his wife, Nélie Jacquemart, a painter. They spent much of their life collecting antiques, with certain of them destined for their Boulevard Haussmann mansion. Monsieur André died in 1894, his wife in 1912, by which time the Haussmann house had become a repository of two types of art: eighteenth-century French and Italian Renaissance. House and collection were left to the Institut de France to be administered as a museum; Président Poincaré officiated at the opening in 1913. There are fabulous treasures here. Downstairs is mostly French, and upstairs is mostly Italian. French paintings alone are memorable, with works by Fragonard, Chardin, Prud'hon, and Greuze among them. Tapestries are rare and beautiful. Eighteenth-century furniture is choice, too. Uccello's *Saint George Slaying the Dragon* is perhaps the most celebrated of the Italian works. But there are pieces by Botticelli, Mantegna, Carpaccio, and Titian as well, with sculpture by Donatello, ceramics by Della Robbia, furniture, and accessories.

Musée National de la Légion d'Honneur et des Ordres de Chevalerie (2 Rue de Bellechasse): A special one, this, for history buffs. It tells the story not only of France's Legion of Honor and its various subdivisions, but of foreign orders of chivalry, as well. (More than 300,000 Frenchmen hold the Legion of Honor, while some 75,000 have been awarded the lesser Order of Merit.) Displays are not only of orders, medals, and ribbons. There are a considerable number of historic paintings, some good, some of historical interest; not to mention sculpture, etchings, drawings, and costumes. And the location is convenient: right opposite the Musée d'Orsay (below).

Musée de la Marine (Palais de Chaillot, Place du Trocadéro) offers perhaps more than a layperson can absorb on matters maritime. Still, going at one's own pace, judiciously skipping here and there, it makes for a diverting visit. Ship models of all eras and ages are minor treasures. There are decorative objects taken from old ships, not to mention paintings, drawings, documents, and flags, evoking the romance of the high seas during the presteam era. Other sections are devoted to later periods; models of the ill-fated, pre–World War II *Normandie* indicate what a masterwork that ship was.

Musée Marmottan (2 Rue Louis-Boilly) had always been a worthy enough destination—a fine home filled with the collection of its late owner, including Empire furniture and Renaissance tapestries. In later years, though, came two groups of paintings by Claude Monet. The second group was so large—sixty-five works—that a special subterranean gallery was built to house it, along with paintings by Monet's contemporaries, including Pissarro, Renoir, and Berthe Morisot. Subject matter is mostly the flowers for which this first of the Impressionists is celebrated, but there is a good deal else: a Trouville beach scene with Monet's wife and cousin, sunset in the harbor of Le Havre, a Tuileries landscape, and, in contrast, smoky Gare St.-Lazare. Among the second group of Monets are many of the water lilies painted at his Giverny home (later counseled as an excursion destination), as well as such diverse subjects as a Dutch tulip field and Rouen Cathedral. A brilliant collection.

Musée de la Mode et du Costume (10 Avenue Pierre 1er de Serbie, just off Place d'Iéna, south of Champs-Élysées) occupies a sumptuous Belle Époque town house that's the ideal foil for its celebrated temporary exhibitions—most extend over a period of some months—which are usually retrospectives of the great Paris-based couturiers, with the *œuvre* of the designers (Lucien Lelong and Pierre Balmain were relatively recent subjects, to give you an idea) displayed on mannequins chronologically, earliest clothes through to later models. Fashion buffs, in this preeminent fashion capital, will be happy here.

Musée de la Monnaie (11 Quai de Conti): You don't have to be a coin collector to enjoy this one, but it helps. For those of us who simply like to spend the stuff, the kicker is the setting—a splendid baroque mansion entered only after you pass through its Cour d'Honneur. Situation is riverfront, on the Left Bank. There are two floors of galleries with displays of French currency from the early Gauls onward, into our own era—at the end of the money trail on the upper floor.

Musée des Monuments Français (Palais de Chaillot, Place du Trocadéro) is an absolutely fabulous put-on; it is surely the only museum—serious museum, that is (I exclude waxworks)—that consists of nothing but fakes. Its exhibits are reproductions of sculpture and painting in the great cathedrals and churches of France. The main floor embraces one enormous arch, doorway, window frame, and saint-in-plaster after another. The museum is late nineteenth century, and the idea was to see it as a teaching tool for students who were unable to get around their country as easily as they can now to see monumental art and sculpture. Anyone who has traveled France will see favorites, Amiens to Vézelay.

Musée National de la Renaissance (Château d'Écouen, Écouen, not far north of Paris, via Métro to Porte de la

Chapelle station, thence via Bus No. 268-C) is a case of taking the city to the country. By that I mean that this double-winged castle, dating to the early sixteenth century—and one of the great Renaissance-era structures of northern France—was put to good use, starting in the 1970s, a decade after a school that had long occupied it moved to another site. The idea—well executed—was to restore it as a museum of Renaissance objects that had long been stored away in Musée de Cluny (The Essential Paris, above) for lack of display space. The ground floor looks once again as it might have when Catherine de Médicis accompanied her husband, King Henri II, on state visits. Completed only in 1988, Écouen's lures—aside from the great building itself—are frescoes surfacing a dozen massive ground-floor chimneys, their themes a mix of the biblical and mythological; a series of ten Brussels tapestries from the same era as the castle—they tell the story of David and Bathsheba—woven with gold and silver thread; and a series of painted leather smaller objects, clocks through locks. Closed for lunch.

Musée National des Techniques (292 Rue St.-Martin): A technology museum in an originally Gothic church complex? You bet. And that's what makes this oddball, oddly underappreciated museum (on scene since a priest founded it in the eighteenth century) so unusual. Exhibits are fun because they're so aged, with subject matter running from physics and optics to robots and turbines, and a mechanical puppet purported owned by Marie-Antoinette. Equally aged *Church of St.-Nicolas-des-Champs* is next door, with a lovely interior whose main altar painting is by the baroque master Simon Vouet. Note that the Techniques is traditionally open only in the afternoon from 1 to 5:30 P.M. on weekdays, longer on Sunday. Check in advance. Near Place de la République.

Musée Nissim de Camondo (63 Rue de Monceau, near Parc Monceau, northeast of the Arc de Triomphe) occupies the mansion—always beautiful, but with its interiors relatively recently restored and refurbished—of the parents of a young man who died while serving as a lieutenant in the French Air Force in World War I. His father and mother left the house as a museum in their son's memory. Though the structure itself is relatively modern, albeit in colonnaded Louis XVI style, interiors are of the eighteenth century. Aside from mostly Louis XVI furniture and accessories, there are exceptional paintings (Guardi, Oudry, Dupléssis, Vigée-Lebrun), gilded bronzework, porcelain, Beauvais and Aubusson tapestries. The most dazzling room is the rectangular Grand Salon—with gold and beige classic-style paneling and a suite of a dozen-odd chairs, all of whose seats are tapestry covered, and a blue-and-gray Savonnerie carpet. Special.

Musée de l'Orangerie des Tuileries (Place de la Concorde)— the elongated, classic-style pavilion at the western edge of the Tuileries—served for many years as the site of short-term exhibitions, much like the Grand-Palais (above). Recent seasons have seen it transformed—after a thorough refurbishing—into the repository of a brilliant collection bequeathed to the French government by Madame Jean Walter, who put it all together over a long period, in collaboration with her first husband, dealer-collector Paul Guillaume, and her second husband, a wealthy architect. It comprises 144 paintings covering the period beginning with the Impressionists and continuing through 1930, either by French nationalists or foreigners who worked in France. It is difficult to fault the collecting trio's taste. There are a full two dozen Renoirs, 14 Cézannes, a dozen Picassos, and almost as many Matisses and Utrillos, with even heavier representation of André Derain. Specifics? How about *Blonde à la Rose* by Renoir, *Odalisque à la Culotte Grise* by Matisse, *Pommes et Biscuits* by Cézanne, *Femmes au Chien* by Marie Laurencin, a Rousseau wedding party, the harbor of Argenteuil by Manet, and Chaim Soutine's *pâtissier*? Lovely.

Musée d'Orsay (Rue de Bellechasse) occupies the onetime main hall and adjacent hotel of Gare d'Orsay, the Seine-front railway station on the Left Bank that went up at the height of the Belle Époque era, in 1900. It came about as a consequence of a decision in the 1970s, when the administration of President Valéry Giscard d'Estaing—looking for a cultural project of consequence that would serve as a monument of the Giscard presidency, in the manner of President Pompidou's Centre Beaubourg and President Mitterrand's subterranean entry to the Louvre—earmarked the station as site of a museum of mid-nineteenth to early twentieth-century art, spanning the period 1848 to 1914. The idea was to transfer exhibits of that era from the overcrowded Louvre and its dependencies, and obtain still other works from other French museums. The space is magnificent and monumental: a 453-foot-long room, barrel-vaulted, glass-roofed, and comprising three exhibit levels created in the refurbishing by a team of six French government–commissioned architects. Exhibits run a broad and beautiful gamut. Take your time at the Orsay, allowing a good half day. Stars of the Orsay show are great Impressionist paintings that had long been exhibited at Galerie du Jeu de Paume in the Tuileries and now are on display in galleries on the top—or third—floor. They include a Van Gogh self-portrait, Renoir's *Le Moulin de la Galette*, Manet's *Déjeuner sur l'Herbe*, Monet's *Rouen Cathedral* and *Tour d'Abane*, Pissaro's *Red Roofs*, Cézanne's *The Blue Vase*, and paintings, as well, by Gauguin, Sisley, Toulouse-Lautrec, Mary Cassatt, Rousseau, and Degas—to name some. Post-Impressionists like Suerat, Signac, and Henri-Edmond Cross are on hand, too, as well as Bonnard and

Vuillard. But there are also sculpture, graphics, posters, and photographs, with architecture and applied arts of the era represented. The range is a 1901 dining room, magnificently paneled, through to Maillol sculpture. To note are such decorative dazzlers of the original station complex as a spectacular waiting-room clock (use it as a landmark as you move about to help from getting lost—it's on the Rue de Bellechasse wall) and the frescoed ceiling of the hotel dining room—now the main museum restaurant and evaluated on a subsequent page—which is supplemented by a terraced café. Sequence? The museum suggests you start with Second Empire displays on the ground floor (don't miss the detailed scale model of Opéra Garnier), moving then via hard-to-find escalators to the top-floor paintings, concluding with art nouveau—among much else—on the second level. Bravo, Orsay!

Musée du Palais de Tokyo (13 Avenue du Président Wilson): Paris visitors who first knew the city some years back and have pleasant memories of the old Musée National d'Art Moderne will recognize this pleasing Art Deco structure. Alas, when much of the building's collection was transferred to the harsh quarters of the Centre Pompidou (above), authorities rechristened this building and displayed a cache of works long in storage. Works by Paul Signac and Henri-Edmond Cross and a goodly group of paintings by Vuillard are among them. These are all on the main floor. But don't leave without a trip to the basement, chock-full of masterworks by the likes of Braque, Picasso, Rouault, and Henri Laurent, whose original donors forbade their being transferred to the Beaubourg.

Musée Picasso (5 Rue de Thorigny): Picasso is hardly a stranger to museums in Paris or the French provinces, for that matter; indeed, the château where he once lived in Antibes, on the Riviera (see *France at Its Best*), displays a

choice cache of his output. And Museo Picasso in Barcelona (see *Spain at Its Best*), with more than a thousand of
his works, embraces major Picasso periods. Still, Paris's
Musée Picasso, opened in late 1985, is hardly to be ignored. Occupying space in Hôtel Salé, an opulent
seventeenth-century mansion in the Marais quarter, which
has been brilliantly restored (and which is not without an
interesting history, having served variously as the Venetian
Embassy and as the residence of archbishops of Paris), the
museum's nucleus is an extraordinary collection of works
from Picasso's estate. It embraces well over 300 of his paintings and sculptures (a riveting 1901 self-portrait is the museum's trademark, but there are memorable works from
principal Picasso periods, including *Les Deux Frères* [1906],
Violon [1915], *La Flûte de Pan* [1923], *Tête de Femme* [1931],
L'Homme au Mouton [1943], and *Vieil Homme Assis* [1971—
two years before his death]), some 3,000 drawings and
prints, as well as ceramics and paper collages. On display,
too, is a clutch of paintings by other masters that Picasso
had collected—Seurat, Cézanne, Degas, Matisse, Derain,
and Rousseau among them. You go as much for the
setting—sculpture-embellished facades, courtyard, grand
stairway, splendidly stuccoed Salon de Jupiter, wrought-
iron furniture and lighting fixtures designed for the various galleries by Diego Giacometti—as you do for the five
levels of art treasures. And the restaurant is worthy of evaluation on another page.

Musée du Petit-Palais (Avenue Winston Churchill, off the
Champs-Élysées) is the fine arts museum of the City of
Paris and is, as well, the site of frequent special shows.
Like its bigger sister, across-the-street Grand-Palais, it's a
souvenir of a turn-of-century World's Fair, elaborate Belle
Époque. Special shows get more public play than the per-
manent collection, although this is an eminently inspect-
able hodgepodge. Range extends from Etruscan and

Egyptian through the Middle Ages and Renaissance, up to the romantics and Impressionists of the last century. There are Maillol and Rodin sculptures; paintings by Toulouse-Lautrec and Cézanne, Courbet, and Delacroix; Beauvais tapestries and Louis XV furniture; Limoges china and medieval manuscripts. Eclectic. *Good* eclectic.

Musée Rodin (77 Rue de Varenne) has one subject: Auguste Rodin and his sculpture. *The Thinker,* his best-known work, is in the garden. Smaller pieces are up a flight, with the ground floor devoted to medium-sized works. What makes this museum at least as inviting as its exhibits is the building itself—a honey of an early eighteenth-century *hôtel particulier.*

Pavillon des Arts (Terrasse Rambuteau, Les Halles) serves as a venue for temporary cultural exhibitions presented by the City of Paris. You'll recognize it by its several-story-high glass walls. Newspapers and *L'Officiel des Spectacles* announce current shows.

EXCURSIONIST'S PARIS:
A SELECTION OF DAY TOURS

Chantilly (23 miles north of town, via Route A1) is the site of a pair of connected castles—originally Renaissance but rebuilt—in the bigger of which are the painting collections of the Condé family. Raphael, Titian, Clouet, Lippi, and Perugino are among artists represented. There is a room full of antique jewels, not to mention ancient illuminated manuscripts and other treasures, as well as a stable that cared for several hundred horses two centuries ago. Grounds and artificial lake are splendid—surprising when one considers that they were laid out by the same Le Nôtre who played a major role in the design of the gardens of Versailles. Lunch is indicated at *Relais du Coq Chantant* (21

Route de Creil; phone 4457-01-28; *First Class*). A visit to
nearby *Senlis* combines well with Chantilly. Special lure is
Notre-Dame Cathedral, a twelfth-century masterwork
with a soaring steeple that dominates the main square and
is among France's finer Gothic specimens—from the
sculpted facade through transept, choir, and side chapels
of the interior. Senlis is not without other monuments of a
rich past (it was a royal seat in medieval times)—remains of
a onetime king's castle, a bishop's palace, a fifteenth-
century town hall, Rue Vieille de Paris (filled with aged
houses), and nearby Maison Haubergier, now the
surprise-packed local museum.

Chartres (50 miles southwest of Paris) is for many visitors
to France the first great out-of-Paris cathedral town. It does
not disappoint. I suspect this is because, tourist traffic notwithstanding, the town itself remains the same provincial
capital it was long before the advent of day-trippers out of
Paris. Approached from the front, with low-slung houses
setting it off, the Cathedral of Notre-Dame reveals its proportions without any pretense. The vastness of the cathedral is immediately apparent. Two steeples—one
Romanesque, one Gothic—flank a magnificent rose window. Length of the building is almost 400 feet, and the
transept is almost half that in width.
    Then one goes indoors to see the globally celebrated
windows. There is no finer stained glass in France; peers
of Chartres are the Cathedral of Bourges and Paris's much
smaller Ste.-Chapelle. Chartres's rose windows flanking
the facade and the transept are only starters; windows of
the long nave are equally lovely. Special, also, are sculptures of the choir: 40 groups and 200 statues portraying
great moments in the life of Christ and the Virgin Mary.
    Beyond, fronting a quiet garden, is the Bishop's Palace; it
shelters *Musée de Chartres*, rich with Renaissance tapestries

and medieval ivories and enamels; and paintings and drawings by such French masters as Teniers, Hugo Robert, Rigaud, Boucher, and Fragonard, as well as foreign greats like Holbein and Zurbarán. Art-rich *Church of St.-Pierre* is nearby, with fine stained glass and a dozen enamels of the Apostles. Old Chartres is of interest, particularly houses on streets like Du Bourg, Du Pont, St.-Hilaire, and Des Écuyers. Lunch is lovely at *La Vieille Maison* (5 Rue au Lait; phone 3734-10-67; near the cathedral; *First Class*); or stop for pastries-cum-tea at *A. Gilbert* on Rue du Cygne.

Compiègne (47 miles north of Paris), given its pedigree, is strangely incognito to most foreign visitors. It has not, to be sure, the beauty of other excursion destinations out of Paris—it is not and never has been Versailles or Fontainebleau—but it remains a place of considerable importance in the history of France: a touristic sleeper of no little interest. At journey's end is a château that knew many medieval and Renaissance kings of France. Charles V built a palace on the site in the fourteenth century. Jeanne d'Arc was taken prisoner nearby in the fifteenth. In the mid-eighteenth century, Louis XV commissioned the very same Gabriel whom he had design Paris's Place de la Concorde to rebuild the Compiègne castle. Its facade is the same today as it was from that time: a great neoclassic expanse with a colonnaded central portico. The whole, viewed from the formal garden it dominates, is not unlike a vastly widened White House.

Compiègne is the last—and newest—of the French royal palaces. From the time of its builders through to the third Napoleon and his empress, of just a century ago, considerable use was made of it. All manner of historic events have taken place within its walls. Louis XV and his grandson, the future Louis XVI, welcomed the young Austrian princess and future queen, Marie-Antoinette, to Compiègne upon her arrival in France in 1770. Napoleon I did likewise, with still another Austrian lady—his second wife-to-be, Marie-Louise, in 1810, concurrently redecorating the sovereigns' apartments in the style of the period. The later Napoleon—the third—and his empress, Eugénie, made Compiègne synonymous with fashion, with their annual autumnal "Series" of house parties. Several generations later, Marshal Foch signed the World War I Armistice on behalf of his country in a nearby wood; he used the castle as his headquarters.

A great part of the palace is given over to *Musée du Second Empire,* an era that the French know—and appreciate— more than does the outer world, particularly the English-speaking outer world, which concentrates on contemporary events across the Channel and calls the age Victorian. The Second Empire of Napoleon III and Eugénie was replete with overdecorated salons and bedchambers and portraits of royalty and beautiful ladies by the very same Winterhalter who painted Victoria.

There are a number of state rooms. Marie-Antoinette's game room is the most charming (along with Empress Eugénie's giddy bedroom). But I like the Napoleon rooms, too—the ballroom, with its crystal chandeliers; and the library, with its Empire-style furnishings and fittings. The castle's biggest draw, with French youngsters at least, is a museum of old cars and carriages. But if your visit is for only a day, skip the antique autos and move on into town. *Hôtel de Ville* is a Renaissance city hall. It contains a museum of toy soldiers—90,000 of them—portraying melodramatic moments in French history. More requisite is the *Musée Vivenel.* It occupies a beauty of an early nineteenth-century house set in a serene garden. Within is a catchall of exhibits—Old Masters drawings, eighteenth-century furniture, ancient Greek pottery, medieval wood carvings, Renaissance enamels, and Limoges china. Lunch is excellent at Hôtel du Nord's *La Rôtisserie,* Place de la Gare (phone 4488-22-30; *First Class*).

Fontainebleau (40 miles south of Paris), although on an equal historical footing with Versailles, is considerably less visited, thanks to a situation that places it farther from the capital than the Sun King's masterwork. This helps make a visit less enervating than a tour of visitor-jammed Versailles, especially in summer. No one would call Fontainebleau intimate. But in contrast to the competition—which was precisely what Versailles turned out to be—it is positively minuscule. It is, after all, the country palace that long preceded Versailles. But it was used concurrently with it. It had been a royal palace since the twelfth century. Louis IX—the same king who built the Ste.-Chapelle in Paris and was later canonized, becoming St. Louis—lived there. Louis XIII was born there. François I, the same who rebuilt the Louvre, largely rebuilt Fontainebleau, with the help of Italian artists and artisans. Succeeding monarchs—including Louis XV, who built an entire wing, and Napoleon I, who created apartments for himself and his empress—made contributions. Today's Fontainebleau, with its darkish, largely Renaissance facade, appears somber to the arriving visitor. But interiors—surrounding several magnificent courtyards—offer glittering surprises, with such rooms as the chapel, theater, François I Gallery, and ballroom (with a parquet floor to end all parquet floors). No soldiers could have clicked their heels in a more elaborate Guard Room. The chamber in which Bonaparte abdicated is among the more memorable. And the Queens' Apartments housed such illustrious royals as Catherine de Médicis, Mary Queen of Scots, and Marie-Antoinette. For lunch, choose *Hôtel Aigle Noir* (Place Napoléon, Fontainebleau; phone 6422-32-65; *First Class*) or the excellent and elegant *Hôtellerie du Bas-Bréau*, at nearby Barbizon (phone 6066-40-05; *Luxury*).

Giverny (45 miles north of Paris): You've seen the monumental collection of the Impressionist painter Claude
Monet at Musée Marmottan in Paris; you've followed that
up with Monet's matchless *Les Nymphées,* at Musée de
l'Orangerie. Now, appetite whetted, you want to make a
pilgrimage to Monet's lovely house at Giverny to the
north, midway between Paris and Rouen. Monet's home
from 1883 to 1926, this classic-style house was opened to
the public after a masterful restoration in 1980; it was an
overnight success. The house, with a pale pink and white
facade—complemented by green shutters at the
windows—is at its best in the rooms hung with the painter's collection of Japanese engravings. His studio, in its
own building, is visitable, as are the gardens that inspired
so much of his work, most especially the Water Garden,
whose weeping willows and pink-blossomed lilies became
the subject matter of his best-loved paintings. You may go
via commercial bus tour, but it's more fun on your own,
via train from Gare St.-Lazare to the station of the little
Seine River town of Vernon, a taxi ride from the Monet
house. Restaurant *Beau Rivage* (13 Avenue Maréchal Leclerc, in Vernon; phone 3251-17-27), is a satisfactory and
Moderate choice for lunch.

Reims (78 miles northeast of Paris) is the city in whose cathedral Charles VII was crowned in the presence of Jeanne
d'Arc, five and a half centuries back—at the conclusion of
the Hundred Years War and following Joan's successful de-
fense of Orléans from the English enemy. This is the city,
as well, where a full two dozen kings of France were
crowned, from an early Louis (the eighth) in 1223 to the final Charles (the tenth) in 1824. Depart early enough so
that you have the bulk of the morning for an inspection of
the *Cathedral* (Place de Six Dadrans). But tarry a bit before
entering. This Gothic work, created between the thirteenth
and fifteenth centuries, is at its most spectacular from

without. The deepset trio of portals—beneath a rose window surmounted by a friezelike gallery of sculpted kings, surmounted by a pair of square towers—makes for one of the most impressive of cathedral entries in France. The apse is flanked by broad flying buttresses and delicate pinnacles delineating them. Only after entering do proportions seem skimpy; Reims Cathedral appears narrow, which is hardly to carp, given the quality of the stained glass (including some by this century's Marc Chagall). The adjacent ex-archbishop's residence, *Palais du Tau*—operated as a museum—displays half a hundred rich medieval tapestries and other treasures of the cathedral proper and boasts an exquisitely scaled Great Hall. Move, then, to *Basilique de St.-Rémi*, a Romanesque-Gothic meld taking the name of the saint after whom the city is called and dating to the eleventh and twelfth centuries; vaulting of both nave and altar stands out. Pause for lunch in the exemplary restaurant of *Boyer-Crayères Hôtel* (64 Boulevard Vasnier; phone 2682-80-80), a decidedly *Luxury* category restaurant in a charming, park-encircled, 16-room hotel affiliated with Relais et Châteaux; the owner-chef's roast baby squab and fish specialties are delicious. In the afternoon, work off lunch by pacing the galleries of *Musée des Beaux-Arts* (a.k.a. Musée St.-Denis), with a group of portrait-drawings by Cranach and a collection of paintings by such masters as Philippe de Champaigne (who was, alas, not a local but from Flanders), Poussin, Boucher, Daumier, Daubigny, Renoir, Monet, Gauguin, Dufy, and—special treat—a substantial clutch of works by Corot. And note that Reims's champagne-producing firms—Krug, Mumm, Pommery, Piper-Heidsieck, Roederer, Ruinart, and Taittinger, among them—cordially welcome visitors to their *caves*. Still other champagne houses in the not-far-distant town of *Épernay* also are open to the public; these include Martel, Moët & Chandon, Perrier-Jouet, and Pol-Roger. *Royal Champagne Hôtel* (in Champillon; phone 2652-87-11), between Épernay and Reims, is a good *First Class* overnight selection, with an excellent restaurant.

Malmaison (10 miles west of Paris) is the country house Napoleon built for his first empress, Josephine, who came from the still-French Caribbean island of Martinique (her Martinique birthplace is a popular visitor attraction). There is nothing *mal* about the sumptuously furnished, pure Empire-style *maison*, except its excessive expense. Josephine remained after her husband, wanting a male heir, divorced her to marry Austrian Archduchess Marie-Louise. Though left well-off by her husband, Josephine still found it difficult to manage. Despite a settlement of more than three and a half million francs from the emperor, she was in debt after two years. But seeing what she spent her money on is easy on the eye. Malmaison is low-slung and set in a flower-garnished formal park. You enter a marble vestibule, full of busts, Roman style. The gilded salon is a maze of Empire-style armchairs. The dining room is simpler, with a black-and-white-checkerboard marble floor and Pompeian decor wall designs. The imperial couple's bedrooms are the most original interiors in the house. Josephine's resembles a luxurious desert chieftain's tent, an exception being her canopied bed topped with a gold eagle. Napoleon's room is the simplest and the handsomest in the house; beige moiré covers the walls and is draped over an unpretentious bed and a half-dozen-odd chairs, as well. Throughout the house, the paintings are knockouts, most especially one of Josephine by Gérard; another of Napoleon as First Consul, arm in vest; and a third of the emperor on horseback, by David—the very same one you've seen in Courvoisier cognac ads. Book lunch at appropriately named (and aptly addressed) *Restaurant Pavillon Joséphine*, 19 Avenue Bonaparte (phone 1751-01-62). *First Class*. Go by R.E.R., an extension of the Paris subway.

Rambouillet (35 miles southwest of Paris) is a little forest-surrounded town whose drawing card is the properly turreted and ever so venerable castle—a part of it dates to the eighth century—that has, since the reign of Napoleon III, belonged to the French government, becoming, at the turn of this century, official summer house of presidents of the republic. When they're not on scene, Rambouillet keeps open hours. Thank Louis XIV, a onetime resident, for the opulent paneling of the series of Assembly Rooms within and his successor twice removed, Louis XVI, for a pair of oddball buildings in the surrounding park—a mock dairy and a house surfaced in shells—that were constructed as gifts for Queen Marie-Antoinette. Oddly unfamiliar to foreign visitors—not many remember that then-President Valéry Giscard d'Estaing hosted a major summit conference in Rambouillet—the château has known historic moments. François I died there. It was from Rambouillet that Napoleon was taken to his initial exile on St. Helena. Charles I abdicated there and—to jump a few centuries—it was from this castle that General de Gaulle directed the liberation of Paris in 1944. *Restaurant Cheval Rouge* (78 Rue Général de Gaulle; phone 3485-80-61) is a reliable lunch choice; *First Class.*

St.-Germain-en-Laye (13 miles west of Paris)—like the earlier recommended Malmaison—is easily reached via the R.E.R. suburban line of the Paris Métro. It's attractive, with a charming core. What brings one to St.-Germain-en-Laye, though, is its castle—a formidable, if substantial, pile, dating to the mid-sixteenth century and largely the work of the builder-king, François I. There is, as well, a pre-François Gothic chapel of uncommon beauty, a park (grand and formal, as how could it not be, what with Versailles's Le Nôtre its designer?), and, as a surprise package, an unusual museum within the château. The exhibits at *Musée des Antiquités Nationales* are very antique, indeed,

going back to the medieval Merovingian dynasty and earlier. The museum was originally a project of Napoleon III,
but it was completely redesigned in 1968 and is now one of
the handsomest in the land, with exhibits set off to advantage in rough-finished plaster-walled galleries. On display
are pottery and metalwork objects. Louis XIV was born at
St.-Germain-en-Laye, in a room of *Pavillon Henry IV* that
had been the oratory of his mother, Anne of Austria, and
that is now the smart, 42-room luxury *Hôtel Pavillon Henry
IV,* where I suggest you have lunch (phone 3451-62-62).

Sèvres (five miles southwest of Paris): Porcelain has been
keeping this town busy since the eighteenth century,
when the crown-sponsored china factory that had been at
suburban Vincennes was moved. The visitor's Sèvres
breaks down into two parts. *Musée de Sèvres* is an eye-
opener for the porcelain-wise traveler. On display are
specimens from the best-known factories of Europe—
England, the Continent, both east and west—and Asia, as
well, including Japan and China, where it all started.
There is, also, the Sèvres factory, where visitors get a start-
to-finish tour.

Vaux-le-Vicomte (30 miles southeast of Paris, near Melun)
is the French country house at its pinnacle: grand in scale
but not so large that it is dizzying to comprehend; brilliant
in decor but never overtly so; splendidly sited—set off by
gardens at once formal and capacious—but not so extensive that they create a feeling of isolation; and, most important, stylish, elegant, and—to this very day—livable.
    Its very construction can be said to have altered the
course of history. The man behind the château was Nicolas
Fouquet (a contemporary of the young Louis XIV), who,
after becoming the king's finance minister, set about building a house befitting his exalted rank. Fouquet was bright
and rich and a friend not only of royalty but of such lumi-

naries as Molière (who performed his plays at Vaux-le-Vicomte) and La Fontaine. To build his house, Fouquet brought together three young geniuses: architect Louis Le Vau, painter-interior designer Charles Le Brun, and landscapist André Le Nôtre. They razed an older house on the site and put up what one sees today: a château in a formal garden that was the inspiration for the Versailles of Louis XIV—the palace that took the court of France out of the capital, isolating it from the people for most of three long reigns, during which time a court style developed that engendered a revolution.

Moreover, the builders of Versailles were the very same who created Vaux-le-Vicomte: the Le Vau–Le Brun–Le Nôtre trio. A visit to Vaux in 1661—the year he attained his majority—inspired Louis to outdo his finance minister. He not only built Versailles as his answer to Vaux, he had Fouquet arrested for embezzlement, to die two decades later in prison. In 1875, the rich Sommier family bought the place and began to restore it.

Vaux is an enchantment—from the moment one steps into the oval, high-ceilinged great hall. Each room—dining room, with its half-timbered Louis XIII ceiling; Muses' Room, with sumptuous Le Brun decor; gilded Games Room; Louis XIV-style King's Chamber-Cabinet-Library— is breathtaking. And the sculpture-dotted gardens are no less so. *Auberge Vaugrain* (1 Rue Amyot, in nearby Melun; phone 6452-08-23; *First Class*), with four-century-old quarters, is a good lunch stop; build your meal around the house veal-stew specialty.

Versailles (a dozen miles southwest of Paris and easily accessible by train [a good, cheap way to go] or bus tour) was the residence of Louis XIV, Louis XV, and Louis XVI and is essential for an understanding of France's history and culture. Go first to Vaux-le-Vicomte (above), which, as I explain, was the inspiration for Versailles. Louis XIV visited it and lost no time in hiring its designers—architect Le Vau, landscapist Le Nôtre, and interior designer Le Brun—to build a castle that would make Vaux, the country house of Fouquet, his finance minister, appear inconsequential in contrast. A half-century went into the building of Versailles. Louis XIV changed architects in midstream, hiring the noted Mansart to replace Le Vau. At one point, more than 35,000 artisans and laborers were at work on the palace and its gardens. Moving-in day meant a lot more than the royal family and servants; something like a thousand courtiers came to call Versailles home, with as many additional settling in the area, the better to be near the powerful Sun King, his favorites, and his patronage. Louis played the divide-and-conquer game. He kept nobles and their wives and families living to the hilt, emulating his elaborate way of life and expensive tastes in food, furnishings, and fashion. And, by concentrating them all in and around Versailles, he could keep his eyes on intracourt intrigues and diversions, the while governing France with minimal interference, if not always maximum wisdom.

A full day is by no means too much time to devote to Versailles. Two days or at least part of two days is even better. Pick midweek days; there will be fewer visitors. Versailles is enormous. Getting about the château complex can be confusing; it is not well signposted, and in warm weather months it is mobbed. I suggest you begin with a *Visite Libre* ticket, which will allow you to follow the crowds to and through *Galerie des Glaces*—the very same Hall of Mirrors where the World War I peace treaty was signed; the colonnaded *Chapelle Royale*, where crown and courtiers worshiped; a number of other seventeenth- and eighteenth-century rooms; *Musée de l'Histoire de France* (pictorial documentation of the seventeenth to nineteenth centuries); and—a fair-sized walk away—*Grand and Petit Trianons*, smaller mansions to which kings and their mistresses got away from the hubbub of the main palace. The Grand Trianon dates to Louis XIV and housed monarchs through to Louis-Philippe. Restored in the 1960s, it shelters official state guests now, much like Blair House in Washington; furniture is essentially Empire. The Petit Trianon is mid-eighteenth century, dating from the reign of Louis XV, and was a project of his first mistress, Madame de Pompadour, with her successor, Madame du Barry, the first tenant; Louis XVI's queen, Marie-Antoinette, was still another. The restoration—with superb furniture—is Louis XVI. Marie-Antoinette's exquisite theater, made of papier-mâché, is nearby, as is the 10-building complex called the *Hamlet*—a mock Norman village where Marie-Antoinette retreated for rustic respite.

Your second, separately purchased ticket will take you on an expertly guided visit (in French or English, as you choose) to rooms of the château that have been refurbished by the French government in recent years at staggering expense and with meticulous attention to historical accuracy—as part of a commendable, ongoing project. These include the king's and queen's private apartments; Madame du Barry's, Madame de Pompadour's, Madame de Maintenon's, and Madame Adelaide's apartments; and Louis XVI's library, the lot constituting interiors of the period—ceilings, mirrors, stuccowork, marble, gilding, paintings, sculpture, furniture, textiles—unsurpassed anywhere in Europe. Allow time for sculptures and fountains of the vast formal gardens. Lunch is recommended in the delightful restaurant of lovely old-school *Trianon Palace Hôtel* (1 Boulevard de la Reine; phone 3950-34-12; *First Class*)—and a splendid overnight spot as well. *Restaurant des Trois Marchés* (3 Rue Colbert; phone 3950-21-21; *Luxury*) is also an excellent choice for a meal—at once atmospheric (it's an eighteenth-century mansion) and delicious (build your meal around braised duck).

Loire Valley Châteaux (a hundred-plus miles south of Paris): In *France at Its Best*, I devote two tightly packed chapters and part of a third to lures of the Loire shores, swinging southwest at ancient Orléans, past history-rich Tours, through charming Angers, to the bustling port of Nantes at its Atlantic estuary. A week is not overlong a period of exploration in this utterly beautiful valley. But you are pressed for time, and your aim is a sampling of the 300-plus eye-filling residences that went up half a millennium back, when nobles and wealthy merchants followed kings—charming, well-educated, meticulously organized François I was the most brilliant—to the Loire, with courtiers whose ranks included painters, writers, musicians, philosophers, architects, landscapists, and, yes, chefs as well as couturiers. They developed a life-style that saw the national culture reach a zenith that to this day evokes admiration and awe; they brought to fruition the French Renaissance.

Ideally, you begin a Loire visit in *Tours,* briefing yourself on what has gone before by means of the 31 three-dimensional dioramas of *Musée Historical de Touraine* (in the venerable Château de Tours), also taking in the great Gothic beauty of the *Cathedral* and the onetime archbishop's palace adjacent to it, which is now the treasure-filled *Musée des Beaux-Arts.* By no means miss an opportunity for a meal at *Luxury*-category *Bardet* (57 Rue Groison; phone 4741-41-11)—one of the best restaurants in the French provinces, and a small but charming hotel, as well, that extends a warm welcome. Then visit as many as you've time for of the Big 7—the Loire's most-visited châteaux. Here they are, alphabetically:

Amboise surmounts a plateau, surrounded by high walls, and is at its most interesting in the suite of state rooms (François I was but one of several resident kings) and a striking Gothic chapel. (Neighboring *Clos Lucé* is the brick manor house in which King François installed Leonardo da Vinci, his imported-from-Italy artist-in-residence, and you may visit the room within in which Leonardo died.) *Azay-le-Rideau*, straddling the Indre River, is sublime in scale and restrained in ornamentation, with handsomely furnished state rooms, and—a special treat—beautiful grounds. *Blois*—part Gothic, part Renaissance, part baroque—embraces four immense wings enclosing a vast courtyard, where the stunner is an octagonal spiral staircase that climbs five intricately sculpted stories. A paneled room inhabited by Catherine de Médicis is among the royal apartments, and there's a bonus of an art gallery chock-filled with French paintings, not to mention nearby Blois Cathedral—Gothic but with a Romanesque crypt.

Chambord—in a walled deer park adjacent to the village taking its name—is the most painted, most photographed, most romantic, and largest of the Loire châteaux, with some 400 rooms. It is François I's jewel—elongated, with a circular tower defining each end, its roof an extravagant jumble of pinnacles and turrets, chimneys and domes. The main staircase is so designed that two spirals are superimposed, with each going its own way, so that if I am going up and you're en route down, we don't see each other. *Chenonceaux* is the most visited Loire château because it is as beautiful without (it appears to float on the Cher River and is set off by formal gardens) as within and because historical figures most associated with it (Catherine de Médicis, Diane de Poitiers, François I) are so well known. The Cher flows under six exquisite arches that support the château's rectangular wing. Interiors—including bedrooms of both Catherine and François, chapel, library, salons—are unsurpassed in the valley, with furniture, paintings, and tapestries sublime throughout.

Cheverny's Grand Salon—with the sumptuously worked panels of its walls and ceiling, its paintings and its Régence furniture—is reason enough for a visit. But this park-surrounded mansion is noteworthy as well for its finely detailed facade, extraordinary central stairway, tapestried walls of its Chambre du Roi, and paintings by such masters as Clouet and Rigaud. *Villandry*'s special treat is its all-Europe ranker of a garden—an extraordinary trio of vast terraces: kitchen garden, fragrant with jasmine and with giant decorative cabbages, lowest down; ornamental garden at mid-level—the most magnificent, with clipped box and yew trees, heart and fan shaped (the theme is love); and, at the top, a maze of moats fed from a central lake and by fountains interspersed throughout.

Creature comforts? Tours, in addition to *Hotel-Restaurant Bardet* (recommended above), has a pair of central *First Class* hotels: *De l'Univers Hôtel* (5 Boulevard Heurteloup; phone 4705-37-12; specify recently refurbished accommodations) and more modern *Bordeaux Hôtel* (3 Place Maréchal Leclerc; phone 4705-40-32). Both have good restaurants, and the Univers is especially nicely staffed. In the country, consider *Luxury*-category *Domaine de Beauvois* (Route de Cléré, near Luynes; phone 4755-50-11), a seventeenth-century manor house with an excellent restaurant (a good lunch stop if you're in the course of exploration), 35 delightful rooms, and an outdoor pool, and which is a member of Relais et Châteaux; *Luxury. Château de Marcay* (outside of Marcay, itself near Chinon; phone 4793-03-47) is a deftly refurbished, twin-turreted, fifteenth-century castle, set in spacious grounds (with a swimming pool that's a joy in summer), 34 attractive, no-two-alike rooms and a quartet of snazzy suites; and an excellent restaurant as reliable for fish (pavé de saumon grillé, for example) as for pastries (warm fig tart is but one species). You could do worse than stop in for lunch in the course of neighborhood exploration. Member, Relais et Châteaux; *Luxury. Château d'Artigny Hotel/Restaurant* (at Veigné; phone 4726-24-24) is elegant and a member of Relais et Châteaux); and *Moderate*-category *Le Grand Monarque Hôtel*

(Place de la République, Azay-le-Rideau; phone 4743-30-38) has an excellent restaurant.

Amiens (74 miles north of Paris) is visitable primarily because its *Cathedral of Notre-Dame* (Rue Henri IV) is not only the largest in France, but one of the most extraordinary; a ravishingly beautiful masterwork, begun in the early thirteenth century and completed more than two centuries later. Pause before entering at the entrance, itself reason enough for an Amiens excursion. Its dazzlers are a trio of portals, their deep frames a veritable museum of sculpture; stone-carved biblical stories appear in rich abundance. Go inside, then. Amiens visitors do not forget their first glance down an exquisitely Gothic-vaulted nave that is 336 feet in length, flanked by rows of elegant columns, 63 on each side. There are three sumptuous rose windows, a pair flanking the transept, another—you must look back—over the entry. The choir is Renaissance, a mind-boggling mass of carved small figures—lay, as well as biblical—several thousand strong. And don't neglect the Treasury. Amiens's *Musée de Picardie* (not far from the cathedral, on Rue de la République) is at its loveliest, for me, at least, with a clutch of eighteenth-century portraits by the likes of Fragonard and Chardin, but there is notable sculpture, as well, and contemporary paintings, too. A good lunch spot is the First Class *Nord-Sud Hôtel Restaurant* (11 Rue Gresset, phone 2291-59-03)—heart of town, near the cathedral, with prix-fixe menus, and a couple of dozen rooms, should you opt to stay overnight.

Rouen (80 miles north of Paris)—an ancient estuary port not far inland from the mouth of the Seine on the English Channel—is, in effect, the port of Paris, linked to the capital by fast and frequent trains and modern highways. I devote a solid chapter to it in *France at Its Best*, a firm believer that its cultural, architectural, and historic lures—not to mention Norman specialties in its restaurants—warrant settling in for a couple of days.

Still, leave on a *very* early morning train, out of Paris, not returning until early evening, and you can get an idea of the reasons behind Rouen's prominence in the evolution of France, from the time when Romans founded it as *Rotomagus*, through its Golden Age—the medieval and Renaissance centuries, from which remain 800 restored houses, more than in any other French city. Base your exploration on Rue Jeanne d'Arc, whose major monument is *Tour Jeanne d'Arc,* the circular tower in which Joan was interrogated prior to being burned alive in 1431, on nearby Place du Vieux-Marché, alongside the ultramodern memorial church bearing her name.

But it is at another church—Rouen's *Cathedral of Notre-Dame*—that you want to start your day. Its Gothic west facade—immortalized by impressionist painter Monet in a series of works—is framed by a pair of towers, with a quartet of delicate pinnacles between them, these surmounting a rose window flanked by three rows of splendidly sculpted saints. Out back, a gracefully extended apse supports a *flèche*, or steeple, soaring into the sky. No cathedral in France, save Paris's Notre-Dame, has a more breathtaking nave. Two levels of arcades edge floor-level arches and half a dozen columns with boldly carved capitals, which delineate the high altar.

There are two other brilliant Gothic churches—*St.-Ouen* and *St.-Maclou*—but from the cathedral I suggest you beeline to *Musée des Beaux-Arts* (Square Verdrel) to take in not only a Monet of the city's cathedral, but also a collection of paintings that is one of the finest in provincial France. The range is from Renaissance French—Clouet and Poussin; and Renaissance Italians—Veronese, Bassano, Bronzino; through later Dutchmen like Steen and Van Ruysdael, and Flemings like Rubens; and on to rococo painters, such as

Fragonard and Nattier, who set the stage for the nine-teenth century; Corot and Daubigny and beyond to such Impressionists as Renoir and Sisley.

Take time out for lunch at *Chez Dufour* (67-bis Rue St.-Nicholas; phone 3571-90-62; *First Class*) or *La Couronne* (31 Place du Vieux-Marché; phone 3571-40-90; *First Class*). In the afternoon, there will be time for the rich collections—furniture, tapestries, jewelry, bronzes—from no-longer-standing Rouen town houses, in *Musée des Antiquités* (Rue Beauvoisine), occupying a former monastery; and a fabu-lous collection of centuries-old wrought iron—a circular stairway through shop signs—in a desanctified Gothic church that is now *Musée Secq des Tournelles* (Rue Jacques-Villon).

3

Paris to Watch

THE CAPITAL AFTER DARK

The Parisian, like the Chicagoan, the Londoner, and the Roman—like residents of all the great cities—can't begin to take in even a portion of the varied diversions available. He or she must pick and choose with discernment. The short-term visitor must also exercise discipline, for the options are virtually limitless. A great deal depends on the time at one's disposal and on one's personal interests.

There are visitors who have been to Paris on a dozen trips and to the opera or ballet at least twice that many times, but have not yet made it to the Folies-Bergère. And they have no plans to. French speakers who are theater buffs return again and again to see Molière performed at the Comédie Française. Music-lovers seek out recitals in Gothic churches or concerts of the Orchestre de Paris, for example, at Théâtre des Champs-Élysées. Still others are happiest people-watching over coffee or a drink in that most Parisian of institutions, the sidewalk café—the De la Paix, perhaps, on Place de l'Opéra, or the Flore on Boulevard St.-Germain.

OPÉRA DE PARIS/GARNIER

Opéra de Paris/Garnier (Place de l'Opéra) is the Second Empire theater, one of the half-dozen world greats, that is earlier recommended architecturally and brought to your attention herewith as home base for Ballet de l'Opéra de Paris—a major European company—that presents performances, as well, by visiting dance troupes, many from abroad. The ballet-only function of this 1,991-seat house, which had been home to the Paris Opéra since it opened in 1875, came about during the administration of President François Mitterrand, when it was determined that a new structure would be built (Opéra de Paris/Bastille, below) for the opera, and that this international landmark would have its function limited to ballet.

Dance—and I speak as an enthusiast—is, to be sure, among the more estimable of the performing arts. And the Mitterrand administration must be praised for neither razing nor otherwise disposing of this Charles Garnier–designed masterwork. Still, Paris is not without citizens—nor, for that matter, visitors—saddened by the transfer of opera to Place de la Bastille, from a theater that gave its name to the busy square, the major Métro station, and the broad avenue it backs.

Withal, Ballet de l'Opéra is a company hardly to be despised. It dates to 1713, with would-be dancers entering its school between the ages of eight and twelve (at that early stage, they're known as *les rats*—the rats), eventually climbing the company's ladder, first becoming members of the Corps de Ballet (they must be no younger than 16) and then moving along (after a three-year minimum period) to higher-level categories—quadrille, coryphée, sujet, premier danseur, and—top-of-the-line (for a select few)—étoile, or star.

It is, of course *les étoiles* whose dancing you want to concentrate on, in the course of a performance—Patrick

Dupond, superstar of the lot; Claude de Vulpian, Monique Loudières, Sylvie Guillem, and Isabelle Guérin—among the ballerinas; Patrice Bart, Laurent Hilaire, Jean Guizerix, and Jean-Yves Lormeau among their male counterparts.

Repertory is nothing if not eclectic, the range of works set to music of the seventeenth century by Jean-Baptiste Lulli through Serge Lifar's *Les Mirages* and Petipas's late nineteenth-century *Raymonda*, in a contemporary version by Rudolf Nureyev (who served during much of the decade of the eighties as the company's *directeur de la danse*), with dances as well by America's Balanchine and Robbins, France's Roland Petit, and beloved classics like *Swan Lake*.

For the first-timer who has never experienced this masterful theater, an evening is an adventure; it should include a stroll in the Promenade Salon, with a pause at a banister of the Grand Stairway to take in comings and goings in the equally spectacular Grand Foyer. The auditorium—multimarbled, and illuminated principally by a three-ton chandelier, with an inappropriate ceiling mural painted by Marc Chagall—embraces orchestra, boxes (*baignoires*), balcony (*balcon*), three higher balconies (called *loges*), the topside *amphithéâtre,* and the even-higher-altitude *stalles de côté.* And English is spoken at the box office.

OPÉRA DE PARIS/BASTILLE

Don't underestimate *Opéra de Paris/Bastille* (Place de la Bastille)—the ever-so-contemporary successor to Opéra de Paris/Garnier as seat of the Paris Opéra. Attention must be paid to a building costing $350 million, occupying a historic square that had not known prominence (except for erection, in the middle of the last century, of the 171-foot-high July column, topped by a statue known as Liberté) since the fourteenth-century fortress-prison whose name it takes was toppled by Revolutionaries in 1789.

Now the square is the core of an art-gallery- and restaurant-dotted quarter with a new populace of young professionals, Opéra Bastille was designed by an Uruguay-born Canadian architect based in Toronto, named Carlos Ott, who set out to design a state-of-the-art structure that would be—and indeed, is—the complete antithesis of traditions of architecture and decor embodied in the Garnier building. Bastille's pale-gray facade—based on a motif of curves, whose only ornament is a pattern of squares—is too often photographed from the side, not as flattering as its directly-on-the-square main entrance, which is like nothing so much as walking through a giant picture frame. Even Ott's restraint, in terms of color, is striking. Lounges leading from the well-proportioned foyer are furnished in black leather. Gray and white, combined with wood trim that emerges as terra-cotta in tone, are the only other hues.

Bulk of the 2,700 seats—and note the exquisite detail of their design—is in the orchestra, with the remainder in two balconies; additional seating is in side boxes and galleries that appear more decorative than functional. Pre- and postperformance and intermission lighting is bright, from fixtures concealed in a glass ceiling, and there are no chandeliers. The drama of the interior results from its splendid scale and contours of the balconies—conveying the impression of giant waves protruding over a sea of faces. The Bastille's second theater is the striking 600-seat Amphithéâtre, blue its dominant color.

There are weak points: Lounges leading from foyer and balconies might be larger. The theater is contemporary enough for there to be escalators (they would not strike an odd note) to supplement steep stairways and invariably crowded elevators connecting various levels. And had I been Ott, I would have razed the next-door building whose ground-floor restaurant's oversized sign fights with the theater's low-key facade.

No opera house has had more contentious beginnings. Indeed, this building's early days constituted a modern-day storming of the Bastille. The first music director is a young Korean-born American (who had been conducting an orchestra in Germany) named Myung-Whun Chung. He replaced earlier-hired (and subsequently fired) Daniel Barenboim at the conclusion of a chain of events that had both the international music and the French political worlds taking sides, either for or against—often vehemently—the dictums of the Opéra's fearless president, Pierre Bergé, head of the Yves St.-Laurent fashion firm. It no longer shares performance time with the Ballet de l'Opéra, which has remained at Opéra de Paris/Garnier, where the opera troupe had been based since the Charles Garnier–designed theater opened in 1875.

Repertory range has been from such favorites as *Madama Butterfly, La Traviata,* and *Così fan tutte,* to such lesser-known works as Lully's *Alceste,* Gluck's *Iphigenia in Tauris,* and Berg's *Wozzek.* A technological feature of the new theater—made possible by a network of secondary performing and rehearsing areas that allow constant use of the main stage—makes a wide-ranging repertory possible. The main stage is surrounded by five identically sized secondary stages that permit quick changes of scenery. And the stage frame, proscenium, and orchestra pit are modular to meet varying specifications, production by production, French or foreign, including symphonic concerts. The main auditorium of this new opera house is the largest such in France built for the performance of opera. Even for longtime fans of Garnier's opera house, this successor to it is at once significant and *sympathique.*

OPÉRA DE PARIS/OPÉRA COMIQUE

Though by no means as grandiose or splendid as Opéra de Paris/Garnier (above), Opéra Comique (a.k.a. Salle Favart,

Rue de Marivaux) is a treasure of a turn-of-century, 1,200-seat theater with a lavish interior that has, traditionally, been the city's principal venue for operetta.

OPÉRA DE VERSAILLES

Recent summers have seen the Versailles Opera Festival—in the gardens of Château de Versailles—become a popular tradition during the second half of July. Two operas with internationally recognized directors and casts are usually presented—*Aïda* and *La Traviata*, for example, with such stars as Placido Domingo, Sherill Milnes, Natalia Troitskaya, and Nelly Miricioiu.

THEATER

There are several score legitimate theaters, albeit with appeal limited to visitors with enough command of the French language to understand offerings—the range Molière through musical comedy. Most significant is the *Comédie Française* (Place du Théâtre-Français, at the foot of Avenue de l'Opéra)—France's most historic theater. Although the present home is *fin de siècle*—and on the button, having opened in 1900—the company itself goes back to the reign of Louis XIV. Napoleon subsidized the troupe, and it remains government-funded, with a repertory based upon classics: Racine, Corneille, Molière, as well as productions, in French, of plays by Shakespeare, Congreve, and Bertold Brecht. The 892-seat house is one of the most beautiful in Europe and reminds me, rather sadly, of the old Metropolitan House—R.I.P.—on New York's Broadway. Productions are styled with considerable panache and, it is surely worth noting, tickets are considerably cheaper than those of the Opéra. Other major theaters include the 1,042-seat *Théâtre National de l'Odéon* (Place Paul-Claudel, on the Left Bank), a nineteenth-century building

that enjoyed contemporary fame during the post–World
War II decades, when its company was led by the gifted
man-wife team of Jean-Louis Barrault and Madeleine Re-
naud; *Théâtre Musical de Paris* (Place du Châtelet, on the
Right Bank near the Seine), an elaborate house specializ-
ing in operettas and musicals; *Théâtre de la Ville* (another
Place du Châtelet old-timer, with a thousand seats, often
used for concerts); *Théâtre du Palais-Royal* (Rue de Mont-
pensier), at the rear of the quadrangular Palais-Royal, with
a handsome eighteenth-century interior, its principal fare
variety and musicals; and the thousand-seat *Théâtre National de Chaillot*, which shares the Art Deco–era Palais de
Chaillot with a trio of museums (above) and gained fame
in recent decades as home base of the *Théâtre National Po-
pulaire*.

What's-on publications: Hotels give away *Allo Paris*—of
limited value. It's well worth going to any news kiosk and
purchasing the inexpensive but extraordinarily comprehensive weekly, *L'Official des Spectacles*.

CONCERTS AND RECITALS

Orchestre de Paris and *Orchestre National de France*, the principal Paris symphonies, are both world-class—and usually
perform in 1,900-seat *Théâtre des Champs-Élysées*, a charmer
of an Art Deco house that is not—take note—on Champs-
Élysées, but on a street leading from it, Avenue de Montaigne. It hosts ballet, too. Concerts are played in several
other halls, including 2,300-seat *Salle Pleyel* (252 Rue du
Faubourg St.-Honoré) and *Salle Gaveau* (54 Rue de la
Boëtie). *Orchestre Philharmonique de Radio France* plays Théâtre des Champs-Élysées. And *Ensemble Orchestral's* concerts take place at Salle Pleyel and Salle Gavreau. *Olympia*
(28 Boulevard des Capucines) is home to rock concerts and
other pop programs, as is huge, 5,000-seat *Palais des Sports*
(Porte de Versailles) at the southwest edge of the city. *La*

Cité de la Musique and *Le Zénith* (Avenue Corentin-Cariou) in the La Villette complex in the northeast corner of town, beyond Gare de l'Est—are venues for concerts, classical and pop. Note, too, that many concerts and recitals take place in beautiful churches—including *Notre-Dame Cathedral* (Île de la Cité), *St.-Germain-des-Prés* (Place St. Germain-des-Prés), *St.-Sulpice* (Place St.-Sulpice), and *St.-Eustache* (Rue Rambuteau), whose fine organ has been completely reconstructed and is used for annual organ festivals.

MOVIES

Parisians adore movies; they line up for hits, just like the rest of us. There are three principal movie sectors: Champs-Élysées, Quartier Latin (in and about Boulevard St.-Michel), and Grands Boulevards (Boulevard de la Madeleine, Boulevard des Capucines, Boulevard des Italiens). When movies are foreign-made, they are sometimes shown with original sound tracks. When that is the case, ads and marquees say "V.O.," for *Version Originale*. This is worth bearing in mind if you've a yen for a movie from home or across the Channel, in its original English.

MUSIC HALLS AND CABARETS

Music halls are places in which you watch a show from a theater-type auditorium, neither eating nor drinking, except at intermissions; cabarets are nightclubs in which you are obliged to eat and/or drink—paying dearly for the privilege—while you watch. Give one or two of the better places a go; shows are, indeed, spectacles—smashing costumes, perfectly beautiful women in the chorus (often with breasts exposed), and productions so elaborate that Las Vegas annually imports several. *Les Folies-Bergères* (32 Rue Richer; phone 4246-77-11) remains the all-time favor-

ite, with good reason—atmospherically Belle Époque—
with long-legged, high-kicking dancers carrying on,
elaborate act after elaborate act, each more gorgeously cos-
tumed than the last. If you limit yourself to one such evening, this should be it; top-balcony seats are inexpensive.
Le Moulin Rouge (Place Blanche, in Montmartre; phone
4606-00-19) is hardly what it was when Toulouse-Lautrec
immortalized it with his paintings, but the cancan still is
danced and the show—performed in a Nevada-style show-
room, with visibility excellent from all over—is probably
the best of all the cabaret offerings; sit at the bar and
you've found yourself a bargain. *Le Lido* (116-bis Avenue
des Champs-Élysées; phone 4563-11-61) is still another
cabaret leader—and pricey. *Crazy Horse* (12 Avenue George
V; phone 4223-32-32), also a cabaret, is the Wild West, or at
least a rather fanciful—and amusing—Paris concept of the
Wild West; as at the Moulin Rouge, it's cheaper sitting at
the bar. *Alcazar* (62 Rue Mazarine; phone 4329-02-20) offers
both dinner (8 P.M.) and 10 P.M. shows. *Au Lapin Agile* (16
Rue de Saules; phone 4606-85-87) must surely have been
around since the Renaissance reign of François I; it has
unlimited staying power, thanks to the surefire formula of
unpretentious Montmartre entertainment that's good-
natured, fun, and less costly than the competition.

4

Paris to Stay

HOTELKEEPING, PARISIAN STYLE

The French, it must be remembered before one checks into a Parisian hotel for the first time, lead systematic, well-ordered lives—and, in the case of the simpler hotels, frugal lives. Everything is done according to systems that have long been perfected. The visitor must be flexible enough to understand this.

If, in modest accommodations, he or she finds but one very tiny bar of soap in the bathroom, rather than separate bars at both tub and sink, it must be appreciated that a few decades back, there would have been no soap at all; travelers in France carried their own. If there are precisely two sheets of writing paper and a matching envelope for each at the desk in the room, it must be realized that there was a time when it would be necessary to ask the concierge for that stationery ration. (In lower-category hotels, that is still the case.)

If, in a smaller hotel without direct-dial phones, the operator tells a guest attempting to place a call, *"Raccrochez l'instrument, Monsieur,''* she means it: "Hang up, I'll call you back," she is saying, and she will. She does not make the call when you hold the receiver, because that is not the system.

Many of these facets of French hotelkeeping are inexplicable. It is like the toast in England—dry and ice-cold at breakfast, warm and buttered with afternoon tea, and no one knows why. One must accept. And when one accepts, one enjoys French hotel life. Concierges, by and large, are helpful and knowledgeable; maids, marvelous; room-service waiters, prompt and efficient. And in the bigger hotels, luxuries promised are luxuries available. Indeed, in no city are luxury hotels more luxurious.

But it is worth pointing out that the *propriétaire* of a small, uncelebrated Paris hotel is invariably quite as conscientious as the *directeur-général* of one of the grander palaces. If his little hotel is good, chances are that he has built up a considerable following, over the years, of repeat clients from, say, Los Angeles, Cologne, or Glasgow, who stay with him whenever they're in town. And if he has a restaurant in connection, they take an occasional meal with him, recommending the place, in the process, to friends and colleagues. Indeed, no great capital—not even Rome (see *Italy at Its Best*)—is able to offer the visitor such an extensive choice of reliable small hotels, family-managed and retaining the character of their neighborhoods.

About the hotels in this book: I have either lived or dined in, and thoroughly inspected the hotels carefully selected for evaluation in these pages; I disregard the complexities of the official French government star system and, as in all books of my *World at Its Best* series, have divided hotels (and restaurants) into three price groups: *Luxury, First Class,* and *Moderate.* Bear in mind that I am fussy. All hotels in my *Luxury* and *First Class* categories, and many in the

Moderate category, have television and minibars (stocked with liquor, wine, soft drinks, and sometimes snacks, for purchase) in all rooms, as well, of course, as private baths even in the great bulk of the *Moderate* category hotels I've selected. Although, I must caution you, *Moderate* category hotels' tubs generally do *not* have shower curtains to protect the rest of the bathroom from the shower's spray while you use the hand or overhead shower. Bathrooms with stall showers replacing tubs (generally cheaper than those with tubs) *do* have shower curtains. (In a small residue of lower-category hotels, a "private bath" might consist of only a sink and a tub—with the toilet a public one, down the hall; happily, not many such arrangements remain, but in modest places it pays to ask in this regard.) It is worth my mentioning, too, that in many instances mattresses of beds in *Moderate* category hotels are lumpy and/or saggy, which means they can take some getting used to, with the first night a kind of indoctrination course, succeeding nights more comfortable. Air conditioning is standard in better modern hotels and many, but not all, traditional-style houses; inquire when booking. The French rank with the very top-rung European hoteliers—Germans, Italians, and Swiss. I want to make clear that, by and large, at least in my not inconsiderable experience, they take as much pride in running modest hotels as in running luxury houses. (This is important to note in the case of Paris, which has more budget hotels than any other European city, with relatively few lemons in the lot.) When a Paris hotel is well operated, everything works well, reception to room service.

Hotels in Paris operated by United States–based international groups include *Leading Hotels of the World*, No. 1 in the capital's luxury sweepstakes with half a dozen hotels, the Plaza Athénée and Ritz among them; *Inter-Continental*, with a pair of hostelries; and *Marriott*, as well as a substantial number of *Moderate* category houses affiliated with *Best*

Western. Britain-based *Hilton International* operates a Paris pair, as indeed does Italy's top chain, *Ciga. Hôtels Concorde* is, on the basis of my experience, the major French chain (its flagship is Paris's Crillon). *Relais et Châteaux,* whose affiliates are individually owned, has more restaurants than hotels in Paris. Other chains on scene include *Altea, Arcade, Ibis, Mercure, Novotel, Pullman International,* and *Trusthouse Forte.* Such leading American hotel representatives as *David B. Mitchell Co., Robert F. Warner, Inc.,* and *Marketing Ahead, Inc.* are also part of the Paris picture.

SELECTED RIVE DROITE/RIGHT BANK HOTELS

Ambassador Concorde Hôtel (16 Boulevard Haussmann; phone 4246-92-63): Consider this attractive, full-facility house, especially if you're a music buff (the Opéra/Garnier is a hop and a skip distant) or a dedicated shopper (top department stores are just down the street). The Ambassador Concorde has 300 rooms, traditional-style, and was relatively recently renovated. There's a creditable restaurant and friendly bar-lounge. Hôtels Concorde. *First Class.*

Arcade Bastille Hôtel (15 Rue Bréguet; phone 4338-65-65) is a good-size link (305 rooms) of the Arcade chain, with Arcade's usual clean-lined rooms (some with double-decker beds) and stall showers sensibly substituting for tubs in each room's bath. The restaurant features buffets at all meals and there's a bar. Just off Place de la Bastille and not far from Place des Vosges and the Marais. *Moderate.*

Astra Hôtel (29 Rue Caumartin; phone 4266-15-15) is middle-sized, elderly, and modernized to the point where every one of its rooms has a bath. Equally commendable is the convenient location—on a street between Boulevard des Capucines and Boulevard Haussmann, with the

Opéra/Garnier to the east and the Madeleine to the west. Restaurant. *Moderate.*

Balzac Hôtel (6 Rue Balzac; phone 4561-97-22) is strategically situated between Faubourg St.-Honoré and the Champs-Élysées. Its aces in the hole are that it's not overlarge (there are 56 rooms and suites with fine baths) and that it's good-looking and professionally staffed. Its Restaurant Sallambier is exemplary and there's a relaxing bar. *Luxury.*

Bastille Speria Hôtel (1 Rue de la Bastille; phone 42-72-04-01) is neat as a pin, with contemporary public spaces (including a welcoming breakfast room—there is no restaurant) and lounge. There are 42 okay rooms, and you're a near-neighbor of Opéra/Bastille. *Moderate.*

Bradford Hôtel (10 Rue St.-Philippe-de-Roule; phone 43-59-24-20) is worth knowing about because it's good value—all 46 rooms have bath—and well located, on a short street just off Rue du Faubourg St.-Honoré, with Champs-Élysées nearby. Breakfast only. *Moderate.*

Brighton Hôtel (218 Rue de Rivoli; phone 4260-30-03) is a comfortable, smallish, smartly located hotel. All 69 rooms have baths, although doubles can be smallish. Breakfast only. *Moderate.*

Bristol Hôtel (112 Rue du Faubourg St.-Honoré; phone 4266-91-45) comes closer to seeming like a palatial town house than any other luxury hotel in town. Public rooms are eighteenth-century; crystal chandeliers illuminate spaces furnished with Louis XV and Louis XVI pieces, some of museum caliber. The Winter Restaurant is an exquisite oval, its oak panels hand-carved in Hungary for the hotel, when it opened in 1924. In summer, the restaurant—

recommended on a later page—moves to an airy, rattan-furnished pavilion, whose glass walls give onto a capacious garden. The bar is dark-paneled, with striped Louis XVI chairs flanking its tables. There are 220 rooms and suites in two buildings, the more recent a onetime convent overlooking the garden and smartly traditional in look, with super marble baths. Remaining is the Bristol's special treat: a honey of a swimming pool on the roof, glass-walled and with a sauna and solarium adjacent. Location, on the smartest shopping street in town, just steps from Palais de l'Élysée, the presidential residence, is inspired. Member, Leading Hotels of the World. *Luxury.*

Britannique Hôtel (20 Avenue Victoria; phone 42-33-74-59) has an easy-to-remember situation: just behind Théâtre du Chatelet, about midway between the Louvre and the Hôtel de Ville. Relatively recently refurbished—there are 40 bath-equipped rooms and breakfast but no restaurant—it had its moment of glory during World War I, when it was headquarters for American relief operations. *Moderate.*

Burgundy Hôtel (8 Rue Duphot; phone 4260-34-12) is fortunate in its location (between Boulevard de la Madeleine and Rue St.-Honoré), its agreeable middling size, and its 90 good-looking rooms, all with bath and in traditional style. There is a restaurant-grill-bar in connection and a capacious lobby. Conscientious owner-management. *First Class.*

Calais Hôtel (5 Rue des Capucines; phone 4261-50-28) is at the corner of Place Vendôme and Rue de la Paix and has been a favorite of mine these many years. The bigger of the 59 rooms, with their own bath, are comfortable and attractive. Breakfast only. *Moderate.*

Cambon Hôtel (3 Rue Cambon; phone 4261-55-20), long popular because of its location on the street distinguished by the rear entrance of the Ritz Hôtel, has upgraded in recent seasons—and tastefully. Public spaces include an inviting bar-lounge and agreeable breakfast room (there is no restaurant), and the 44 rooms have been brightened, too, with the larger among them noteworthy. *First Class.*

Castiglione Hôtel (38 Rue du Faubourg St.-Honorê; phone 4265-07-50) is enviably well situated on the city's smartest shopping street, diagonally opposite the British Embassy. This is an attractive 120-room house whose public spaces include Le Callione Restaurant and a bar-lounge. Proportion of suites is high, but double rooms, some with balconies, can be very nice, too. *First Class.*

Castille Hôtel (37 Rue Cambon; phone 4261-55-20)—recommended in earlier editions of this book—is no longer counseled. On my most recent inspection visit, I was rudely received at reception, and ultimately shown but one of the 100 rooms—a duplex suite that wanted refurbishing. Readers have reported similarly uninviting accommodations. Despite its being restaurant-equipped and with a good location just opposite the rear entrance of the Ritz, I do not suggest staying here. *First Class.*

Caumartin Hôtel (27 Rue Caumartin; phone 4742-95-95): Enviably well positioned between Opéra/Garnier and Madeleine, this is a worth-knowing-about house in contemporary style, with brown leather sofas in the lobby-lounge and light and airy looks to the 40 rooms, all with bath. Breakfast only. *Moderate.*

Centre Ville Matignon Hôtel (3 Rue de Ponthieu; phone 4387-55-77) is indeed *centre ville*, or heart of the city, on a street that parallels Champs-Élysées at its lower end, near

Rond-Point, so that you can do a great deal by foot in every direction. This is a well-equipped house with 23 bath-attached, nicely maintained rooms; restaurant and bar. *Moderate.*

Choiseul-Opéra Hôtel (1 Rue Daunou; phone 4261-70-41) has location as a major plus; it's on a short street just off Avenue de l'Opéra near Place de l'Opéra. There are 42 well-maintained, bath-equipped rooms. Breakfast only. *Moderate.*

Concorde-Lafayette Hôtel (Place du General Koenig; phone 4758-12-84) occupies a strikingly designed, 34-story tower adjacent not only to Palais des Congrès—Paris's principal convention center—but, of more immediate interest, also next door to Porte Maillot Air Terminal, from which buses depart for and arrive from de Gaulle Airport quarter-hourly. A kingpin of France-wide Hôtels Concorde, along with the landmark Crillon on Place de la Concorde, the Concorde-Lafayette embraces a thousand pastel-colored rooms and suites, agreeably contemporary, full-facility and with many absolutely fabulous views, especially those at the summit embracing the Top Club—premium-tabbed with extra amenities. There's a trio of restaurants (the range is from haute-cuisine L'Étoile d'Or to casual Les Saisons), and as many bars, with that on the picture-windowed roof—all Paris lies below—an especial treat. And there's a bonus of shops—60, all told—adjacent. *Luxury.*

Continent Hôtel (30 Rue du Mont Thabor; phone 4260-75-32) bases its decor motif on the style of Louis XVI. There are 28 rooms of varying sizes, the lot with okay baths or showers. Location is super; you're on a street leading from Rue de Castiglione, just below Place Vendôme, with the Tuileries also a hop and a skip. Breakfast only. *Moderate.*

Crillon Hôtel (10 Place de la Concorde; phone 4265-24-24) is an intrinsic and original component of a monumental Paris square, with its next-door twin housing a ministry of the French government. It is surely the only hotel extant with one of its original rooms—a rococo boudoir—moved in toto for permanent display in a world-class museum (New York's Metropolitan Museum). Like Place de la Concorde, both hotel and Ministère de la Marine date to the eighteenth century when, in 1758, King Louis XV commissioned architect Jacques-Anges Gabriel to design the north facade of the square; along with Place Vendôme and Place des Vosges, it is the loveliest such in Paris. Some years after its construction, the building served as a residence of the Spanish ambassador. In 1788, it was purchased by Comte de Crillon, whose name it took and in whose family it remained until the turn of the present century. In 1909, along with two adjacent buildings, it became a hotel, passing relatively recently to control of the Taittinger family, producers of the esteemed champagne bearing their name and proprietors of Hôtels Concorde, of which the Crillon is flagship. The Taittingers have invested more than $10 million in a splendid refurbishing. Walls of the lobby, Grand Salon (a smart venue for tea and cocktails), and Restaurant Les Ambassadeurs (an appropriate name, what with the American Embassy just next door) are sheathed in gold-hued marble, a perfect foil for illumination provided by a network of crystal chandeliers and sconces. There's a snappy cocktail lounge paneled in warm walnut, its chairs covered in the same red velvet as those of the adjacent Obélisque, an informal grill with quick but stylish service. (I evaluate both Crillon restaurants on later pages, but at this point let me urge you to try the buffet breakfast at Les Ambassadeurs, even if you're staying in another hotel.)

Rooms? A brilliantly proportioned formal staircase leads up a flight to the quartet of Grands Appartements—high-ceilinged and with broad terraces giving onto Place de la

Concorde. They have been painstakingly refurbished—
Louis XV and XVI furniture, Aubusson carpets, Flemish
tapestries, original stuccowork and sculpture; there is
nothing else quite like them in France and if you're a guest
in the hotel with a special interest in interior design, furniture, and accessories of the rococo era, I suggest you ask
the head concierge if at some point during your stay, when
one or more of these suites—each a national treasure—is
between occupants, you may have a peek. The group includes Salon des Aigles with Bohemian crystal chandeliers
and extraordinary gold leaf; Salon Marie-Antoinette, in
which the queen whose name it takes is believed to have
taken music lessons and with a terrace framed by Corinthian columns; Salon des Batailles, with exceptional parquet flooring and Louis XV furnishings; the Imperial and
Royal suites (Rooms 101 and 158), with painted panels after originals now on display in Paris's Chilean Embassy,
Vermont's Middlebury College and, I note above, Manhattan's Metropolitan Museum; and the space that was for
long the Crillon family's chapel, again as it was in the
eighteenth century. Smaller suites—all told, there are 40—
are hardly to be despised; with 140 bedrooms, no two
quite alike, that are stunning in their simplicity:
Eighteenth-century-style furniture is set against pale-
hued, paneled walls; high windows are hung with sumptuous draperies, and baths are elaborately equipped and
marble-walled. The Crillon is one of a kind: a unique experience. Member, Leading Hotels of the World and Relais et
Châteaux. *Luxury.*

Duminy-Vendôme Hôtel (3 Rue du Mont Thabor; phone
4260-32-80) is nicely situated on a convenient street a step
or two from Place Vendôme. There are just under 80
traditional-style rooms with brass beds and marble baths,
and a friendly bar. Breakfast only. *Moderate.*

Edouard-VII Hôtel (39 Avenue de l'Opéra; phone 4261-56-90): Paris abounds in hotels named for British royals. I counsel on other pages hostelries called after George V, his son Edward VIII (when Prince of Wales), and George's wife, Queen Mary. The Edouard-VII, whose title honors George V's papa, occupies a building dating to the Edwardian—or early twentieth century—era, with just a hundred tastefully mod-look rooms, popular-with-Parisians Restaurant Delmonico, busy bar, and strategic situation just down the avenue from Opéra/Garnier, corner of Rue d'Antin. *First Class.*

Élysée-Park Hôtel (5 Rue de Ponthieu; phone 4359-70-36) is positioned on a street that parallels the Champs-Élysées; besides its convenient location, it offers 30 well-kept rooms with bath. Breakfast only. *Moderate.*

Étoile-Maillot Hôtel (10 Rue du Bois de Boulogne; phone 4500-42-60) is a winner, just off Avenue de la Grande-Armée, which is Champs-Élysées with a new name, substituted when it goes beyond Étoile. Rooms, all with bath, are spacious and tasteful, and there are some suites, good to know about if your Paris stay will be for some time and will involve entertaining. Breakfast only. *Moderate.*

Excelsior-Opéra Hôtel (5 Rue La Fayette; phone 4874-99-30) is a near-neighbor to the Opéra, for which it is partially named. Behind its busy Belle-Époque facade are half a hundred mod-look rooms, all with bath, and a bar-equipped lobby-lounge. Friendly. Only breakfast is served. *Moderate.*

Family Hôtel (35 Rue Cambon; phone 4261-54-84) is, as far as I can tell, the least expensive of the Rue Cambon hotels that more or less cluster across from the rear entrance of the Ritz. This is a long-admired, heavily repeat-clientele old-timer, with baths attached to 18 of its functional rooms, and showers in the case of the remaining 8. Friendly and good value. Breakfast only. *Moderate.*

France et Choiseul Hôtel (239 Rue St.-Honoré; phone 4261-54-60) is a heart-of-town oldie near Place Vendôme. There are 135 rooms, all with bath, although some appear smaller than one might like in a hotel of this caliber. Public rooms are traditional, Louis XV mostly. There's a bar-lounge, and an agreeable patio. *First Class.*

George V Hôtel (31 Avenue George V, just off Champs-Élysées; phone 4723-54-00) is a grand hotel in the grand manner, handsomely furnished (and recently, extensively, and superbly refurbished) in eighteenth-century style, with the genuine articles—tapestries, paintings, sculptures, clocks, boiserie—scattered about to add authenticity to the ambience. The restaurant moves to the lovely court-yard in summer. The bar is one of the most engaging in Paris, particularly at day's end, when it's time for an aperitif—or a scotch or dry martini. But what really makes the George V, when all is said and done, is service: skilled and quick, and that includes concierges, room-service waiters, chambermaids, doormen, and bellmen. The George V is a part of Trusthouse Forte's Exclusive Division and a member of Leading Hotels of the World. *Luxury.*

Le Grand Hôtel (2 Rue Scribe, with entrances also on Boulevard des Capucines and Place de l'Opéra; phone 4268-12-13) is, to understate, accurately named. It was a key part of the master plan for the reconstruction of Paris during the reign of Napoleon III, in the mid-nineteenth century, by the innovative architect Baron Haussmann. An immense Belle-Époque triangle, whose three sides surround a court the size of a football stadium, it is quite the oldest of the city's landmark luxury hotels, constructed as such.

Work began in the spring of 1861, and in July 1862 Empress Eugénie toured the completed building, remarking at the time that its splendor put her in mind of the pair of palaces she called home. (*"C'est absolument comme chez moi, je me soie crue à Fontainebleau ou à Compiègne."*) Alas, a succession of managements over the succeeding years did not do justice to the Grand's interiors. We must be grateful that the original, brilliantly decorated restaurant, now called Salon Opéra and used for private parties, has mercifully been left intact; the same Charles Garnier who would later create the next-door opera house was one of its designers. And we must appreciate, as well, that the relatively recent landlord, Inter-Continental Hotels, which realizes that it has a national treasure on its hands, undertook an intelligently conceived program of restoration and refurbishing. This is a big house, but as the eighties became the nineties all 515 rooms and suites had been refurbished albeit in traditional style (when booking, request a room overlooking the Opéra/Garnier; the view is fabulous, and public spaces—main lobby, bar, glass-roofed Cour d'Honneur with stylishly recreated restaurant—were tastefully renewed as well. The Grand's celebrated Café de la Paix, a history-laden Paris institution (about which I write more in a later paragraph), thrives as always, but the hotel's Restaurant Opéra, one of the ranking luxury-hotel eateries in town (and reviewed on a subsequent page) is underappreciated. *First Class/Luxury.*

Inter-Continental Paris Hôtel (3 Rue de Castiglione; phone 4260-37-80): Talk about felicitous name changes: If your Paris experience extends back a couple of decades, you'll remember the Continental Hotel—one of the great Second Empire houses. When Inter-Continental took over in the 1970s, all they had to do was add the prefix *Inter* to the original title. Not unlike the same chain's Le Grand Hôtel (above), the Inter-Continental dates to the Belle Époque, when Napoleon III and Empress Eugénie reigned. Its architect, Paul Blondel, was a son-in-law of Charles Garnier, designer of the nearby opera house taking his name. The hotel opened in 1878 to immediate plaudits. In 1883, it was the site of a banquet to honor Victor Hugo, turned 80. Come 1887, and it was advertising in magazines as *"le plus confortable, le plus vaste et le plus élégant des hotels du continent,"* with room tabs beginning at four francs per night. By 1892, it was a favorite of guidebook authors, with *Guide Joanne* lauding its five-franc lunches, 600 bedrooms, and the elevators connecting the bedrooms to a lavish lobby. Empress Eugénie liked the Continental well enough to settle in for an entire month in the spring of 1898, occupying a suite overlooking the Tuileries. By the time of World War I there were 300 bathrooms for the 600 rooms—an exceptionally high proportion. During World War II, playwright Jean Giraudoux was based in the hotel, heading the government's information office. The early 1960s saw the first of several extensive refurbishings, the most recent of which, in the early 1990s, was coordinated by general manager Fred de Roode—U.S.-born, French-speaking, Swiss-trained—who, when I first met him, was at the helm of the Inter-Continental on Maui (see *Hawaii at Its Best*). The current $65 million facelift had as highlights reduction of the room total (long since reduced from the original 600 to 450) to 365 (with small rooms considerably enlarged), and a restyled La Terrasse Fleurie Restaurant (reviewed on a later page) occupying space in the fountain-centered courtyard—to which horse-drawn carriages pulled up in the early decades. But the hotel's trio of historic public rooms remain as officially protected monuments, in all their nineteenth-century glory—Salon Imperial, the frescoes of its ceiling gilt-framed; Salon Napoléon, Corinthian columns surrounding its crystal chandeliers; and Salon Aiglon, richly carved and ornamented. They're used today for private parties and meetings, but management is proud of them, and I'm sure that if, as a guest, you express an interest in seeing them, the concierge will see that you have a peek. The traditional look and contemporary amenities of rooms and suites are top-of-the-line, there are a pair of additional restaurants, busy bar, staff at once alert, skilled, and congenial. Location is heart-of-town. *Luxury.*

Lancaster Hôtel (7 Rue de Berri, just off Champs-Élysées; phone 4361-59-43) is surely among the more engaging of the deluxe hotels—bedrooms are mostly as big as the hotel is small; ditto, the baths. There is a cozy bar and *First Class* restaurant that in summer is transferred to what may well be Paris's prettiest courtyard-garden. And public spaces are old-school handsome. Skilled management, too, which is not surprising; the century-old Lancaster is a part of the London-based Savoy Hotels group. *Luxury.*

London Palace Hôtel (32 Boulevard des Italiens; phone 4824-54-64) has no discernible connection to the British capital (except that there are Brits among its guests) and it is hardly a palace. Still, this is a functionally updated house—I wish that the favored color was not orange—with comfortable lounge and 50 clean-lined rooms each with bath or shower. Situation is exemplary; you're on one of the *grands boulevards* within shouting distance of Place de l'Opéra and with the Boulevard Haussmann department stores perhaps almost too close to your quarters, at least if you're a compulsive shopper. *Moderate.*

Lotti Hôtel (7 Rue de Castiglione; phone 4260-37-34) is a long-on-scene neighbor of centrally situated Rue de Castiglione hotels like the Inter-Continental Paris, Meurice, and Vendôme. Recent seasons have seen it tastefully and thoroughly refurbished by its current landlord, Italy-based Jolly Hotels, a chain I have come to know through research for *Italy at Its Best.* The Jolly people have wisely retained the quietly traditional look of the Lotti, starting with its attractive lobby-lounge and small but reliable restaurant, beyond to the 131 rooms and suites, many of them good-sized, and the nicest with views of Rue de Castiglione and the Tuileries beyond. *First Class.*

Louvre Hôtel (Plaza André-Malraux; phone 4261-56-01): Talk about being heart-of-Paris: the Louvre is just opposite the Comédie Française, just down the avenue from Opéra/Garnier, adjacent to the Palais-Royal, and an immediate neighbor to the Tuileries and the Louvre. There are 220 rooms, a chatty cocktail lounge, and the commendable Brasserie Tuileries, whose terrace-café lies under arcades of the Palais-Royal. *Historical note:* This is a hotel with roots to New York Harbor's Statue of Liberty, because it was at an 1875 banquet in the Louvre Hôtel that the Franco-American Union was created, for the purpose of presenting the statue to the United States on the hundredth anniversary of its independence in 1886. Members of the committee included the Colmar-based sculptor of the statue, Bartoldi, and a chap named Gaget, whose company manufactured miniatures of the statue, which were sold to raise funds for its construction; Monsieur Gaget's name was the inspiration for the word *gadget*, in both the French and English languages. Hôtels Concorde. *First Class.*

Lys Hôtel (23 Rue Serpente; phone 4326-97-57) is venerable seventeenth-century, furnished with old French Provençal pieces and loaded with atmosphere. All 18 of its rooms have baths. Breakfast only. *Moderate.*

Madeleine-Palace Hôtel (8 Rue Cambon; phone 4260-37-82) is a fair-sized oldie that has been, as its management succinctly put it, *entièrement rénové.* That means all of the

116 rooms have their own baths, and there is a bar. Location is middle-of-everything. Breakfast only. *First Class.*

Marriott Prince de Galles Hôtel (33 Avenue George V; phone 4723-55-11) began life as the just plain Prince de Galles (doesn't *Prince of Wales* sound nice in French?) in 1929, as a next-door neighbor of the hotel (above) named for the father (George V) of the then Prince of Wales, who was to reign so briefly as Edward VIII. Though the Prince de Galles is considerably smaller than the George V (it has just over 170 rooms and suites, in contrast to its neighbor's near 300), their facades are both of the Art Deco era, and both have gracious inner courts. The Marriott chain, which purchased the "Prince" in 1984, completed an extensive and masterful renovation the following year. The look of the hotel is now essentially early nineteenth century, Directoire and Empire, with careful attention paid to luxurious textiles, wall-coverings, and lighting fixtures. (Bravo, interior designer Robert Lush, who also directed renovation of the Carlton Inter-Continental in Cannes.) Amenities include a striking-looking peach- and ivory-hued, marble-accented restaurant (which moves to the flowering courtyard in summer and which is evaluated on a later page) and a bar-lounge beloved of Parisians and visitors over the years, refurbished to be sure, but still with its original handsome paneling. *Luxury.*

Mayfair Hôtel (3 Rue Rouget-de-Lisle; phone 4260-38-14) has an inspired location on a tiny street between Rue de Rivoli and Rue du Mont-Thabor just below Place Vendôme. This is a lovely 53-room house, with a capacious lobby, handsome bar-breakfast room, accommodations mostly based on Louis XVI-style furnishings, decor in tones of gray, excellent baths. The staff is delightful. There's no restaurant, but the Mayfair is otherwise *First Class.*

Mercure Montmartre Hôtel (1 Rue Caulaincourt; phone 4294-17-17)—not far from Place de Clichy—adheres to the Mercure chain's formula: compact but nicely fitted-out modern rooms with good baths (there are 308 all told), copious buffet breakfasts, and a bar. Montmartre's landmark Sacré Coeur Basilica is not far north. *Moderate.*

Mercure Paris Étoile Hôtel (267 Avenue des Ternes; phone 4766-49-18) pleases visitors who enjoy the Étoile–Arc de Triomphe area at the termination of Champs-Élysées. It's a block north of the arch, occupying a modern building, with 56 smallish but well-planned rooms with plenty of surface space, good baths (as is customary in hotels of the Mercure chain), and—also typically Mercure—breakfasts (no other meals) from a generous buffet. Cocktail lounge. *Moderate.*

Meurice Hôtel (228 Rue de Rivoli; phone 4260-38-60), with its inspired locale—as beautiful as it is convenient—at the intersection of Rue de Castiglione and Rue de Rivoli, steps from Place Vendôme and the Tuileries, was built the year Napoleon abdicated, and the ambience remains at once elegant and low-key, so meticulously have Italy-based Ciga Hotels (famous as the chain that includes such houses as Rome's Excelsior, Venice's Gritti Palace, and others I evaluate in *Italy at Its Best*) carried out a major restoration. The lobby and its most spectacular lounge, Salon Pompadour— still with original gilded paneling strikingly patterned— and crystal chandeliers remains one of the great Paris public spaces, and a wise choice for a drink or afternoon tea. Accommodations are super, carefully and authentically refurbished by Ciga, along with upper-floor corridors. Suites, mostly overlooking the Tuileries, are Louis XV and Louis XVI with antiques of that era among their furnishings. Standard rooms are smart, too, often generous-size with excellent baths, and overlooking Rue

de Castiglione or an inner court; you must specify preference. Ciga very wisely moved the restaurant from the
basement to the high-ceilinged, chandelier-hung, gilt-
embellished Salon Tuileries, facing arcaded Rue de Rivoli;
and the hotel's main entrance (formerly on Rue du Mont-
Thabor) is now on Rue de Rivoli, adjacent to the restaurant. The Meurice takes its name from its founder, whose
aim, in the early decades of the last century, was to estab-
lish a hotel that would meet standards of the upper-class
British, then the dominant upscale travelers on the Continent. By 1819, but three years after opening, Monsieur
Meurice advertised "his sincere thanks to the English who
have kindly honoured him with their patronage [and for
whom he opened] four new apartments in front of the
Tuileries Garden." The original Meurice was succeeded by
a second hotel in the mid-nineteenth century (Queen Victoria was among guests) and, subsequently, a third
(Spain's Alfonso XIII stayed, as a young man—bringing his
own furniture—and again years later, after he abdicated,
pre–World War II). *Luxury.*

Ministère Hôtel (31 Rue de Surène; phone 4266-21-43) is a
pleasant selection in the central Madeleine quarter. Rooms
can be smallish, but those with bath (24 of 32) are comfortable. Management is accommodating; service, personal.
Breakfast only. *Moderate.*

Molière Hôtel (21 Rue Molière; phone 4296-22-01): A hotel
named for the playwright simply has to have something
going for it, and the Molière does. It has an excellent location near the Opéra/Garnier and good-looking rooms, all
with bath, be they single, twin, or suite. Breakfast only.
Moderate.

Montana Tuileries Hôtel (12 Rue Saint-Roch; phone 4260-
35-10) has location as a secret weapon. Rue Saint-Roch,

taking its name from a landmark church situated where it intersects Rue St.-Honoré, leads into Avenue de l'Opéra, but is, as well, a hop and a skip from Rue de Rivoli and the Louvre. Those of the 25 rooms I have either inhabited or inspected are generous in size, all with bath—and, in some cases, relatively recently refurbished. The lounge opposite reception doubles as breakfast room, and service is sprightly. A good deal. *Moderate.*

Mont-Thabor Hôtel (4 Rue du Mont-Thabor; phone 4260-32-77) is smack in the heart of things on a street that lies between Rue de Rivoli and Rue St.-Honoré, near Place Vendôme. The lobby and bar are agreeable; and those bedrooms I've inspected, likewise. Clientele is an interesting mix of South and North Americans and Japanese. *First Class.*

Normandy Hôtel (7 Rue de l'Échelle; phone 4260-30-21) is situated on a short thoroughfare leading from Avenue de l'Opéra to Rue de Rivoli and the Tuileries. It's a fine, traditional-style house that's well maintained, with 140 no-two-alike rooms with good baths; attractive restaurant in Louis XVI style; paneled cocktail lounge with leather chairs encircling well-spaced tables. *First Class.*

Novotel Paris–Les Halles (8 Place Marguerite-de-Navarre; phone 4221-31-31) is a contemporary high-rise (gained by Rue des Halles) that's part of the international, French-origin Novotel chain. I wish the link in New York (see *New York at Its Best)* was as good-looking. Lobby is clean-lined and high-ceilinged, there's a rambling cocktail lounge, a high-tech restaurant under a glass roof, and 285 ever-so-contemporary rooms with good baths. To be happy, you have to want to be this far east—near vast Forum des Halles shopping center and the Beaubourg. *First Class.*

Orion Paris Les Halles (4 Rue des Innocents; phone 4508-00-33) is a kind of apartment-hotel, modern as can be, in the Halles area, near the Beaubourg. All accommodations are kitchen-equipped (including dishes and utensils), with bath, and rates by day, week (cheaper), or four-weeks-plus (cheapest). Take your choice of studios (of which there are 134, accommodating one to three persons) or one-bedroom suites (of which there are 55, accommodation 1 to 5 persons). *First Class.*

Pavillon de la Reine Hôtel (28 Place des Vosges; phone 4277-96-40): If you've longed to stay directly on beautiful Places des Vosges—and in style—this might well be your hotel choice. Half of its 50 handsome rooms overlook a garden, the others a courtyard. The look is essentially seventeenth-century, what with a beamed lobby, paneled, fireplace-centered lounge, and handsome rooms (alas, doubles can be smallish) with excellent marble-counter baths. With a full-service restaurant (there is limited-menu room service, including breakfast) and bar, this hotel could be Luxury category, but it's *First Class.*

Place du Louvre Hôtel (21 Rue des Prêtres Saint-Germain-l'Auxerrois; phone 4233-78-68) is on a street that you wouldn't normally pass by, but that's convenient and easy to locate: directly behind the eastern facade of the Louvre in the direction of Hôtel de Ville and paralleling the Seine. There are 20 neat rooms with bath. Breakfast only. *Moderate.*

Plaza-Athénée Hôtel (25 Avenue Montaigne; phone 4723-78-33) is, not unlike the George V, a relatively modern building with a fashionable off-Champs-Élysées location, perfectly beautiful eighteenth-century interiors (Relais Grill and the Bar Anglais are contemporary-look exceptions), and an inner patio that becomes a restaurant in summer. A special feature is Les Gobelins, a long gallery connecting the extraordinarily handsome Restaurant Régence with the lobby, which sees service as a tea lounge in the afternoon. Suites are sumptuous, but ordinary guest rooms are attractive, too; all are in the style of Louis XV or Louis XVI, with luxurious baths, and face either the quiet street or the courtyard; specify preference. Lavish attention to detail is evident throughout, with the budget for fresh flowers in excess of that for electricity—to give you an idea. A Trusthouse Forte Exclusive Division hotel that's also a member of Leading Hotels of the World. *Luxury.*

Princesse Caroline Hôtel (1-bis Rue Troyon; phone 4380-62-20) is named for the sister of Napoleon who married Joachin Murat, King of Naples. But I digress. This hotel, just north of the Étoile, on a street leading from Avenue Wagram, has a nice sense of style, with a paneled Louis XVI–inspired lobby, Bar Le Murat—named for Caroline's husband—and 63 rooms, some of whose baths have double sinks set into wide counters. Breakfast only. *Moderate.*

Pullman Windsor Hôtel (14 Rue Beaujon; phone 4561-04-04) occupies a turn-of-century building in a tranquil quarter between Étoile and Parc Monceau and is among the more comfortable links of the Pullman chain at which I've stayed, France-wide. Public spaces—generous-sized lobby, cozy bar, excellent, weekdays-only Restaurant Clovis—are a deft meld of contemporary and Belle Époque, while those of the 135 rooms I've seen, including some big ones, are gracious old-school. Lovely service. *First Class.*

Queen Mary Hôtel (9 Rue Greffulhe; phone 4266-40-55) could have been named for Mary Queen of Scots, who was, after all, queen of France before she was queen of Scotland. But I suspect it was named after the more recent wife of the late George V. The only royal picture in the lobby is of none of these sovereigns, but of Edward VII, instead. At any rate, this is a smallish, nicely managed and located hotel (the Madeleine is nearby) that has been recently refurbished with a Louis XVI salon off the lobby. All 16 rooms have bath. Breakfast is served, but there is no restaurant. *Moderate.*

Regina Hôtel (2 Place des Pyramides; phone 4260-31-10) is *fin de siècle,* albeit updated as regards baths and the like, but has retained its original decor. There is a long gallery of a lobby, cozy restaurant-bar, which extends into a patio in summer, and some of the best-looking bedrooms and suites in town. (The bedsteads are inevitably old-fashioned brass.) Those with a view of the Tuileries are special (and more costly, of course). Location is noteworthy on a square bisected by Rue de Rivoli, almost opposite the Louvre. *First Class.*

Résidence du Bois Hôtel (16 Rue Chalgrin; phone 4500-50-59) is a townhouse kind of hotel on a residential street just off fashionable Avenue Foch, which is one of the arteries leading from the Étoile. The 20 suites and rooms and public rooms are period style and luxurious; you have the feeling that you're in the country. *First Class.*

Résidence St.-Honoré Hôtel (214 Rue du Faubourg St.-Honoré; phone 4225-26-27): You might not think of this fashionable shopping street as the site of a well-priced hotel (admittedly, near its western end). But the Résidence St.-Honoré is worth knowing about, what with 91 comfortable, bath-equipped rooms and a bar-lounge. Breakfast only. *Moderate.*

Ritz Hôtel (15 Place Vendôme, with an entrance, as well, on Rue Cambon; phone 4260-38-30) has not, to its great credit, been content to rest on the laurels of a global reputation; it's the "original" Ritz, founded by the legendary César Ritz in 1898. Acquired by a new management team in the late 1970s, it has undergone a long-range multimillion-dollar renovation—undertaken with extraordinary imagination, taste, and skill—that has been more a case of renewing and enhancing original decorative elements than of replacing them. The Ritz occupies one of the original eighteenth-century Place Vendôme palaces and extends through to an early twentieth-century Rue Cambon addition. The opulent Vendôme-side bar-lounge is a splendid choice for afternoon tea or cocktails. But then you walk through the arcade that connects Vendôme with Cambon buildings, alongside a block-long series of windows displaying luxury goods from Paris shops (with a *vendeuse* on hand during daytime hours to take orders), and there is still another bar, the Hemingway, intimate, named for a one-time resident, and with black leather surfacing stools and chairs surrounding the tables. Restaurant Espadon (which I review on a later page) moves from Louis XV–inspired winter quarters to the sculpture-accented, lantern-hung garden in summer. The relatively recently created Ritz Health Club is a capacious subterranean installation of especial beauty. Its swimming pool, edged by a full-meal-service café on its balcony, just has to be the handsomest in France, and is supplemented by not one but a pair of gyms (men's and women's), squash court, saunas, Turkish baths, and a health center and facial service that are open evenings. Noteworthy, too, are the Ritz Club, softly lighted and good-looking, which welcomes hotel guests for traditional-cuisine meals, drinks, and dancing into the wee hours; and École de Gastronomie Française Ritz-Escoffier, a somewhat unwieldy monicker for the hotel's cooking school, with wine, pastry, and table-setting among specialties, and course durations ranging from two hours to three months. Accommodations? There are just 200 suites and rooms. The suites—

including one with a bed that was Marie-Antoinette's, and with museum-caliber eighteenth- and early nineteenth-century furniture and accessories in most—constitute, in my view, the most beautiful of any that I know of in any hotel in Europe. But ordinary rooms, minimum singles as well as standard doubles—at least those I have stayed in or inspected—are superbly appointed as well. Member, Leading Hotels of the World. *Luxury.*

Royal Monceau Hôtel (37 Avenue Hoche; phone 4561-98-00): Long reputed as one of Paris's smarter hotels—it is located on one of the very grand avenues that radiate, like spokes, from Place Charles de Gaulle—the Royal Monceau joined the crack Italian luxury chain, Ciga, a few seasons back and has emerged handsomer than ever as a consequence of a $15 million renovation. There are close to 200 rooms and nearly 30 suites—decorated in the style of the Empire and the Directoire—good-looking lobby, welcoming bar-lounge, and pair of noteworthy restaurants. One, Le Jardin, is surmounted by a glass dome in the hotel's garden; the other, Carpaccio, is authentically—and deliciously—Italian. You may work out, too; there are both a swimming pool and a gym-cum-sauna. *Luxury.*

Royal St.-Honoré Hôtel (13 Rue d'Alger; phone 4260-32-79) is a satisfactory smaller house, with a situation that is nothing if not convenient—on a short street between Rues St.-Honoré and Rivoli, just east of Place Vendôme. There are 78 traditional-style rooms with good baths, a pleasant lobby and lounge. Breakfast only. *First Class.*

St. James et Albany Hôtel (202 Rue de Rivoli; phone 4268-31-60) went up, in part, toward the end of the seventeenth century as the *hôtel particulier* of Duc de Noailles. Half a century later, Marquis de Lafayette married a daughter of the Noailles clan, on premises; and not long thereafter,

Queen Marie-Antoinette welcomed Lafayette at Château de Noailles upon his return from America. Later dubbed Hôtel St. James, the earlier structure was combined with the adjacent Hôtel d'Albany in the mid-nineteenth century, to open as a commercial hotel, which it has been ever since. The early 1980s saw refurbishing—traditional interiors, alas, became acceptable, if undistinguished, contemporary (each of the 145 units—some two-room suites, some duplex suites—has a fridge and electric plate, should you want to make coffee or tea). The restaurant moves to a pretty courtyard in summer, and there's a bar. But, in the process of renovation, there was a name change. The longtime stubbornly plural Hôtels St.-James et d'Albany became the singular Hôtel St. James et Albany, and the preposition preceding Albany disappeared in the process. *Alors*, such is *le progrès*. *First Class*.

St. James's Club (5 Place Chancelier Adenauer; phone 4704-29-29) is a counterpart of the London original (see *London at Its Best*), where I've enjoyed staying. But the Paris club is far less central and far posher than its northerly counterpart. (Its vice-president, Jane Eland, told the American magazine *Architectural Digest* that "the key to turning Paris's 'little Fontainebleu' into Paris's finest club is to make sure the right sort of people come." Tut, tut. I do not devote space to private clubs in my books and make mention of this one for the same reason that I do of the London cousin: you may stay the first time without being a member, as you would at any hotel, deciding after that if you'd like to join.) The Paris St. James's occupies a restored mansion way out near Bois de Boulogne, with a fountain in the garden and interiors by the same Andrée Putnam responsible for the severe black-and-white Morgans Hotel in New York (see *New York at Its Best*). Madame Putnam relaxes a little here—beige, with green plants in the lobby, a bit of warmth in the bar, graceless upholstered chairs in rooms and suites that are, to their credit, Art Deco-patterned; and a salmon-draped restaurant, perhaps the handsomest room in the house. *Luxury.*

St.-Paul le Marais Hôtel (8 Rue de Sévigné; phone 4804-97-27) is an aged house that has been deftly transformed into a contemporary hotel of considerable style and is nicely located between Places des Vosges and Musée Carnavalet. There's a nifty main-floor lounge, breakfast room in the barrel-vaulted cellar, and 27 beamed-ceiling rooms that are otherwise pale-hued and contemporary with good baths. There is no restaurant. *Moderate.*

St.-Petersbourg Hôtel (33 Rue de Caumartin; phone 4266-60-38) is no more Old Russian—the name notwith-standing—than it is Old English. It is, however, an elderly house that has been spruced up to the point where all 120 rooms have baths. There is a neat little lobby, a convenient restaurant, and a dark-paneled bar that calls itself Anglais, perhaps because it sports a framed photo of Queen Elizabeth II and Prince Philip. The location, between the Madeleine and the Opéra, is good. *Moderate.*

St.-Romain Hôtel (5 Rue Saint-Roch; phone 4260-31-70) charms with its good looks. Relatively recently refur-bished, it offers 33 rooms with marble baths, bar-lounge, and breakfast in the old cellar—whose stone walls are barrel-vaulted. I should add that—unusual in Moderate-category French hotels—there's a printed breakfast menu from which you may order not only the usual boiled egg, but fried eggs with bacon, cereals, cheeses, and yogurt, all as à la carte extras. Location is a convenient street between Rue Saint-Honoré and Rue de Rivoli. *Moderate.*

San Régis Hôtel (12 Rue Jean Goujon; phone 4359-41-90)—on a street leading from Avenue Franklin Roosevelt, near the Étoile—is a looker, as smartly furnished and accessorized in its 33 rooms (including 4 suites—all with fine baths) as in public spaces, which include a stained-glass-ceilinged restaurant and bar. *First Class.*

Scribe Hôtel (1 Rue Scribe; phone 4742-03-40) is in the heart of the busy Opéra area. It's a big, comfortable old-timer that has been intelligently, expensively, and tastefully refurbished in appropriate Louis XVI style, in the course of recent seasons. The high-ceilinged bedrooms are a highlight. There's a congenial bar-lounge and reputed restaurant in the basement. *Luxury.*

Sydney-Opéra Hôtel (50 Rue des Mathurins; phone 4265-35-48) is a honey—smallish, with a convenient Madeleine-Opéra location and 40 rooms, no two alike, each delightfully decorated and with bath. Breakfast, but no restaurant. *Moderate.*

Touraine Opéra Hôtel (73 Rue Taitbout; phone 4874-50-49) is aptly named. It is indeed in the neighborhood of Opéra/Garnier, north of Boulevard des Italiens. There are 38 well-equipped rooms with bath. Breakfast only. *Moderate.*

Trémoille Hôtel (14 Rue de la Trémoille; phone 4723-34-20) is intimate and quiet—on the serene street for which it is named, off Champs-Élysées, parallel with Avenue Montaigne. Public rooms are Louis XV and furnished with elaborate boiserie and tapestries. There is a dining room–bar-lounge, and the 112 bedrooms are capacious and comfortable. A Trusthouse Forte Exclusive Division hotel, affiliated with Leading Hotels of the World. *Luxury.*

Tuileries Hôtel (10 Rue St.-Hyacinthe; phone 4261-06-94): The Tuileries is on a tiny street that gives onto more-substantial Rue Marché St.-Honoré, lying midway between Place Vendôme (to the west) and Avenue de l'Opéra (to the east), with Rue St.-Honoré a bit south. This is a gracious, late eighteenth-century mansion converted with panache, in the style of the epoch when it was built, into a 30-room hotel. Breakfast only. *Moderate.*

Vendôme Hôtel (1 Place Vendôme at Rue de Castiglione; phone 4260-32-84) occupies a house designed by Hardouin-Mansart, the architect who took over Versailles from Le Vau at midpoint and completed it for Louis XIV. The front facade of the Vendôme is original; the rest of the building, although less venerable, is hardly unimpressive. This is a smallish hotel. The intimate bar-café doubles as a restaurant, making a specialty of full-meal service in the 40 high-ceilinged bedrooms (all of whose beds are super brass ones). And location is A-1. *First Class.*

Warwick Hôtel (5 Rue de Berri; phone 4563-14-11): A step or two off Champs-Élysées, the Warwick is decorated in contemporary tones, with traditional accents adding warmth. There are just under 150 rooms and suites, including a suite-cum-garden-terrace that looks out on the city, La Couronne Restaurant, bar-lounge, and a bountiful breakfast buffet. *Luxury.*

Westminster Hôtel (13 Rue de la Paix; phone 4261-57-46) went up a couple of centuries back as a convent and became a hotel in the nineteenth century. Located on a legendary, heart-of-town street (Cartier adjoins its entrance), it has been extensively remodeled by its owners, Warwick Hotels. A fifth of its hundred units are suites, and bedrooms are antiques-accented, with updated baths. Neighborhood locals keep the hotel's Le Céladon Restaurant (evaluated on a later page) humming, and the bar-lounge (go for afternoon tea or a wee-hours' drink) is mock-Renaissance, with a fireplace as high as its two-story ceiling. *Luxury.*

SELECTED RIVE GAUCHE/LEFT BANK AND ÎLE ST.-LOUIS HOTELS

Abbaye St.-Germain Hôtel (a.k.a. Hôtel de l'Abbaye; 10 Rue Cassette; 4544-38-11) occupies what had been a convent, not far east of Boulevard Raspail, with Boulevard St.-Germain-des-Prés a fairish walk north. Relatively out-of-the-way situation notwithstanding, the Abbaye has built up a loyal following, thanks to the good looks of its lobby, bar, and garden and the marble baths of its 45 smartly traditional rooms. Breakfast only. No credit cards are accepted. *Moderate.*

Académie Hôtel (32 Rue des Sts.-Pères; phone 4548-36-22) boasts a location on a Rive Gauche mini Hotel Row. There are 32 rooms with bath and pleasant public spaces. *Moderate.*

Angleterre Hôtel (44 Rue Jacob; phone 4260-34-72) is no more English than the Quartier Latin street on which it is situated. It is a typical Parisian inn; all rooms have bath or shower. Breakfast only. *Moderate.*

Arcade Montparnasse Hôtel (71 Boulevard de Vaurigard; phone 4320-89-12) embodies major aspects of the successful formula of the national chain of which it's a link: small but contemporary rooms (with as many as four beds, some double-decker, but with standard doubles available as well), restaurants featuring copious buffets for all three meals, and bar. This one's smaller than most with just over 30 rooms. Near skyscraping Tour Main-Montparnasse and Gare Montparnasse as well. *Moderate.*

Beaugency Hôtel (21 Rue Duvivier; phone 4705-01-63) has the dubious distinction of having the smallest-in-size rooms (30 all told) of any hotel of its category with which I am familiar in all France; it was obviously designed for French business travelers on quick overnight stays, with little more than a briefcase for baggage. Staff is minimally cordial and the location, near École Militaire some blocks south of Tour Eiffel, is inconvenient. Breakfast only. I can't recommend this one. *Moderate.*

Bellechasse Hôtel (8 Rue de Bellechase; phone 4551-52-36) is core-of-Rive Gauche on a street that intersects Boulevard St.-Germain. Lobby is clean-lined and appealing, rooms—relatively recently renovated—likewise. There are 32, all with bath. Breakfast only. *Moderate.*

Bersoly's St.-Germain Hôtel (28 Rue de Lille; phone 4296-32-34) is nicely located on the same street as the Musée d'Orsay and convenient to the Right Bank. The lobby is unprepossessing, but those of the 16 rooms I've inspected, though small and with narrow twin-beds, are otherwise agreeable. Breakfast only. *Moderate.*

Bonaparte Hôtel (61 Rue Bonaparte; phone 4326-97-37) is an unpretentious, worth-knowing-about oldie on a core-of-St.-Germain street that leads to the Seine. All 29 rooms are bath-equipped (the smaller ones have showers instead of tubs). Breakfast only. *Moderate.*

Claude-Bernard Hôtel (43 Rue des Écoles; phone 4326-32-52) is a neighbor of the Sorbonne and Collège de France. It is simple but adequate; most rooms have private baths. Breakfast only. *Moderate.*

Colbert Hôtel (7 Rue de l'Hôtel-Colbert; phone 4325-85-65) lies on the short street taking its name, between Boulevard

St.-Germain and the Seine. It's a charmer, with 40 no-two-alike rooms in the style of Louis XV and Louis XVI (including a honey of a suite with views of Notre-Dame), bar-lounge, and atmospheric breakfast room in a basement *cave.* There's no restaurant, but *Moderate*-category Le Cour Colbert is just opposite. *Moderate.*

Danube St.-Germain Hôtel (58 Rue Jacob; phone 4260-34-70), strategically situated at the intersection of Rues Jacob and Sts.-Pères, boasts a winsome inner patio and lounge. Management is pleasant; 30 of the 45 rooms have baths. Breakfast, but no restaurant. *Moderate.*

Derby Hôtel (5 Avenue Duquesne; phone 4705-12-05) has a fin-de-siècle facade—and ambience within as well—on an attractive street near the École Militaire, the Invalides, and UNESCO, from whose global membership it draws much of its clientele. Virtually all of the 36 good-looking rooms have baths. Breakfast only. *Moderate.*

Deux-Îles Hôtel (59 Rue St.-Louis-en-l'Île, on Île St.-Louis; phone 4326-13-35) is center of the Île St.-Louis action, on its principal street. The lobby is attractively antique-accented, and although no two of the 17 rooms are quite alike, they're pleasant, and all with bath. Breakfast only. *Moderate.*

Fleurie Hôtel (32 Rue Grégoire-de-Tours; phone 4329-59-81) occupies quarters in an eighteenth-century house splendidly facaded. The 29 rooms tend to be small (although there are a few pricier larger-size chambers) but all have marble-accented baths. Situation is half a block from Boulevard St.-Germain. This is an attractive, relatively recently renovated house. Breakfast only. *Moderate.*

Grand Hôtel des Balcons (3 Rue Casimir-Delavigne; phone 4634-78-50): A hotel with ten of its 55 rooms without private baths is not grand in the accepted sense. Withal, if you land a room *with* bath you can be happy indeed. Near Place de l'Odéon and Jardin de Luxembourg. Breakfast only. *Moderate.*

Grands Hommes Hôtel (17 Place du Panthéon; phone 4634-19-60) Use the dome of the neighboring Panthéon as a landmark and you'll have no difficulty in locating the Grands Hommes, a pleasant house with 32 bath-equipped rooms. Breakfast only. *Moderate.*

Hilton International Paris Hôtel (18 Avenue de Suffren; phone 4273-92-00) was considered a sassy Yank upstart by the locals when I covered its opening. It was the first completely new hotel in Paris for decades. At first, the French tended to be patronizing about the *Eel-tohn,* but they soon realized that it represented contemporary luxury hotelkeeping. And so this hotel has thrived, despite a location that is more romantic than convenient (its next-door neighbor is the Eiffel Tower) and a look that is more functional than beautiful. There's a restaurant called Le Western beloved of the Parisians for its U.S.-style steaks; and a Gallic-accented coffeeshop. And I'll say this for the location: During my first visit, I made up my mind to take no taxis; I wanted to master the Métro. With the system map in hand, I took it everywhere; and have been a Métro fan ever since. *Luxury.*

L'Hôtel Guy-Louis-Duboucher (13 Rue des Beaux-Arts; phone 4325-27-22)—despite, or possibly because of, small capacity (there are but 27 no-two-alike, antique-accented rooms, each with a marble-surfaced bath)—has achieved a certain snob status. There is no denying its good looks, convenient location, or interesting past (Oscar Wilde died on the premises). Still, I have found its reception staff un-welcoming and its restaurant more attractive than deli-cious. *Luxury.*

Jeu de Paume Hôtel (54 Rue St.-Louis-en-l'Île, on Île St.-Louis; phone 4326-14-18) went up as a tennis court (its name, in the French language) in the eighteenth century and, relatively recently, was transformed, with considera-ble style, into a honey of a 32-room-with-bath, antique-accented hotel, with inviting public spaces (including a bar). Location is Île St.-Louis's principal thoroughfare, abounding in restaurants. Breakfast only. *First Class.*

Latitudes St.-Germain Hôtel (7 Rue St.-Benoît; phone 4261-53-53), situated between Boulevard Saint-Germain and the Seine, is at once good-size (117 bath-equipped rooms in a variety of color schemes) and good-looking, with wood-paneled, marble-accented lounges, *fin-de-siècle* bar-lounge Art Deco reading room, and a greenhouse in which breakfast is served. *Moderate/First Class.*

Left Bank Hôtel (9 Rue de l'Ancienne Comédie; phone 4354-01-70) is, despite its English-language name, authen-tically Rive Gauche, occupying a seventeenth-century house, with antiques and tapestries dotted about, 31 beamed-ceiling rooms with modern baths sporting marble counter sinks, and an agreeable breakfast room. Location is core of the area for which the hotel is named. Best West-ern. *Moderate.*

Lenox Hôtel (9 Rue de l'Université; phone 4296-10-95) suc-cessfully employs a traditional-contemporary mix, with re-spect to decor; there's a convenient bar and all 34 rooms are bath-equipped. Quartier Latin location is convenient. *Moderate.*

Lutèce Hôtel (65 Rue St.-Louis-en-l'Île; phone 4326-23-52): To stay in this charming house—there are but 31 pleasant rooms—is a distinct pleasure. Breakfast only. *Moderate.*

Lutétia Hôtel (46 Boulevard Raspail, at Rue de Sèvres; phone 4544-38-10), with its brilliant, carved-stone facade, is an Art Nouveau landmark of Paris and has been since it went up in 1910. Hôtels Concorde, its proprietors, have refurbished it stem to stern, and, to their great credit, they illuminate that one-of-a-kind facade every evening. There are 315 rooms and suites, with the ones to ask for those with views of Les Invalides and the Eiffel Tower. There are a pair of restaurants; I am partial to the popularly priced Brasserie, reviewed on a later page. The bar is congenial. And the situation is super. *First Class.*

Madison Hôtel (143 Boulevard St.-Germain; phone 4329-72-50) has a good location opposite the church of St.-Germain-des-Prés, with a view of it from the front. All 55 rooms have baths. Breakfast only. *Moderate.*

Marronniers Hôtel (21 Rue Jacob; phone 4325-30-60) is strategically situated on an atmospheric Quartier Latin street about midpoint between the Seine and Boulevard St.-Germain. There are 37 neat rooms with bath. Breakfast only. *Moderate.*

Montalembert Hôtel (3 Rue Montalembert; phone 4548-68-11) is an old-school house of fairish size, with an equally agreeable core-of-Left-Bank situation. All 60 rooms have been modernized and have baths. Breakfast only. *First Class.*

Notre-Dame Hôtel (1 Quai Saint-Michel; phone 4354-20-43) is, to be sure, accurately titled. By that I mean there are views of the great Paris cathedral from all 26 of its bath-equipped rooms, relatively recently refurbished. Breakfast only. *Moderate.*

Pas-de-Calais Hôtel (59 Rue des Saints-Pères; phone 4548-78-74) is conveniently situated in the heart of the Left Bank, on one of its most attractive streets. It is smallish, spotless, and inviting. All 41 rooms have baths. There's a spacious lounge, congenial management, and breakfast (but no restaurant). *Moderate.*

Pont-Royal Hôtel (7 Rue de Montalembert; phone 4544-92-07) is located on a pleasant Quartier Latin street just off Boulevard St.-Germain. The look is spiffy traditional—lobby, paneled bar with green leather chairs, terraced Les Antiquaires Restaurant—as well as 80 comfortable rooms and suites with good baths. Very nice, indeed. *First Class.*

Quai Voltaire Hôtel (19 Quai Voltaire; phone 4261-50-91) has a location that is nothing less than inspired, on the Seine, right across from the Louvre, between Pont Royal and Pont du Carrousel. This is a nicely freshened-up old building. There are fewer than 35 rooms, a good proportion with private baths. Breakfast only. *Moderate.*

Relais St.-Germain Hôtel (9 Carrefour de l'Odéon; phone 4329-12-05) is, in a nutshell, small but smart. By that I mean 9 rooms only, each with a fabulous marble bath with double sinks, plus an antique-accented suite. Location is between Place de l'Odéon and Boulevard St.-Germain. Breakfast only. *First Class.*

Ste.-Beuve Hôtel (9 Rue Ste.-Beuve; phone 4548-20-07) has but 22 rooms, but they're attractive, not unlike the rest of the house—and popular. Only breakfast is served, but you're only a hop and a skip from the celebrated La Coupole Restaurant (below). *Moderate.*

St.-Germain-des-Prés Hôtel (36 Rue Bonaparte; phone 4326-00-19) is an aged building that has been imaginatively refurbished, with a paneled lobby, Louis XIII-style lounge, fresh flowers at every turn, beamed ceilings, tapestried walls, and 30 rooms, mostly with papered walls, all with bath, and for the most part good-sized. Location is super—steps from the church of St.-Germain des Prés and the boulevard taking its name. Breakfast only. *Moderate.*

St.-Grégoire Hôtel (43 Rue de l'Abbé Grégoire; phone 4548-23-23): I don't know of a hotel the interior designer David Hicks has created in his native Britain. But he is responsible for the decor—beige, pale rose, yellow in a setting of beamed ceilings and abundant jumbo-size vases of flowers—of the St.-Grégoire. There are just 20 rooms, each with touches unique to it and a good bath, and one with its own terrace. Only breakfast is served, but the hotel's management owns the neighboring La Marlotte Restaurant, which provides room service. Near Rue de Rennes and Boulevard Raspail. *Moderate/First Class.*

St.-Louis Hôtel (75 Rue St.-Louis-en-l'Île; phone 4634-04-80)—on Île St.-Louis's busy main drag—shelters 21 bath-equipped rooms and serves breakfast (no other meals) in its medieval cellar. Nice. *Moderate.*

St.-Simon Hôtel (14 Rue St.-Simon; phone 4548-35-66), flanking a short street just off Boulevard St.-Germain, is a case of good things in small packages—just under 30 rooms, all with bath, and a welcoming management. Breakfast only. *Moderate.*

Solferino Hôtel (91 Rue de Lille; phone 4705-85-54) is a long-on-scene favorite with considerable repeat clientele, thanks to its convenient location (near Musée d'Orsay), and functional rooms, most of which (27 of 33) have baths. Breakfast only. *Moderate.*

Splendid Hôtel (29 Avenue de Trouville; phone 4551-24-77), a neighbor of École Militaire, UNESCO, and the Invalides, has 45 simple but pleasant rooms with bath. There's an inviting lobby-lounge with a bar but no restaurant, although breakfast is served. *Moderate.*

Tour Notre-Dame Hôtel (36 Rue St.-Jacques; phone 4354-47-60) is an interestingly restored *hôtel particulier* that's a neighbor of Musée de Cluny (above), at the corner of Boulevard St.-Germain. There are just under half a hundred ultra-mod rooms with marble baths and, in some cases, balconies, from which there can be views of Notre-Dame. There's a cozy bar and breakfast, but no restaurant. Nice. *Moderate.*

Trianon Palace Hôtel (1-bis Rue de Vaugirard; phone 4329-88-10) is fair-sized—120 rooms—and situated near Boulevard St.-Michel and the Jardin du Luxembourg. Most rooms have baths, and breakfast is served. *Moderate.*

Université Hôtel (22 Rue de l'Université; phone 4261-09-39) is a long-popular, attractively furnished charmer, with 27 no-two-alike, bath-equipped rooms and convenient situation. Breakfast only. *Moderate.*

Verneuil St.-Germain Hôtel (8 Rue de Verneuil; phone 4260-82-14) is a pleasure. It's a tastefully updated eighteenth-century house between Rue du Bac and Rue des Sts.-Pères, with 26 attractive, bath-equipped rooms, two of which are living-room-attached suites. Breakfast only. *Moderate.*

La Villa Hôtel (29 Rue Jacob; phone 4326-60-00): Starkly contemporary hi-tech design—once you leave major monuments like the Beaubourg—is the departure rather than the rule in Paris, and when, relatively recently, the former Hôtel d'Isly, in a centuries-old house core-of-Quartier-Latin, was gutted and replaced with a decidedly contemporary interior—well, Parisians took notice. The look is leather and unembellished wood, and all 35 rooms sport ultra-mod baths. Bar in the basement (the music is jazz) and breakfast. *Moderate.*

STAYING AT THE AIRPORTS

Paris Orly Airport Hilton Hôtel (phone 4687-33-88) has the great advantage of being directly opposite Orly's main entrance. It is, of course, soundproofed and air-conditioned, with 366 comfortable French-modern rooms, moderate-tab coffee shop, smart La Lousiane Restaurant, bar-lounge, and amenities, including business center, dozen-plus meeting rooms, barber and beauty parlor, and gratis bus service to and from the terminal. *Luxury.*

Holiday Inn Roissy Hôtel (Allée du Verger, Roissy; phone 3429-30-00) is typically Holiday Inn functional, with 250 rooms, each with a shower-equipped bath; convenient restaurant, comfortable bar-lounge, and a location adjacent to de Gaulle Airport. *First Class.*

Altea Paris-Roissy Hôtel (Zone Hôtelière, Allée du Verger, Roissy; phone 3429-40-00), among the newer hostelries serving de Gaulle, is low-slung and well appointed, with just over 200 pleasant rooms (including 8 suites and a good-sized clutch of premium-tab, extra-amenity Club rooms). There are both dressy and brasserie-style restaurants, congenial bar, and business services including fax and telex, as well as meeting rooms. *First Class.*

5

Paris to Eat and Drink

FRANCE'S CUISINE IN FRANCE'S CAPITAL

The Paris restaurant scene is the most extraordinary of any city in the world. It is not alone the quantity; New York, London, Rome, and other great cities have thousands of restaurants, too. It is the concentration of the practitioners of the art of French cuisine in the French capital—a city that appreciates them, knows how to enjoy the fare they present, and does so frequently, arguing and debating their merits and demerits, endlessly and relentlessly.

Ideally, the visitor to Paris approaches food as the visitor to Madrid does bullfighting. Or the visitor to Milan does opera. Or the visitor to Kyoto does the tea ceremony. This is the specialty of the town. In no city of the planet does gastronomy play a larger role. Paris, at least for a substantial portion of one's stay, must be regarded as a very special source of meals.

This is hardly a locale for grabbing a bite on the run. (Although, it must be pointed out, Parisians have taken to the concept of the quick burger in ever-multiplying McDonalds and, moreover, of French imitators of that imported-from-America chain.) Transatlantic visitors, however, do not cross an ocean for Big Macs. Ideally, both budget and time should be allotted for interesting lunches and dinners. Compensate, as the French do, with a minimal breakfast (see below) so as to be really hungry for the two major meals of each day. Restaurants selected might be a mix—a couple of the grand-luxe places; substantially more first-class restaurants, the great stronghold of the Paris restaurant scene and dealt with at length below; and the rest inexpensive spots, of which there is—rest assured—no dearth, as you will find as you read on.

TRADITIONAL VS. CONTEMPORARY

France's nouvelle cuisine—emulated transatlantic, north of the English Channel, in much else of Europe, and at other points planetwide—has given up its maiden name (the term *nouvelle* is rarely applied any longer, at least in France) and grown up. A better term is *contemporary*. By that I mean that ambitious young chefs—cooks who name restaurants after themselves, hire publicists, compile cookbooks, demonstrate on the telly, and charge high tabs—still are an intrinsic part of the French—and, of course, the Paris—restaurant scene.

But they are, by and large, no longer wild-eyed radicals of the kitchen. They remain creative—and more power to them, in this respect. But they have come to appreciate that diners paying enormous sums (there are no Moderate and few First Class restaurants with contemporary cuisine) want the dishes set before them to be recognizable, not without familiar ingredients (the potato, historically France's most popular and most-consumed vegetable, has blessedly returned from banishment to contemporary restaurants) served in decent-sized portions (the old nouvelle invariably appeared in skimpy servings). While not without welcome innovations, even surprises, they currently appear devoid of absurd and bizarre combinations that focused on oddball mixes of sweet and savory.

The influence of nouvelle has been stronger than some of us like to admit. Presentation of cuisine, always important to nouvelle chefs, has become more sophisticated—surely there are influences of artfully arranged Japanese dishes—in restaurants of all persuasions, both in France and abroad. Desserts, again emulating early nouvelle sweets, are often served on near-dinner-size plates in precise symmetrical designs. Vegetables—still too often, for this diner—arrive shredded, sliced, and wrapped in spherical shapes, even tied in knots, awaiting demolition by the diner's fork. Bread, still somewhat suspect, instead of being produced by the basket, is served a tiny roll at a time so that, often, you must ask for seconds.

Withal, we must—it seems to this devotee of what is, when all is said and done, the world's greatest cuisine—be glad that its classic and traditional influences again are accorded the respect they deserve. French sauciers—whose output, when skilled, was never "heavy," despite old nouvelle criticisms—again are acclaimed. French ingredients again are respected. French appetites again are being satisfied in posher places, although it must be emphasized that even during the nouvelle vogue's flightiest years, traditional restaurants, wherein the overwhelming majority of French men and French women dine—Paris-wide and nationwide—never stopped producing dishes that made their national cuisine celebrated. And still do.

A glory of French food is that it has never been necessary, even in the most diehard brasserie, to overindulge. France has never neglected foods that are today standbys of healthy eating—salads (who does them more justice?) and seafood (where are fish and mollusks prepared in more infinite variety, from bivalves on the half-shell in tandem with lemon slices, through to simply broiled fish?), poultry (the roasted chicken is a French masterwork), and green vegetables (who knows better than the French how to simply cook, say, string beans or broccoli?). For that matter, in what land did fresh fruit gain currency as a dessert? In which cuisine (certainly not American) is bread served without butter—except in distinctly pricey temples of gastronomy? Again, where (certainly not the United States) is coffee never served with rich cream, and even with milk only at breakfast?

You will find some of the outstanding contemporary-cuisine restaurants on pages following. By and large, though, I make a special point of concentrating on restaurants easier to reserve for, with more realistic prices, and that serve the kind of food that the great bulk of visitors from across the Atlantic have crossed over to experience on home ground. A typical meal will open with hors d'oeuvres or soup, go on to an entrée of meat or fish or a seafood dish, with a green salad dressed with oil, vinegar, salt, and pepper following; thence, cheese selected from a platter, fresh fruit or dessert, and coffee. If the meal is un-festive, one wine will accompany it—red, if with meat; white, if with fish. The French have far less aversion to the consumption of water than do, say, the British. Feel free to ask for tap water (*une carafe d'eau*) and if you prefer bottled water, rather than ordering Perrier (which the French tend to regard as too effervescent to drink with food), order their favorite mealtime *eau gazeuse*, Badoit; Évian leads the bottled nonbubblies.

MEAL HOURS

Meal hours are sensible; lunch service in restaurants starts between noon and 12:30 P.M., continuing until about 2:00 P.M.; between 8:00 and 10:00 P.M. is the preferred time for dinner, although restaurants begin serving between 7:00 and 7:30 P.M. It's advisable to *reserve in advance*, except in simpler places (hotel concierges will do this for you, or phone yourself), noting that many restaurants observe a weekly closing day, as well as a *fermeture annuelle,* or annual vacation.

MENU SPECIFICS

Hors d'oeuvres might include relishes like scallions and radishes, black and green olives, and celery *rémoulade.* There might be, as well, eggs-mayonnaise, lentils or beans, tiny shrimp or other shellfish, and snails served piping hot in their shells, with a parsley-butter and garlic sauce; various *pâtés* and *terrines,* and, the supreme opener, *foie gras*—poached fattened duck or goose liver. *French soups*—the widely exported onion, of course, but even simple *potages du jour*—are invariably delicious, as, indeed, are creamy *bisques* based on lobster or crab.

Meats are masterfully prepared. Beef appears as steak (*entrecôte, châteaubriand*), roasted on skewers, and in stews as *ragoûts* and *daubes. Blanquette de veau* is the veal stew par excellence. But look also for veal *escalopes,* as well as chops (*côtelettes*), sweetbreads *(ris de veau),* and brains *(cervelles).* Lamb appearing roasted, as *gigot d'agneau avec flageolet*-type beans is a favorite. Pork specialties are no less good, from *charcuterie* (sausage and specialty pork products) to *jambon* (ham) and roasts.

If simply grilled with a squeeze of lemon or accompanied by a delicate sauce, *fish* in France is a winner. Likewise, such seafood as crab, crayfish, lobster, and oysters. Nowhere is *poultry* more imaginatively prepared; chicken, of course, but duck and goose as well. If you haven't tried frog's legs *(grenouilles),* you're missing a treat. Fresh *vegetables* are rarely, if ever, overcooked.

The *cheese* course is important in France. You know Camembert, Brie, and Roquefort, but try Pont l'Évêque, Reblochon, Port-Salut, Chèvre (goat cheese, several species of which often appear on a single tray), and any number of others, varying by region, not unlike wine. *Pastries* are at their most enjoyable mid-morning or mid-afternoon, with coffee or tea in a *pâtisserie* that doubles as a *salon de thé,* or simply purchased by the bag from shops whose windows prove irresistible. They're always available as *desserts,* along with gargantuan *ice cream* sundaes, called *bombes* or *coupes,* hot *soufflés*—chocolate, lemon, vanilla, Grand Marnier—and *crêpes,* the thin pancakes of Breton origin. French wines rate a section of their own.

THE FRENCH BREAKFAST

Petit déjeuner is nothing more than the term (translated as "little lunch") implies. Unless you specify otherwise, it will consist of *café au lait*—a pot of intense black coffee served with an equal-sized jug of hot milk, the idea being that you mix the two, more or less half and half. Accompanying the coffee will be a *petit-pain* (crusty roll), a *croissant* (by and large, flakier in Paris than in provincial France), and/or a *brioche,* along with butter and jam. This is a *café complet,* or Continental breakfast, upon occasion served with fruit juice. Where that is not the case, juice, as well as eggs, bacon, and ham may be ordered additionally, at least at better hotels. Breakfast is generally not included in room rates at better hotels, where it can be expensive; neighborhood cafés are less pricey options for, say, croissants and coffee. (If a Parisian ever has anything more than *café complet,* it is a single boiled egg served *à la coque*—in the shell— with salt, but rarely pepper, which must usually be specially requested). In virtually all cases, no matter how simple the hotel, breakfast is served in bedrooms, as well as in the hotel's dining or special breakfast room. And in certain instances, hotels offer the option of breakfast buffets; those of Paris's Crillon and Ritz hotels are quite the grandest such of any that I know in France.

AN ABBREVIATED CULINARY GLOSSARY

For menu-reading purposes, here are some dishes and terms that may be helpful:

Agneau: lamb
À la mode: "in the style of"
À point: medium-rare, as with steak
Asperges: asparagus
Au gratin: not only with cheese, as in the United States, but also sprinkled with crumbs and baked brown
Au naturel: simply prepared
Baguette-Jambon: ham sandwich on slim French bread, cut lengthwise—a good café snack
Beurre: butter
Bien cuit: well done, as with steaks or roasts
Biscuits: cookies, crackers
Blanquette: light meat in cream sauce, as blanquette de veau (a veal stew)
Bleu: rare, as with steaks (*saignant* is *very* rare)
Boeuf: beef
Brioche: a type of breakfast pastry, muffin-shaped
Café: coffee
Café au lait: breakfast coffee, a pot of black and a pot of warm milk to be mixed with it by you
Café filtre: after-dinner filtered coffee
Canard: duck
Champignons: mushrooms
Chaud: warm
Chou: cabbage
Chou-fleur: cauliflower
Choux de Bruxelles: Brussels sprouts
Confitures: preserves, jam
Coupe: ice cream dessert, sundae; a *bombe* is similar
Crêpes: pancakes
Croissant: flaky breakfast pastry, crescent-shaped

Croque-monsieur: grilled-cheese sandwich

Crudités: raw vegetables—carrots, radishes, tomatoes, celery, green peppers—served as hors d'oeuvres

Daube: stew

Dinde: turkey

Eau: water

Eau glacé: ice water

Eau minerale: mineral water (Badoit, Perrier, Évian, Vittel, Vichy, Célestin are leading brands)

Eau minerale avec gaz: bubbly

Eau minerale sans gaz: plain

En brochette: skewered cubes of meat

En coquille: usually seafood in a fake-shell container

En papillote: cooked in oiled paper or aluminum foil

Entrecôte: smallish steak

Entrée: first course (as distinct from main course)

Épinards: spinach

Escargots: snails

Farci: stuffed

Flageolets: tiny lima beans usually served with roast lamb

Foie: liver; *foie gras* is fattened liver of *oie* (goose) or *canard* (duck)

Fond: bottom

Frit: fried

Froid: cold

Fromage: cheese—varieties include Boursin (mild, creamy), Brie and Camembert (soft-ripened), Pont l'Évêque and Port-Salut (semisoft), Chèvre (goat cheese), Roquefort and Bleu (tangy, crumbly, blue-veined), and Emmenthaler (what we call Swiss). There are about three hundred others.

Fruits: ananas (pineapple), cérises (cherries), citrons (lemons), fraises (strawberries), framboises (raspberries), groseilles (currants), oranges (oranges), pamplemousse (grapefruit), pêches (peaches), pommes

(apples), poires (pears), prunes (plums), Reine-Claude
(greengage)
Fumé: smoked
Garni: garnished
Gâteau: cake
Glace: ice cream, but also ice
Glacé: frozen, iced
Haché: chopped or sliced
Haricots verts: green (string) beans
Huile d'olive: olive oil
Jambon: ham
Jardinière: mixed vegetables
Julienne: thin strips of meat, cheese, vegetables
Lait: milk
Légumes: vegetables
Lyonnaise: cooked with onions
Macédoine: mixture of fruits or vegetables
Menu: bill of fare (also *carte*), but also set meal, prix-fixe,
    as, for example, menu touristique
Oeufs: eggs: à la coque (boiled); sur le plat (fried);
    brouillés (scrambled); pochés (poached)
Oie: goose
Pain: bread; petit-pain (roll)
Périgourdine: cooked with truffles
Petits pois: green peas
Poisson: fish
Porc: pork
Potage: soup (also sometimes *soupe*)
Poulet: chicken
Provençal: cooked with tomatoes
Quenelles: dumplings
Ragoût: stew
Rillettes: a coarse type of pork pâté
Rôti: roast
Saignant: very rare, as with steaks

Sandwich: sandwich
Saucisse: sausage
Thé: tea
Tournedos: filet steak
Veau: veal
Véronique: cooked with grapes
Viande: meat
Vinaigrette: the genuine French dressing or marinade: oil
   and vinegar, with salt, pepper, and possibly other
   seasonings
Volaille: poultry

WINES OF FRANCE

BY MAX DRECHSLER

Wine in Paris, as, indeed, throughout France, is a facet of
daily living—the natural accompaniment to food. As such
—except for rarified vintages sought out by connoisseurs—
it is not something to be reverenced with awe. It is true, of
course, that some of France's wines are the greatest and
most noble in the world. But it is by no means necessary to
be an expert to enjoy drinking wine in the course of a Paris
sojourn. Although some wines are drunk as aperitifs, by
and large they augment and enhance meals.

   Always ask to see the wine list; read it over. You learn a
lot from these carefully prepared compilations as you go
from restaurant to restaurant. Conscientious restaura-
teurs—even in smaller places—give a great deal of thought,
attention, and consideration to their wine lists. And lists of
bigger restaurants are frequently publications deserving of
far more careful reading than can usually be devoted to
them in advance of a restaurant meal. If your interest in
wine is such that you would like one of these lists, don't
hesitate to ask, offering to pay for it, if it appears to have
been costly to produce.

As far back as the Middle Ages, the French recognized the need for legal controls to offer guarantees of origin and method of production. But it was not until 1935 that the government created the world's first comprehensive wine legislation. Termed *Appellation d'Origine Contrôlée* (A.O.C.), or Controlled Place of Origin, it covers every aspect of wine-making from soil and vine to bottle. Though not necessarily a guarantee of quality, A.O.C. regulations ensure that the consumer knows what goes into the bottle he or she may purchase, where it came from, and how to identify it; there are some 400 A.O.C. wines. In addition, there are two categories of wines that meet less rigid classifications: *Vins Délimités de Qualité Supérieure* (V.D.Q.S.)— developed in 1945—and the even more recent *Vin de Pays*. Wines in these two last-mentioned categories are worth trying and can be very good value. There remains *vin de table*—not officially designated—made in vast quantities around the Mediterranean and often with little but its low price as a plus. In all events, it's the label that tells the story. Don't hesitate, in a restaurant of any quality, to ask to see several different bottles before making a decision; when in doubt, pose questions to the waiter, captain, or *sommelier*—the specialist wine-server (wearing a silver necklace containing a *tastevin*, or wine-tasting minicup), to be found in better spots. Invariably they're happy to be helpful. French table wines—reds and whites in quantity, fewer rosés—are usually dry, fruity, or flowery, but never sweet. Here's a breakdown by principal areas:

Alsace's wines are almost entirely white. Alsace is unique among French wine regions in that all its wines are sold under the name of the grape from which they're made and with but one A.O.C. (Alsace), albeit broken down as *Riesling* (dry, clean taste, rich bouquet), *Gewürtztraminer* (spicy, fruity, pungent, with a flowery bouquet), *Sylvaner* (agreeable, fruity, and dry), and *Tokay* (not to be confused with the sweetish Hungarian Tokay, dry and full-bodied).

Bordeaux has been a wine center since the beginning of the Christian era. It's regarded as the area of the planet that produces the greatest wines (although Burgundy partisans might quarrel with this). This southwestern region, dominated by the city of Bordeaux and bisected by the Garonne River, divides itself into sectors that have given their names to the various types of Bordeaux. The *four major areas* are *Graves, St.-Émilion, Médoc,* and *Pomerol;* from these come the most noted red and white table wines. A fifth, *Sauternes,* produces the most celebrated of the French sweet whites. There are two additional types of Bordeaux. One, named for an area called *Entre-Deux-Mers,* is a type of dry white wine. The last is *Bordeaux Rouge*—moderate-priced reds that come from throughout the Bordeaux area.

There are two broad types of bottled Bordeaux: château-bottled and regional-bottled. *Château* designates wine produced on the estate of a specific château or grower (a real castle may or may not be part of the grower's estate). *Château-bottled* wine is entirely a product of that vineyard— the grapes have been grown and tended there, then harvested and processed into wine, and finally bottled and labeled on the premises. Among the most expensive and famous are Château Latour, Château Margaux, Château Lafite, and Château Mouton-Rothschild; but there are 84, all told. *Regional-bottled* wine comes from a broader area rather than a single vineyard; they include Graves and St.-Émilion. Wines are taken to various shippers' cellars in the city of Bordeaux, processed, and bottled. Besides the name of the area of production on the label, that of the shipper is indicated (rather than the individual vintner or château owner-grower). Quality tends to be good—and consistent.

Bordeaux *reds* are usually firm and delicate, yet sturdy when young, and mellow and full-bodied when mature. They grow better as they age—traditionally 10 years, sometimes sooner. At their best, they are subtle, with elegant flavor and brilliant color, the while being generous but neither heavy nor strong. Among the more important reds from the left bank of the Garonne River are Médoc, Haut Médoc, Moulis, Listrac, St.-Julien, St.-Estèphe, Pauillac (home of three of the five Premiers Crus—or top rankers— Château Lafite, Château Latour, and Château Mouton-Rothschild), Margaux (noted for Château Margaux), and Graves Rouges (noted for Château Haut Brion). Important right-bank reds include St.-Émilion, Pomerol (smallest of the leading Bordeaux districts), Fronsac, Côtes de Blaye, Côtes de Bourg, and Premières Côtes de Bordeaux.

Bordeaux *whites*—constituting about half the region's total output—include Graves and Entre-Deux-Mers, noted for light, crisp vintages; and—continuing south, where wines are less dry and more mellow—Premières Côtes de Bordeaux, Graves de Vayres, and St.-Macaire. The sweet Sauternes dessert wines (Château d'Yquem is the most noted) and those of Barsac are the most southerly; these last double as aperitif wines and go well with *foie gras frais*.

Burgundy/Bourgogne, southeast of Paris, produces some of the greatest of the world's wines, with its reds full, elegant, vigorous, big, and complex. Geographically, from north to south, it embraces *Chablis* (with France's most celebrated whites), *Côte d'Or* (divided into northerly *Côte de Nuits* and southerly *Côte de Beaune),* *Mâcon,* and *Beaujolais.* Originally attached to monasteries, the region's vineyards were secularized after the French Revolution and subdivided; the system of small owners prevails. In the Côte de Nuits–Côte d'Or area, they include Fixin, Gevrey-Chambertin (with eight Grand Cru vineyards), Morey St.-Denis (with four Grands Crus), Chambolle-Musigny, Clos Vougeot, Vosne-Romanée (with the ranking Romanée-Conti, La Tache, and Richebourg), and Nuits-St.-Georges. Some of the best-known Côte de Beaune wines are Aloxe-Corton (only Grand Cru of Côte de Beaune), Savigny, Pommard, Meursault, and Chassagne-Montrachet (lighter reds); Santenay and Côte de Beaune-Villages. Mâcon produces some light reds but is known mainly for whites. Beaujolais, at Burgundy's southern tip, produces one of the best-known red wines—light and fruity and at its best when young and slightly cooled. Beaujolais Nouveau is drunk in the fall just after being made; the better Beaujolais include Brouilly, Chénas, Chiroubles, Côte de Brouilly, Fleurie, Morgon, and Moulin-à-Vent. Beaujolais is the favorite wine of Lyon, France's gastronomically reputed No. 2 city.

Best whites? Those of Chablis—crisp, fruity, extremely dry, with a refreshing acidity—embrace four categories: Petit Chablis (drunk young), Chablis (green-tinged, fruity), Chablis Premier Cru, and Grand Cru (with such labels as Blanchots, Les Preuses, and Valmur). Côte de Beaune ranking whites include Aloxe-Corton (Grand Cru Corton-Charlemagne), Meursault, Puligny-Montrachet, Bâtard-Montrachet, and Montrachet (considered one of the best dry whites extant). Mâcon whites—Mâcon, Mâcon Supérieur, Mâcon Villages, Pinot-Chardonnay-Mâcon— are invariably light, crisp, and good value. The best-known Mâcons are Pouilly-Fuissé (slightly green-tinged, very dry), Pouilly Vinzelles, and St. Véran.

Champagne—from the region based on Reims that constitutes the most northerly of France's A.O.C. areas— produced still wines until, in the seventeenth century, a Benedictine monk (of course, you will have heard of Dom Pérignon) began corking bottles, the better to keep the bubbles therein for an indefinite period. All champagne is blended wine, and most of it is nonvintage. Each of the firms in the area has created its particular *cuvée*, or characteristic blend, and knowledgeable champagne drinkers choose by the producer's name. Champagne may be called champagne—in France at least—only if it's from Champagne (otherwise, if made in the same manner, it is *vin mousseux*, created by the *méthode champenoise*). The French are sticky about this. According to how dry it is, it is categorized Brut (driest of the lot, and for most champagne drinkers the preferred type), Extra Dry (next to the driest, despite its always-in-English designation), Sec (medium sweet), Demi-Sec (even sweeter), and Doux (the sweetest). Champagne is the all-occasion wine, and Brut champagne is the one wine that is good served throughout a meal, with each and every course (omitting the salad, with which no wine is preferable). There are close to a score of top-rank champagne firms, with Moët et Chandon, Mumm, Piper-Heidsieck, Taittinger, and Veuve Clicquot among the best known; all adhere to rigid standards set by Comité Interprofessionel du Vin de Champagne (C.I.V.C.).

Languedoc-Roussillon—the Mediterranean area around Montpellier—produces red, white, and rosé, but the best are reds: Corbières, Minervois, Côtes du Roussillon, Fitou, and Costières. There is an exceptional white—Clairette du Languedoc.

Loire Valley output includes white wines (both still and sparkling and accounting for three-quarters of the production), reds, and rosés. Better-known wines include such whites as Muscadet, Quincy, Sancerre, Saumur, Pouilly-Fumé—clean, dry, crisp, and occasionally fresh and fruity; such sparkling whites as Vouvray and Saumur; such reds as Chinon, Bourgueil, Sancerre, and Saumur-Champigny; and two pleasant rosés: Rosé d'Anjou and Rosé de Cabernet.

Provence provides a fascinating array of white, rosé, and red wines—with rosés especially celebrated and including Bandol (of which there are reds and whites, as well), Cassis (not to be confused with the black currant liqueur of Burgundy and a good white wine, as well), and Bellet (red and white, as well as rosé). Also worth trying (and not widely available beyond the area of production): Côtes de Provence, a red with rosé characteristics.

Southwest: Beyond Bordeaux is a less famous wine region, but one that produces large quantities of very drinkable wines, especially well suited to the local cuisine. Reds include Bergerac, Côtes de Bergerac, Côtes de Duras, Pechermant, Madiran, and Cahors—the excellent "black" wine, so called because of its dark hue. Southwest whites of consequence include Montravel, Côtes de Haut-Montravel, Bergerac, Rosette, and Montbazillac—an excellent Sauternes-like, sweet wine, good with dessert.

Savoie and Jura—the Alpine regions: Savoie wines have the tang of their bracing environment. They are mainly whites, which can be excellent—such as Crépy and Seysel (both still and sparkling). Reds and rosés include Arbin and Cruet. Jura is famous for its *vin jaune*, or yellow wine, as well as Château-Chalon—reminiscent of sherry; L'Étoile—a sparkling white; and the sweet, highly alcoholic *vins de paille*, or straw wines.

Côtes du Rhône may well have been the very first region of France in which grapes were cultivated for wine, and production was spurred by the medieval popes' seat in Avignon; indeed, the most famous Rhône red—Châteauneuf-du-Pape—the Pope's New Castle—celebrates the Provence papacy. That wine—strong and pungent—is the best known of the area's southern vineyards, along with Côtes du Rhône and Côtes du Rhône Villages (both red and white) and Tavel and Lirac (fine rosés). From the region's northern vineyards come Côte Rotie (red, white, and rosé), Hermitage and St. Joseph (red and white), Cornas (red), and Condrieu (white).

Cognac and Armagnac are the most noted of French brandies, which is to say, the best extant. Like champagne—which may be so called only if it is from Champagne—cognac may be so designated only if it is from the well-defined Cognac region, based on the little town of Cognac, north of Bordeaux. Cognac is made in traditional stills from Charentes wine and matured in oaken casks. There are several categories, designated by stars and, in the case of the finest, with initials VSOP, for Very Special Old Pale. Armagnac comes from the Gascony region of the south-west around Auch; like cognac, it is protected by government controls. Best type is bas-armagnac. But all armagnacs are made from distilled grapes by an ancient process that continues largely to ignore the machine. To experience it is to enjoy it. *Marc,* less known abroad, is a robust brandy, emanating principally from Burgundy and—somewhat more refined—from Champagne. It takes getting used to.

Eaux-de-Vie are highly distilled brandies made, by and large, from fruits of Alsatian orchards. They are clear and colorless and served icy cold as digestifs—after meals—with positively irresistible aromas redolent of the fruits from which they derive. Not unlike ice cream, they come in a variety of flavors, including framboise (raspberry), poire (pear), fraise (strawberry), mirabelle (plum), and kirsch (cherry).

Aperitif wines—nowhere better than in France—are worth becoming acquainted with, particularly if one is to follow the cocktail hour with a meal that will include wine and that may be followed by still additional variations on the alcoholic theme. It is not for nothing that Europeans prefer them to the transatlantic custom of more potent premeal cocktails. Best known is *vermouth*—excellent on the rocks with a twist of lemon. Popular, too, is *vermouth cassis*—the cassis being black currant syrup out of Burgundy. Noilly Prat, Boissière, and Martini are among the leading vermouth brands. (Note: *un Martini* means simply a glass of vermouth; *martini-gin* is what you ask for when you want a dry martini cocktail—and then only in better-category hotel bars accustomed to American and British tastes.) *Kir*—the most popular aperitif with the French—blends the earlier-mentioned cassis syrup with white wine; *Kir*

Royal—esteemed by those French with higher drink budgets—substitutes champagne for the white wine. *Pastis* is the French national café drink—a Gallic variation of the Turks' raki and the Greeks' ouzo, anisette in flavor and so constituted that it turns cloudy when diluted with water; Pernod and Ricard are the leading makes. *Dubonnet, Byrrh, St. Raphael,* and *Lillet* are aperitif wines of the vermouth family—sweetish but not cloyingly so, and good on the rocks and/or with soda.

Liqueurs: Orange-based *Grand Marnier,* widely exported, is known to many visitors in advance of arrival, as are *Bénédictine* and less-sweet *B & B*—brandy and Bénédictine combined; it emanates from the Norman town of Fécamp. *Chartreuse,* which comes in two colors (green and yellow), is the only liqueur still made by monks. Which leaves. . .

Bière: Foreigners are often surprised to learn that beer is popular with the French. Draft is cheaper than bottled; to order it, specify *à la pression.* Top brands, mostly out of Alsace, are Kronenbourg, Mutzig, Champigneulles, and Kanterbrau. Imports, too.

Water: Feel perfectly free to order *une carafe d'eau* (a carafe of water) or *un verre d'eau* (a glass of water) in restaurants or cafés. If you prefer bottled water, bear in mind that the French generally consider *Perrier* too effervescent for consumption with meals; they drink it as an aperitif or as a café pick-me-up, favoring less bubbly (but still *gazeuse*) *Badoit* or *non-gazeuse Évian* to accompany food.

SELECTED RIVE DROITE/RIGHT BANK RESTAURANTS AND CAFÉS

Ambassade d'Auvergne (22 Rue du Grenier-St.-Lazare; phone 4272-31-22) offers specialties of south-central Auvergne, rarely encountered in Paris. The prix-fixe dinner, to give you an idea, might embrace soupe aux choux (a cabbage potage), petit salé aux lentilles (a hearty pork

dish), and the difficult-to-describe but delicious aligot—
with a mashed-potato base. Mousse au chocolat is a favored dessert. *First Class.*

Les Ambassadeurs (Crillon Hôtel, 10 Place de la Concorde;
phone 4625-24-24): The approach to this restaurant—an
all-Paris leader—is hardly to be despised. Place de la Concorde for starters, with the Crillon lobby following. You
pass, then, up a couple of steps, to the hotel's high-
ceilinged Grand Salon, where you could do worse, if it's
evening, than to pause for a predinner drink in one of the
city's handsomest environments. The salon leads to Les
Ambassadeurs: marble-walled, hung with crystal chandeliers, massed with great bouquets of flowers, its tables
flanked by black-upholstered armchairs, with the staff
swift, skilled, and tuxedo-clad. Splurge with foie gras or
smoked salmon to start. Seafood is special at Les
Ambassadeurs—sole meunière or, more spectacular, a
whole lobster in a coriander-infused bouillon. Beef entrées
are top of the line; ditto breast of chicken, crisp-skinned in
a light ginger-honey sauce. And so are braised sweetbreads. Chocolate desserts are irresistible, none more so
than one termed Dôme Chocolat Noisettes Croquantes et
Nectar de Cacao—alone worth a pilgrimage to this restaurant. Don't fail to peruse the eighteen-page wine list, outstanding not only for Bordeaux (how about a $2,500
Château Mouton-Rothschild '61?) but for a selection of
Burgundies that's one of the most extensive I've encountered, with no less than three dozen types of champagne
(half a dozen from the House of Taittinger, the Crillon's
proprietors), and—among digestifs for postmeal
relaxation—two dozen cognacs and armagnacs. Note that
there's a multicourse menu at lunch and that the Crillon's
own chocolates offered at meal's end with coffee (I think,
the best in town) may be purchased by the box through the
captain, or in the hotel's shop. *Luxury.*

L'Ambroisie (9 Place des Vosges; phone 4278-51-45) is surely the smallest (there are just a dozen tables in a compact, cozy space) and least pretentious (principal decor is a giant vase of flowers and a tapestry-surfaced wall) of Paris's costly ranking restaurants. Time to go is midday for the prix-fixe lunch, which might open with chef-propriétaire Bernard Pacaud's jellied duck terrine or lobster minestrone, followed by, say, braised turbot, basil-scented lamb, or game in season, with a Pacaud-created sweet to conclude—his fig melba, perhaps. Apple strudel as you've not had it previously, or a fabulous frozen concoction based on pear sherbet. Dinner—à la carte only—is considerably pricier. Wines are ordered from a relatively small but top-of-the-line list, staff is cordial, and no location in town—setting is a venerable Place des Vosges *hôtel particulier*—is more romantic. *Luxury.*

André Faure (40 Rue du Mont-Thabor; phone 4260-74-28): You are not going to lose weight as a consequence of an André Faure meal. But it will have been worthwhile. This is a smallish place on a street leading from Rue de Castiglione, near Place Vendôme. You go for the warmth of the welcome and the satisfying à la carte, composing a meal that might, to give you an idea, start with a dozen snails, continue with coq au vin or a rich duck confit in the style of the southwest, and conclude with a Norman-origin tarte tatin. *Moderate.*

Androuet (41 Rue d'Amsterdam, near Gare St.-Lazare; phone 4874-26-93). The name of the Androuet game is cheese, glorious cheese. Its ground floor is a shop selling nothing but, in infinite variety. Up a flight you go—for a meal; I suggest you order "Le Grand Plateau." A hundred and fifty types of cheese are presented (they take up space on seven trays), with wine and bread to accompany. I know of no better introduction to the cheeses of the world's No. 1 cheese country. *First Class.*

Angelina (226 Rue de Rivoli) is for afternoon tea deluxe. China is fine Limoges. Decor is Belle Époque. Clientele is an amusing mix of ancien régime and younger Parisians. In what other tearoom might you see two handsome, albeit on in years, ladies order splits of champagne to revive them from the rigors of the boutiques? Mind, the waitress will bring only tea or coffee. Another staffer—a *pâtissier*—is the source of the irresistible pastries. *First Class.*

Auberge de France (1 Rue du Mont-Thabor; phone 4260-60-26) is worth knowing about when you seek a core-of-Rive-Droit restaurant. The prix-fixe meal centered on grilled entrecôte, nicely garnished, with dessert, is tasty and fairly tabbed. Pleasant service. *Moderate/First Class.*

Au Chien Qui Fume (33 Rue du Point Neuf; phone 4236-07-42) had been a mainstay of sustenance in the old days when the area in which it's situated was the site of Les Halles produce markets. Alas, the markets have moved, but this restaurant, on scene for something like three-quarters of a century albeit updated, stays on. A shellfish shucker is on duty at the entrance (oysters are a specialty). Or open with the house's own smoked salmon or duck foie gras. Entrées include roast lamb, thyme-scented. A don't-miss sweet is profiteroles au chocolat. The menus are good value. Traditionally open until 2 A.M. *First Class.*

Au Dauphin (167 Rue St.-Honoré, phone 4260-40-11) An upstairs table by the windows affords a view of the Comédie Française, the staff is cordial, and the price is right, but there's not too much that can be said in favor of the food, other than that it's so-so. The menu might open with house terrine and feature roast pork with mustard sauce as an entrée. *Moderate.*

Au Lyonnais (32 Rue St.-Marc; phone 4296-69-04), with cozy, *fin-de-siècle* dining rooms on two floors, is proficient at preparing the fare of Lyon. Start with hot sausages, go on to lamb with flageolet-type beans or coq au Beaujolais, making certain that you do not fail to order a portion of gratin Dauphinois, the tastiest of potato casseroles. Drink Beaujolais—the wine of Lyon. *First Class.*

Au Petit Riche (25 Rue le Peletier; phone 4770-68-68) observed its 110th birthday in 1990. It's a lively atmospheric brasserie, with good things to eat and drink, peppy service with a *sourire*, and an enviable location just north of Boulevard Haussmann not far from Opéra/Garnier. The three-course menu offers a choice of six oysters on the half-shell or nine Burgundy-style snails to open, lamb fricassée or beef filet among entrées, and delicious pastry among desserts. Grilled sole is a good à la carte choice, and a bottle of the house's Vin Bistrot is sound value, with a big list to supplement it. *First Class.*

Aux Petits Pères (8 Rue Notre-Dame-des-Victoires; phone 4260-91-73) is not, at first glance, prepossessing. What attracts you is the address: a street named for the neighboring Church of Notre-Dame-des-Victoires (Ecclesiastical Paris, chapter 2), just off a similarly titled—and fashionable—square. The staff out front is feminine and charming, the chefs are gents and talented. Walls are half-timbered, with postcards received from *copains* of the *direction* tucked neatly into edges of mirrors. You order from the à la carte, opening, perhaps, with eggs delicately poached in a Bordeaux sauce, continue with an exquisite duckling, prepared Rouen style, or a sautéed veal chop served with braised endives. The house Bordeaux is sound and well-priced; have assorted cheeses with what remains of it. Or a house-created sweet. *First Class.*

Au Trou Normand (9 Rue Jean-Pierre Timbaud; phone 4805-80-23): In Normandy, a *trou Normand* refers to the opening in one's face—the mouth—into which is ingested, between courses of a traditional meal—a snort of Norman-origin Calvados. This restaurant is something else again: a source of entrecôte and other grills (a dozen entrées, all told) teamed with socko frites, preceded by a wide choice of tasty openers, the lot exceptional value, albeit à la carte. Near Place de la République, northeast of the Beaubourg. *Moderate.*

Bistro de la Gare (38 Boulevard des Italiens; phone 4828-49-61) is a Parisian success story, thanks to its ingenious simplicity: an inexpensive menu embracing but a handful of combinations, that of steak (or broiled chicken) with frites, preceded by a salad, the most popular. Setting is bright, welcoming, and cordial; service, efficient. (A competing operation, *Hippopotamus*, which also has several Paris outlets and is in the provinces, too, is diagonally opposite, and Bistro de la Gare has several other locations.) *Moderate.*

Brasserie Bastille (14 Place de la Bastille; phone 4343-42-76)—though without the excitement, exceptional looks, or celebrated cuisine of Brasserie Bofinger, below—is worth knowing about, given its location on a square shared with Opéra/Bastille. Go for lunch in connection with a matinee or pre- or postperformance in the evening. Fare is traditional—oysters and terrines, substantial beef and other entrées, wicked sweets. *Moderate/First Class.*

Brasserie Bofinger (5 Rue de la Bastille at Place de la Bastille; phone 4272-87-82) calls itself the oldest brasserie in town, dates to 1864, and can well be proud of its smashing good looks—stained-glass ceilings, elaborate marquetry, oversized turn-of-century ceramic sculptures, paintings dating to the restaurant's founding years, and quick-as-a-wink waiters. Choucroute garnie, the classic Alsatian dish wherein a mound of sauerkraut is topped by assorted meats, sausages, and boiled potatoes, is, with reason, the most noted specialty, but there's a good value three-course menu (embracing oysters on the half-shell, navarin d'agneau—France's famed lamb stew—with floating island for dessert) to supplement the à la carte. *First Class.*

Brasserie Flo (7 Cour des Petites-Écuries; phone 4770-13-59) is worth a detour from the visitor-trafficked part of town around Place de l'Opéra to a street midway between it and Gare de l'Est. Lure is an authentic *fin-de-siècle* brasserie—Art Nouveau carved wood, lavish oil paintings, exuberant stained glass, and stick-to-the-ribs fare, including oysters by the dozen served on elegantly elevated metal stands, foie gras frais, and choucroute garnie, Alsace's sauerkraut masterwork. Convivial. *First Class.*

Brasserie Vaudeville (29 Rue Vivienne, not far east of Avenue de l'Opéra; phone 4271-90-75) is not a whit less atmospheric—agreeably high decibel count, massive proportions, waiters in long, white aprons, carved-wood-cum-stained-glass decor—than Flo (above). Seafood is excellent, but you do at least as well with a dinner that might run to onion soup and steak with sauce Bordelaise accompanied by frites, with cheese to conclude, washed down by what remains of a bottle of the house's Côtes du Rhône. Swift and smiling service. *First Class.*

Bristol Hôtel Restaurant (112 Rue du Faubourg St.-Honoré; phone 4266-91-45): Go in winter, and the setting is an oval room superbly paneled and chandelier-hung.

Go in summer, and you'll be seated in a rattan-furnished pavilion giving onto the Bristol's capacious garden. The menu blends traditional with contemporary. You may, for example, begin with smoked Norwegian salmon or lobster bisque, among the familiar starters, or a more innovative salad built around duck breasts and crayfish; continuing with roast lamb or filet of beef, among old-school type entrées, in contrast to, say, escalope of turbot cooked with sauternes or confit of sweetbreads prepared with wild mushrooms. Desserts rate a separate card. And you need not go thirsty: 70,000 bottles are stored in the Bristol's cellar. Splendid service. *Luxury*.

Cafés: Of the Right Bank cafés, most requisite is *Café de la Paix* (Place de l'Opéra), which has been a Paris institution for nearly a century and a quarter—from the time when Le Grand Hôtel went up alongside the Opéra, as part of Baron Haussmann's reconstruction of Paris. Nary a visitor, celebrated or not, who has passed through Paris over that long period has missed stopping for coffee, a drink, or a bite to eat, the better to take in action on the square. (Relais Capucines, adjacent to the café, is a proper restaurant counseled in a later paragraph.) *Café Royal Concorde* (7 Rue Royale) is a super spot to sit for a spell, observing broad Place de la Concorde, just beyond. *Café Pény* (3 Place de la Madeleine) is strategically situated, with the colonnaded Church of the Madeleine and the square's pedestrians as subject matter. If you're hungry, order salade Niçoise or an assiette froide while seated at an outdoor table. *Fouquet's* (99 Avenue des Champs-Élysées) is as much restaurant as café, but it's to the tables out front, spilling around onto Avenue George V, that I direct you for observation of ambulatory action in this quarter. *Café Les Tours de Notre-Dame* (23 Rue d'Aréole): Take a table in the shadow of the cathedral's gargoyles; socko views. *Café Wepler* (Place de Clichy) and *La Mère Catherine* (Place du Tertre and later recommended as a restaurant) are for people-watching in Mont-martre. *Café Royal Vosges* and *Café Ma Bourgogne* are well situated on beautiful Place des Vosges. And *Café Flore en l'Île* (42 Quai d'Orléans) doubles as a creditable restaurant, but its ace-in-the-hole is an Île St.-Louis location affording extraordinary vistas of Notre-Dame's flying buttresses and apse. *Café de la Plage* (Rue de Charonne near Place de la Bastille) is the ideal spot to become acquainted with the newly popular Bastille quarter, now heavily populated with artists, art-gallery entrepreneurs, and architects. All the foregoing, when utilized as cafés, are *Moderate*.

Café Tuileries (Inter-Continental Paris Hôtel, 3 Rue de Cas-tiglione; phone 4260-37-80) is called to your attention as a source of tasty, well-priced sustenance, breakfast into the evening; menus at lunch and dinner are good buys; onion soup is always a good bet; and there's an entrance on Rue de Rivoli. *Moderate/First Class*.

Capucine (39 Boulevard des Capucines; phone 4261-14-71) makes for a perfect mid- or late-afternoon pause, with your object tea accompanied either by pastry or one of the house's irresistible coupes, or sundaes. You'll be in the company of neighborhood regulars, mostly mature—and gossipy—ladies. Pleasant. *Moderate*.

Cartet (62 Rue de Malte, north of Place des Vosges; phone 4805-17-65) is a smallish, narrowish place with tables packed together. You go for the food. Order a bottle of Côtes du Rhône and start with a selection of house terrines and sausages. There are half a dozen fish choices. Main courses? If you're two, order gigot d'agneau and wait for the arrival of an entire leg of lamb perfectly roasted, with pommes de terre gratinées in tandem. Or try saucisson de Lyon chaud or daube of beef. You'll be in no shape for a sweet, but persevere. Your options include profiterole aux fraises, a choco-strawberry sensation; tarte au citron; or gâteau au chocolat, with pears in its central regions. Memorable. *Luxury.*

Caveau des Chevillards (1 Rue St.-Hyacinthe; phone 4261-19-74): Down you go, to the vaulted seventeenth-century cellar of an elegant house a bit north of Rue St.-Honoré and due east of Place Vendôme. Time to go is evening, when candles illuminate smartly set tables, and you sit on Louis XIII chairs, feasting on such traditional dishes as seafood mousse or a salad based on confit of duck, trout prepared the house's way, half a dozen beef dishes, or roast lamb, garlic-scented. Menu at lunch is *First Class;* dinner, à la carte, comes closer to *Luxury.*

Le Céladon (Westminster Hôtel, 13 Rue de la Paix, with its own entrance on Rue Daunou; phone 4261-57-46) is—not surprisingly—decorated in pale celadon green. Ambience is intimate; fare, a sensible traditional-contemporary mix (open with an extravagant lobster-caviar salad, if you're flush, opting for entrées of, say, grilled salmon or roast lamb, concluding with a coffee-sauced sundae); and location conveniently central. Prix-fixe menus are well priced. *First Class/Luxury.*

Charcuterie St.-Roch and *Pâtisserie St.-Roch* (Rue St.-Honoré neighbors at Rue St.-Roch) are brought to your attention as examples of satisfying sources of the makings of a picnic (or hotel-room) meal. Select from a big selection of salads, sliced meats, and other victuals, which might be termed French deli, at the charcuterie, following with sandwiches if you like, but certainly cake and/or pastry from the pâtisserie. Depending, of course, on what you order, and how much of it: *Moderate/First Class.* I selected these two places for this entry because they're so central—and neighbors. But you may duplicate this kind of scene all over town, especially at such charcuteries as *Chedeville* (12 Rue Marché St.-Honoré) and the charcuterie section of *Fauchon* (26 Place de la Madeleine)—with pastries, as well.

Chartier (7 Rue du Faubourg Montmartre; phone 4740-86-29) has Folies Bergère as a neighbor and is nicely combined with the Folies, of an evening. This is a big turn-of-century eatery with a small army of white-aproned waiters darting about with trays full of good things to eat—as for example Burgundy-style snails or steak tartare as openers, hearty beef or poultry entrées, perhaps fresh strawberries with crème chantilly for dessert. *Moderate.*

La Chaumière (38 Rue du Mont-Thabor, near Place Vendôme; phone 4544-67-91) is mobbed at lunch with workers of the area, tucking into its good-value menus. Three courses typically include such entrées as chicken and steak. Cheerful service. *Moderate.*

Chez Gabriel (123 Rue St.-Honoré; phone 4233-02-99) comes through with flying colors by means of a three-course menu with a grilled veal chop and a mound of crisp frites indicated as the entrée choice. Old-fashioned in look; ditto, the smiling service. *Moderate.*

Chez La Vieille (a.k.a. Chez Adrienne, 37 Rue de l'Arbre Sec; phone 4260-15-78) is, to summarize in three words, eccentric albeit exceptional. It's not going to win a beauty contest, given a setting that consists of but two plain rooms, the larger main floor adjacent to an entry passage dividing it from the kitchen, the smaller annex up a flight. It does not serve as the setting for a leisurely dinner because it serves only lunch. It has no business card, as do most restaurants in most countries, the better for you to retain name, address, and phone. And more significant, it has neither menu nor posted prices. You take what you're served (there's a choice of entrée) and pay, in cash, what you're asked, at meal's end. Madame Adrienne, the chef-propriétaire, speaks only French, pops in from the kitchen only if she's curious about an arriving party, or is already familiar with its personnel (the restaurant draws smart, sometimes celebrated Parisians), and appears more interested in cooking well for you than charming you with chit-chat. Her sister, Madeleine, the chief waitress/hostess (who also speaks only French), is, however, cordial, and the third visible member of the enterprise is a woman who serves but neither speaks (except when addressed) nor smiles. The drill here (location is a street running north from the Seine, near Pont Neuf) is Adrienne's old-fashioned food, starting with generous-size portions of the day's hors-d'œuvre, ladled on your plate one selection at a time, and including, on one visit, rillettes (chunky pork pâté from the Loire valley), poultry-based pâté de volaille, deliciously stuffed tomatoes, pickled beets (rarely encountered in France's restaurants, or those of any country, for that matter), superbly sauced mussels, the best celery ré-moulade you will have consumed, and Adrienne's master-ful version of ratatouille, Provence's eggplant-onion-tomato meld bound in olive oil. Entrées can be anti-climactic after the gargantuan first course; they include roasts of pork and lamb, sautéed veal chop (the only less-than-spectacular dish that I have tasted), and superbly prepared duckling. Chocolate mousse is a winner among desserts, Beaujolais popular as a wine choice. As for mineral water, Chez la Vieille is the only restaurant of consequence I recall encountering in France that does not stock the mildly *gazeuse* Badoit (the country's No. 1 mealtime water); you must be content with nonbubbly Évian, hardly a sacrifice, given the extraordinary flavor and excitement of your lunch. *First Class.*

Chez Marcel (7 Rue St.-Nicholas; phone 4343-49-40) is a Bastille-area institution—a no-nonsense bistro with delicious country pâté and sausages, fresh fruits (strawberries in season are super), and fruit pastries, with old-fashioned bistro cooking—steak/frites, boeuf bourguignon, coq au vin—in between, and a fine selection of wines, aperitifs, and digestifs. Lots of neighborhood regulars. *First Class.*

Chez Pauline (5 Rue Villedo; phone 4296-20-70) straddles a short street just east of Avenue de l'Opéra, just north of the Comédie Française. It is at once small and smart, with paneled walls and silk-shaded table lamps. You are heartily welcomed and well fed; a dinner might run to jambon persillé (one of the best such I've had in France) or bisque de homard, continuing with boeuf bourguignon or the house's deservedly reputed stuffed cabbage. Super sweets. *First Class.*

Chicago Meatpackers (8 Rue Coquillière; phone 4028-01-83) is the very same you may recall from London or Glasgow (see *Britain at Its Best*). It's indicated at the onset of a sinking spell—when you're a little homesick for, say, baby back ribs, a bowl of chili, or a bacon cheeseburger. Don't neglect side dishes: coleslaw, baked potatoes, onion loaf, or the desserts: mud and pecan pies, cheese and carrot cakes. You may begin with a dry martini, Harvey Wallbanger, piña colada, or Scotch; and Michelob is among the beers. There are California as well as French wines. And where else on the Continent are you going to find Diet Coke? Location is Les Halles, near the Church of St.-Eustache (above). *Moderate.*

La Chope des Puces (122 Rue des Rosiers) is just the ticket on a day when you're exploring Marché aux Puces (Flea Market) and you crave a seat and some sustenance. Build your lunch around moules marinières—mussels in white wine—the specialty of the quarter, and be prepared for live musical accompaniment from an ensemble of long-on-scene gypsy guitarists. *Moderate.*

La Chope des Vosges (22 Place des Vosges, phone 4232-64-04): You've been touring the Marais of a morning and have just come from, say, Musée Victor Hugo. You're ready for lunch. At La Chope, it might consist of soupe du jour (usually a vegetable potage), a nicely grilled brace of lamb chops with frites, and a glass or carafe of the house red. With a view of the square as a bonus. *Moderate.*

Cochon d'Or (31 Rue du Jour; phone 4236-38-31) is about midway between Palais Royal and the Beaubourg, in the shadow of St.-Eustache Church. Stop in after a Beaubourg morning for a hearty—and delicious—lunch that might open with jambon persillé or a snail casserole. Filet of pork and roast lamb are indicated entrées. Very small, very friendly. *First Class.*

Coconnas (2-bis Place des Vosges; phone 4278-58-16) pleases first with its location—in a centuries-old house fronting one of the city's great squares, and with outdoor tables for warm weather—and is satisfactory, as well, when your meal arrives. The three-course menu might open with rabbit terrine, proceed with sautéed veal, and conclude with chocolate mousse. *Moderate-First Class.*

Le Coin de Caviar (62 Rue Bastille at Rue des Tournelles; phone 4272-32-39) translates—accurately—as Caviar Corner. It is just that. You're seated at pink-linen-covered tables—set against teal velvet walls—for a Russian-accented meal that, if you order à la carte, might open with the four-caviar platter. There are well-priced lunches, seafood-accented, with blinis or fish-based rillets among openers, the day's fish as entrée, pastry or sherbet to conclude. Fun. *First Class.*

Coupe d'Or (316 Rue St.-Honoré at Rue 29 Juillet) is accorded valuable space in this book only because it typifies many modest-looking cafés with outdoor tables where, to order anything to eat as an accompaniment to say, coffee or tea, can result in an astonishing *addition*. Two teas with two pieces of pastry and service can add up to the price of a prix-fixe lunch (admittedly for one) in an unassuming restaurant. Better to enjoy your tarte au citron as the concluding course of a meal, or purchased from a pâtisserie for consumption on the street as you move along, or in your hotel room. *First Class.*

La Cour St.-Germain (19 Rue Marbeuf, off Avenue George V near Champs-Élysées; phone 4723-84-25—with other locations at 156 Boulevard St.-Germain, phone 4726-85-49, and Gare de Lyon, phone 4343-35-48) is a good-value chain that has made its fame with a two-course *formule*, or menu, centered on a substantial entrée, usually of beef and well garnished. *Moderate.*

La Crémaillère (15 Place du Tertre, phone 4335-43-88) is a Montmartre old-timer that could, at least in the course of my most recent sampling, do with a sprucing up and a new chef. Even a standard menu embracing onion soup and boeuf bourguignon was disappointing. But service proved engaging. *Moderate/First Class.*

Le Drouot (103 Rue Richelieu, just off Boulevard des Italiens; phone 4296-68-73): There's a neon sign on the corner to guide you to the Drouot's unimpressive entrance, which leads to an equally unimpressive stairway, which you ascend, to find yourself in a noisy, cavernous, utterly unpretentious space. I don't know if this restaurant dates to the turn of the century, when Toulouse-Lautrec painted. Had it, he would surely have been on scene to record this panorama of working-class Paris. The lure is so-so bistro food (the standard is nothing like what it was a few years back) at rock-bottom prices—the lowest such of any I know in Paris. Open with céleri rémoulade, tomato or cucumber salad, a dozen snails, mayonnaise-dressed avocado, or an omelet. Your entrée might be roast chicken, choucroute garnie (which I counsel), or beef any number of ways. Cheeses are okay; so are pastries and ice cream. Ditto the house wine. Service may—or may not—be cordial. Caveat: No credit cards. *Moderate.*

La Durée (10 Rue Royale) has been baking cakes and pastries—the while creating tempting chocolates—for some nine decades. If your hotel is near Place de la Madeleine, it's ideal for a croissants-and-coffee breakfast. Later in the day, stop in for something sweeter. Attractive. *Moderate.*

L'Écluse (64 Rue François 1er, near Champs-Élysées; 15 Place de la Madeleine; and several other locations) just has to be the definitive Paris wine bar. Decor varies according to locale, but in each case tables are tight; decibel count, high; waiters, more efficient than you would dare hope, given the impression of turmoil at mealtime; and food, tasty. Bar signs identify principal wine choices; order *au verre* (by the glass), *à la bouteille* (by the bottle), or *en carafe.* Accompany with the assiette charcutière, a delicious cold meat platter; and a generous order of smoked salmon, cold roast beef, or the house's pâté. End with cheese—preferable to L'Écluse's chocolate cake. *First Class.*

Entracte Opéra (1 Rue Auber; phone 4742-26-25) is easy to pass by, hovering, as it does, in the shadow of the Opéra/ Garnier. But locals working in the neighborhood patronize it with good reason: tasty food at good prices, with service on its two floors smiling and snappy. In summer, consider a range of salads and cold platters. At any time, onion soup is the indicated starter; then zero in on saucisson chaud, grilled sausages-cum-potatoes, with a coupe—or sundae—to conclude. *Moderate.*

Espadon (Ritz Hotel, 15 Place Vendôme; phone 4260-38-39) has been a personal favorite since a long-ago summer lunch, hosted by the late Charles Ritz, in the garden. At other seasons, Espadon occupies high-ceilinged quarters within, its arched walls the palest green and tables pink-napped, with red roses and gleaming crystal. Franco, Espadon's Italian-born director, rarely removes his eye from a vividly animated scene—tuxedoed captains and waiters and white-jacketed busmen looking after a clientele that's a marvelous mix of dark-suited Paris execs, modishly attired Parisiennes, affluent gentry in from the provinces, Ritz guests, and transient diners from around the world. It works beautifully. So, indeed, does the kitchen. Classics like foie gras, caviar, and smoked salmon are among starters—with the house's own lobster and artichoke salads as well. The Ritz has never stopped serving gratinée à l'oignon, Paris's beloved onion soup. Fish are fabulous, as for example grilled turbot in tandem with sauce Béarnaise. Red meats tempt, too—rack of lamb, tournedos, sautéed veal medaillons. Ask for the dessert cart to be wheeled to your table. If you've any interest in wine, request the full—not the abbreviated—*liste des vins;* it constitutes a course in oenology. And note that there's a multicourse menu to supplement the à la carte. *Luxury.*

Fauchon (26 Place de la Madeleine): The city's most reputed fancy-food shop is a lunchtime magnet for Parisians who pack its self-service buffet. There are hot dishes—the moussaka is as savory as it is in its native Greece—along with sandwiches, salads, the celebrated Fauchon pastries, and sublime chocolate sodas. To order: Decide what you want, pay the cashier, *then* take the cashier's receipt to present to the counter attendant in exchange for your grub. And expect crowds. *Moderate/First Class.*

La Fermette du Sud-Ouest (31 Rue Coquillère, phone 4236-73-55)—not far from Pont Neuf—charms from the moment of entry. You find yourself in a venerable stone-walled house, with blanched-wood tables set with white linen on two levels, a bar at the rear. Chef-propriétaire Jacky Mayer serves up what his restaurant's title suggests: cuisine of the southwest. You order à la carte from a limited bill of fare, opening perhaps with chunky, tarragon-accented terrine of rabbit, smoked ham, Monsieur Mayer's own terrine of foie gras frais or—exceptional, this—the stuffed-snail specialty called cassolette de petits gris charentaise. Entrées please, too; cassoulet, the bean-based casserole with southwest origins, is as good as I've had it anywhere in France. Confit de canard aux cèpes, preserved duck-cum-mushrooms—is delicious. And there are memorable pork and quail specialties, with floating island and tarte Tatin the dessert rankers, and Cahors, a southwest red, among vintages. A ranking restaurant. *First Class.*

Galeries Lafayette (Boulevard Haussmann): Lunch is invariably a pleasure at this behind-the-Opéra/Garnier department store. No. 1 locale is the handsome *Lafayette Grill* on the sixth floor—a proper restaurant with a well-priced menu (salad, entrée, cheese, or help-yourself dessert buffet). The same floor's *Relais des Galeries* is a good-value cafeteria. And in the separate building housing Galfa Club (the men's store) is the up-a-flight *Le Pub*, with steaks the specialty and *plats du jour*, as well. *Moderate/First Class.*

Garnier (111 Rue St.-Lazare; phone 4387-50-40): It's odd how rarely visitors venture north of Boulevard Haussmann to the Gare St.-Lazare quarter—unless they're catching a train. Garnier, just below the station, is smart, its banquettes a mix of tan leather and chrome, its staff expert and cordial, its prix-fixe menu—oysters or snails, grilled sole (or other fish) with beurre fondu or Béarnaise sauce, with dessert following—the ideal way to become acquainted with the offerings of a premier seafood house. *First Class.*

La Grande Cascade (Bois de Boulogne; phone 4506-33-51): It's a glorious day, with the sun bright and clouds billowy. Why not lunch in the park, on the terrace of this delightfully Belle Époque restaurant? Open with a refreshing salad, concentrate on tournedos or roast partridge as entrées, and end with one of the Cascade's made-on-premises sherbets. *First Class.*

Le Grand Louvre (Musée du Louvre; phone 4020-53-41) takes its name from the expanded and refurbished art museum in which it is located—at the foot of the spectacular stairway leading to the subterranean lobby from which visitors take off to inspect collections in the various wings. Look of the restaurant—priciest and most formal of the museum's eateries—is severe, albeit not unattractive, with gray walls setting off tables whose white napery is accented by bowls of orchids. Cuisine, with commendable southwest inspiration, is selected from a relatively limited menu, available as either a main course and dessert prix-fixe, or a costlier three-course prix-fixe. Smoked trout and an unusual leg of goose ballottine combined with foie gras are among openers; grilled half duck, tournedos, and lamb specialties are examples of entrées. Pavé au chocolat sauce café—a chocolate-and-coffee masterwork—is counseled to conclude, but other sweets are satisfying, too.

Southwest wines—Jurançon among the whites, Cahors among the reds—are worth a try, but there are others. Even though you're in a jam-packed museum, service is smiling. And it is worth noting that this part of the Louvre (including shops) is open evenings, so that you may go for dinner as well as lunch or afternoon snacks (terrines, cheese platters, salads, ice cream) or a set afternoon tea. *First Class/Luxury.*

(There are considerably less costly sources of sustenance in the Louvre, including *Cafétéria du Musée*—self-service, with salads, hors-d'œuvre, burgers or franks with frites, pastries including a mean tarte aux pommes—with the chairs at the tables copies of the metal seats you rent to sit upon in parks; *Café Richelieu*, for sandwiches, coffee, and ice cream; and *Café du Louvre*, the smallest. This aforementioned trio is *Moderate.*)

Le Grand Véfour (17 Rue Beaujolais; phone 4296-56-27): Louis XV was king when Le Grand Véfour opened in 1760. Its location then—fronting gardens at the rear of Palais-Royal—was one of the choicest in town; two centuries later, it still is. The walk across the quadrangular garden is a joy at midday or in the evening, with myriad lamps lighting the way. For long, bailiwick of the celebrated restaurateur Raymond Oliver—whose faded sign on the windows, "Sherry Cobblers, Lemon Squash, English Spoken," was an amusing put-on—the restaurant in recent seasons was acquired by the Taittinger champagne interests and exquisitely refurbished. (Alas, my only quarrel with the decor is the elimination of M. Oliver's window sign.) The menu, formerly grandly traditional, is now a happy mix of the conventional and the creative. Beneath the painted glass panels of the ceiling and from tables set with cut glass and old Limoges, you lunch or dine exceedingly well, opening with vichysoisse, mushroom-flecked poached eggs, a foie gras terrine, or escalope of salmon in aspic. Roast duck or tournedos—among traditional entrées—are super, but there are contemporary veal and sweetbread dishes that go down very well, indeed. Conclude with either hot apricot tart or chocolate mousse. *Luxury.*

La Guirlande de Julie (25 Place des Vosges; phone 4887-94-07) is indicated for midday sustenance in the course of Marais exploration. The three-course menu—which includes wine—is good value and features an unusual duck ragoût among entrées, another of which is a tasty filet de bœuf. Attractive. *First Class.*

Hippopotamus (Boulevard des Italiens at Rue Louis-le-Grand; Avenue Franklin-Roosevelt near Champs-Élysées; Place de la Bastille at Rue Bastille, other locations) is an estimable chain whose success is based on attractive interiors, efficient and sometimes even smiling service (a plus considering the crowds), and well-priced steaks, lamb and pork chops appropriately sauced (Béarnaise with the beef), and accompanied by good-sized portions of frites, and, extra of course, inexpensive wines. *Moderate.*

L'Incroyable (26 Rue de Richelieu; phone 4296-24-64) is, indeed—to translate its title—unbelievable, or at least its prices seem so, for what you get: a three-course menu that might run to soup or escalope of veal or grilled pork chop, nicely garnished, as well as cheese or pastry. Just east of Avenue de l'Opéra. *Moderate.*

Juvenile's (47 Rue de Richelieu; phone 4297-46-49)—a street extending from Avenue de l'Opéra is nothing if not memorably titled. Its game is wine by the glass in copious variety, with minimum-tabbed labels inexpensive; substantial sandwiches, steak especially, to accompany. If your wine is among the less costly: *Moderate.*

Lasserre (17 Avenue Franklin-Roosevelt; phone 4359-53-43): Time was, not so many seasons back, that when you wanted to dine at this gala and gorgeous spot, you picked up the phone and booked a day or two ahead. Recent seasons have seen the matter of booking become so complex and long-range that one wonders if it's worth it; there are, after all, countless outstanding restaurants in Paris, most of them considerably less pricey than Lasserre and willing to let you pay for a high-priced meal with a credit card. That is not the case here. Should you be among the chosen, you'll be impressed by the show, although the attitude toward foreigners, in my experience, can be patronizing and the atmosphere distinctly chilling. Setting is a sumptuous town house. You have a drink in one of the ground-floor lounges. When the table is ready, poof! You're escorted upstairs to the dining room, whose roof—in summer at least—slides open to reveal the heavens. Food can be anticlimactic after all of this splendidly staged drama. Which is not to say it is not creditable; such classic standbys as foie gras, rich terrines, grilled lobster, and game birds are elaborately prepared. Remember now, have a wad of franc notes or traveler's checks; no credit cards. *Luxury.*

La Main à la Pâte (35 Rue St.-Honoré; phone 4236-64-73): French cuisine is so masterful, distinguished, and distinctive that when foreign-cuisine restaurants open in the French capital, like it or not, they tend to take on Gallic characteristics, whereas in other countries—America and Britain, for example—they retain the flavor of their country of origin. La Main à la Pâte was recommended to me by an Italian who really knows both his own and French cuisine—Franco, the director of L'Espadon in the Ritz Hôtel. If you forget the decor—the restaurant proper is a flight up from a street-level bar and is an outrageously corny and plastic reproduction of a massive grape arbor—you can be reasonably content here. Despite French headings on the menu and translations into French of Italian (not considered necessary in Italian restaurants of the major American and British cities), fare is reasonably authentic. You do okay with pasta, cannelloni and lasagne through agnolotti and maccheroni quattro formaggi. Osso bucco is creditable, as can be veal chops variously prepared. And note that prices are surprisingly high. *Luxury.*

Marriott Prince de Galles Hotel Restaurant (33 Avenue George V; phone 3723-55-11)—though no less elegant than the handsome hotel (Paris to Stay, above) in which it is situated, and with summer service in the hotel's courtyard—is the venue of an exceptionally well-priced menu. It's available at dinner only (expense-account execs fill the restaurant midday). The meal might open with the egg masterwork from the southwest called pipérade, feature roast loin of lamb, herb-scented, as an entrée, completing the meal with the dessert you choose from a trolley wheeled to table. Super service. At any time other than dinner with this menu (which is *First Class*), the Marriott's restaurant is *Luxury.*

Maxim's (3 Rue Royale; phone 4265-27-94) is hardly without attributes. Staying power is No. 1; it goes back to the turn of the century when *Le Tout Paris* populated it. Decor is No. 2; its original Art Nouveau environment—splendidly carved wood, elegant brass, superb stained glass, richly hued paintings—is so special that the French government has declared it a protected historic site. No. 3 is the enormous staff—by and large (forgetting the occasional lemon), cordial and fluent in English. Fare—stubbornly classic style—can be competent but, in my experience, hardly more so than that of any number of *brasseries* that are similarly aged (see Flo and Vaudeville, Right Bank, above, and Lutétia, Left Bank, below), albeit with tabs easily a third that of Maxim's. Still, if the present *patron*, Pierre Cardin, should invite you to be his guest for, say, a meal embracing terrine de canard, médaillons de veau, and tarte Tatin—when he's not off opening a clone-Maxim's in such unlikely spots as Peking, Mexico City, or Singapore (not to mention Manhattan's Madison Avenue)—well, of course, accept. If you're on your own, though, note that those bottles of champagne in ice-filled buckets, on each table, are for sale; they're not offered with Pierre's compliments. One specialty you won't want to miss is pommes Maxim's—thinly sliced potatoes baked in generously buttered pans. Though à la carte only, like dinner, lunch is somewhat less costly. *Luxury.*

La Mère Catherine (6 Place du Tertre; phone 4606-37-69), a Montmartre institution for generations, shows no sign of slacking. It remains a congenial locale for a dinner up on the hill. A pastis in the forward room—all red-and-white-checked cloths and lampshades—is for premeal. Dinner out back is served to musical accompaniment and embraces an unchanging menu: appetizer, chicken or steak, cheese, dessert, and wine. *First Class.*

Monoprix (21 Avenue de l'Opéra): The up-a-flight eatery of this outlet of the nationwide budget-price department-store chain is a good bet for lunch on the run. (And note that the *Monoprix* on Boulevard Haussmann—tucked into the facade of Galeries Lafayette, the department store whose management owns both chains—has a main-floor take-away counter that's convenient when you're hungry and on the run with, perhaps, limited time for last-minute shopping; satisfactory sandwiches and cold drinks. *Moderate.*

Le Moulin du Village (Cité Berryer—a tiny street tucked between Rue Royale and Rue Boissy d'Anglas, just off Rue du Faubourg St.-Honoré; phone 4265-08-47) is a neat little exercise in white, with walls and linen of that hue set off by good contemporary art, and tables surrounded by bentwood chairs. There's a cozy bar at the entrance (the restaurant is operated by wine importers who also operate the Blue Fox wine bar in the next building) and a tasty three-course menu, which might open with the day's potage (soup au pistou is good) or mushroom-stuffed ravioli, with such entrées as braised beef accompanied by Yorkshire pudding (the latter is a manifestation of the propriétaires' British origins); and a choice of sweets to conclude. If one of the bosses is on hand and you're a wine buff, talk over the interesting cellar before ordering your bottle. *First Class.*

Mövenpick (12 Boulevard de la Madeleine; phone 4742-47-93) is accorded space here only because it's traditionally open until midnight, and because you may have encountered outlets of this chain in Switzerland, its nation of origin, as have I, with satisfaction. The Paris version is something else again: a garish succession of connected basement spaces that makes an attempt at standard dishes like chicken, steak, and paillard de veau, without success. Environment and fare are coffee-shop caliber, albeit with steepish tabs and service that can be disagreeable. *First Class.*

Musée Picasso Café (5 Rue de Thorigny) is no less handsome than the relatively recent museum (above) of which it is a part. Look is smartly severe—white walls hung with framed museum posters, black-metal tables and chairs. You may go for as little as a cup of coffee or a glass of wine. But the food is good enough to consider starting—or concluding—your museum visit with a lunch that might embrace a seafood terrine or the day's soup; a hot spinach, chicken, ham, or chicken-liver tart, or the day's meat entrée; and pastry or cheese. Service is swift and smiling. *Moderate.*

Les Noces de Jeannette (14 Rue Favert; phone 4296-36-89) teams up well with a performance at the just-opposite Opéra Comique. This is an upstairs spot with somewhat excessive Second Empire décor. It's popular with groups and has reliable fare—coquilles St.-Jacques or a pot of rillettes (pork pâté) to begin, a chicken entrée or steak marchand de vin following, served as part of a prix-fixe menu that is sound value. *First Class.*

L'Obélisque (Crillon Hôtel, 10 Place de la Concorde, with its own entrance on Rue Boissy d'Anglas; phone 4265-24-24) is the less expensive—and more recent—of the Crillon's restaurant pair. This is a snappy grill room, all red velvet chairs and Lalique-like chandeliers, with wines offered by the glass or bottle and delicious comestibles, the lot of them speedily—and cheerily—served; the range salads and omelets, pasta and *poisson* (there's always a fish of the day), smoked salmon and steak, with gratin Dauphinois the potato specialty, a super cheese board, and luscious desserts. Lots of locals and staff members from the next-door American Embassy are regulars. *First Class.*

L'Oeuf à la Neige (16 Rue Salneuve; phone 4763-45-43) is, in a word, Alsace transported—gastronomically, at least—to the Arc de Triomphe. There are lovely things to eat here, as you may remember them from Strasbourg. By that I mean a meal that might embrace a savory hot tarte to commence, bäckoffe—an Alsatian masterwork with a preserved-duck base—or the pork entrée known as pâté Lorrain; and rich desserts to conclude. And of course there are Alsatian whites in the cellar. The prix-fixe is good value. *First Class.*

Opéra (Le Grand Hôtel, 2 Rue Scribe; phone 4268-12-13) is so overshadowed in the public mind by the same hotel's historic Café de la Paix (above) that its premium restaurant—beautifully paneled and chandeliered, with a crackerjack kitchen and serving staff—is perhaps the least appreciated of the important hotel restaurants. Pity, this. You want to book for a dinner that might embrace the best vichyssoise in town or smoked Norwegian salmon served with Russian blinis, roast lamb, the house's chicken-breast specialty, with poached pears in a Poire William-flavored sabayon sauce as a festive finale. *Luxury*.

Opéra de Paris/Bastille (Place de la Bastille): Because it's relatively new, I make mention at this point of the stand-up bars at this sleekly contemporary theater (Paris to See, above) should you wonder if you may have something to eat before or during the performance. Of course, the answer is in the affirmative: rather skimpy sandwiches at prices less expensive than you might expect for the republic's most talked-about theater. Coke, Perrier, wine, and champagne by the glass. Fare and facilities are similar at *Opéra de Paris/Garnier* (Place de l'Opéra). *Moderate/First Class*.

Patachou (9 Place du Tertre; phone 4251-06-06): A smart and stylish restaurant in tourist-trod Montmartre? Don't fight it. Relatively recently installed Patachou—despite its location on a square packed with vendors of souvenirs being grabbed up by mostly German customers—is a class act. Its principal space, tile-floored and furnished in Louis XV style, has three walls of paneled wood, with the fourth—overlooking Paris below and beyond to the Eiffel and Montparnasse towers—a massive pane of glass. And just beneath it is a capacious terrace, an enviable spot for a warm-weather lunch or dinner. Go at midday for the good-value menu, based on the day's catch, nicely prepared poultry or a meat entrée, with ice cream or pastry (a specialty here) as dessert. *First Class.*

Paul (15 Place Dauphine with another entrance at 52 Quai des Orfèvres; phone 4354-21-48) lies in the shadow of Paris's Palais de Justice on a quiet square—the site of its front door; its back door being on a quai edging the Seine. Locals are bowling on the green as you enter for a meal—everything is à la carte—that might open with a tomato salad dressed with a perfect vinaigrette or a platter of super sausages that go well with the house's excellent bread. The plat du jour may or may not please (sautéed veal chop, for example, can disappoint) but always-available roast chicken is a winner. *First Class.*

Le Petit Ramoneur (74 Rue St.-Denis; phone 4236-39-24) has the solitary Tour St.-Jacques, edging the Seine, as its nearest landmark. Lamb, with France's (and my) beloved flageolet beans, and beef are among entrées on the bargain-tabbed menu, which includes half a carafe of wine and pastry. Expect crowds. *Moderate.*

Pharamond (24 Rue de la Grande Truanderie; phone 4233-06-72)—in a house of yore that exudes ambience, near the Beaubourg—is a touch of Normandy in the capital. You may not want to go so far as to order the Norman standby, tripes à la mode de Caen, but there are such satisfactory dishes as duck terrine and marinated salmon salad, scallops prepared with Norman cider, filet of veal in a rich sauce, and roast lamb. Pear charlotte, bathed in raspberry sauce, is the indicated sweet. *First Class.*

Pierre Traiteur (10 Rue de Richelieu; phone 4296-09-17; a hop and a skip from Palais-Royal) is intimate in scale, unspectacular—paintings of no special discipline punctuate pinky-buff walls—and staffed by a team of congenial waitresses uniformed in neat black and white. The menu is limited, but everything I have tasted is commendable. Starters include asparagus sauce mousseline, poached eggs in a piquant sauce, or a delicious soup à l'ail glacée, which is Pierre's answer to Spain's gazpacho. Steak au poivre and gigot d'agneau are favored entrées, and, in all events, you must order the house's potato winner, gratin Dauphinois. Baked-on-premises fresh grapefruit tart is, to understate, unforgettable. *First Class.*

La Poularde Landaise (4 Rue St.-Philippe-du-Roulle; phone 4359-20-25) is a charming spot between Champs-Élysées and Boulevard Haussmann, with a homey, chintzy look and kind waitresses in attendance. Specialties are of the southwest—confit de canard (preserved roast duck) especially. It's served with sautéed potatoes and a salad, but it is not, I caution you, as good as you'll get in the area of origin. *First Class.*

Printemps (Boulevard Haussmann, diagonally to the east of the Opéra/Garnier), one of the preeminent department stores, is a spectacular setting for lunch, thanks to the situation of its complex of eateries—restaurant, grill, *salon de thé*—on the sixth floor of its Nouveau Magasin building (one of a trio that's closest to the Opéra), beneath an absolutely fabulous (and immense) stained-glass dome. *Moderate.*

Relais Capucines (Le Grand Hôtel, Place de l'Opéra entrance; phone 4268-12-13) is the often neglected restaurant section of the Grand's celebrated Café de la Paix (above). It's a Belle Époque space adjacent to the outer café, with an extensive brasserie menu; the range from oysters, soups, fish, and meat entrées to cold plates, hamburgers, and a selection of coupes, or sundaes; not to mention a half-dozen changed-daily *plats du jour. Moderate/First Class.*

Le Roi du Pot au Feu (34 Rue Vignon; phone 4742-37-10): Any number of national cuisines have a boiled beef dish in star position. None surpasses France's pot-au-feu, a soup that's a meal (or vice versa). In this restaurant, which translates as King of Pot au Feu, it's the specialty you want to order—nicely served at tables laid with red-checked cloths, in an agreeable setting not far from the Madeleine. But there are other options on the à la carte, roast chicken and grilled steak among them. *Moderate/First Class.*

La Samaritaine (Rue du Pont Neuf, between Rue de Rivoli and Quai du Louvre) is a multibuilding, budget department store that has put its riverfront location to good use with *Restaurant Terrasse* on the tenth floor of Building No. 1. Lures are cold-plate lunches offered in combination with truly spectacular vistas of Paris. *Moderate.*

Self-Tuileries (205 Rue de Rivoli, east of the Meurice Hôtel) is a long-on-scene cafeteria, adequate for a snack or casual meal on the run. No credit cards. *Moderate.*

La Table de Jeannette (12 Rue Duphot, entered through a courtyard just south of Place de la Madeleine; phone 4260-05-64) is comfortably Louis XIII in look—brass chandeliers, wood-burning fireplace that's put to use in winter, draperies matching the upholstery of high-back chairs surrounding generously spaced tables. Perfectly delicious food comes served on Haviland Limoges porcelain. The rich cuisine of the southwest is the name of Madame Jeannette's game. And she plays it well. Build your meal around entrées either of confit de canard accompanied by pommes Sarladaise or an authentically hearty cassoulet, making sure you conclude with the apple tart, doused with crème fraîche. *First Class.*

Taillevent (15 Rue Lamennais; phone 4563-39-94) has had so much praise quite literally heaped upon it in recent years that prospective customers must set to work weeks in advance to gain entry, only to have to lay out considerable cash (or traveler's checks) for the privilege. When innumerable other restaurants of good repute are so glad of one's credit-card business, it's questionable if the effort is worthwhile. In a setting of oak-paneled walls, crystal chandeliers, and caned Louis XVI chairs, the ambience, to be sure, is engaging. Food is taken very seriously, indeed, and there's no denying that service can be impeccable, with the menu a meld of contemporary and traditional. A Taillevent lunch or dinner might embrace foie gras or truffled seafood sausage, a guinea-hen pot-au-feu, and a dessert representing the handiwork of the house's *pâtissier. Luxury.*

Tartempion (15-bis Rue du Mont-Denis; phone 4606-10-40) is an agreeable alternative to La Mère Catherine (above) for a Montmartre meal. Setting is a charming old house; lure is well-priced menu based on beef and poultry entrées. *Moderate.*

Terrasse Fleurie (Inter-Continental Paris Hotel, 3 Rue de Castiglione; phone 4260-37-80) is a pavilion sheathed in glass—the better to take in the playing fountain and greenery of the Inter-Continental's splendid courtyard—that's become one of the smartest—and tastiest—restaurants in town. There is an extensive à la carte at both lunch and dinner, with caviar and crayfish among hors-d'oeuvre, filet of sole and pan-fried char among fish, Aberdeen Angus beef and breast of pigeon among meats, wild strawberry soufflé among sweets. And there is, as well, an excellent five-course-and-coffee menu, which might run to a salad embracing foie gras, string beans, shallots and mushrooms, or bisque de homard; filet of beef or champagne-sauced sweetbreads; a selection of cheeses from an enormous tray and a likewise generous choice of sweets from a *chariot* wheeled to table; with coffee to conclude. Wines are from a ranker of a cellar (Inter-Continental knows its vintages). And service at once congenial and professional. *Luxury.*

Le Train Bleu (Gare de Lyon; phone 4343-09-06): Wow! That's what you say when you climb the steep flight from Gare de Lyon's main floor to this turn-of-century restaurant that is surely among the great Belle Époque environments in the republic. A series of ravishing circular murals, framed in heavy gold, embellish the ceiling. Additional murals are embedded in the walls, elaborate frames setting them off. You are not surprised to learn that it was the president of France who inaugurated this restaurant in 1901, nor that it is still going strong. Start with potage cressonière or smoked filet of mackerel and continue with gigot d'agneau, duckling à l'orange, or braised Provençal beef. Don't skip the cheese platter, nor, for that matter, a fruit tart to conclude. And turn the menu over; an excellent wine list is on the reverse. *First Class.*

Le Vieil Écu (166 Rue St.-Honoré, phone 4260-20-14): There are times, in Paris as elsewhere, where that old bromide—You Get What You Pay For—holds true. Le Vieil Écu is a case in point. It packs in neighborhood workers seeking a substantial lunch bargain-tabbed. And if you get a table—even with a reservation—on one of the two nondescript floors, you count your blessings and make an effort to command the cheaper of the two menus, grateful for a reasonably satisfying meal of the day's soup, steak/frites, a wedge of cheese, or a simple sweet. Service is neither kind nor smiling. I can't recommend this one. *Moderate.*

SELECTED RIVE GAUCHE/LEFT BANK AND ÎLE ST.-LOUIS RESTAURANTS AND CAFÉS

Allard (41 Rue St.-André-des-Arts, off Place St.-Michel; phone 4326-48-23) is an old-timer with staying power. The look is Congested Quartier Latin; you enter a cramped bar-room; there are low-ceilinged dining rooms on either side, with tables at close quarters. Old-school waiters are gracious. Fare is unpretentious—Paris bistro cooking at its delicious best, including the casserole that is cassoulet, an estimable coq au vin, a masterfully prepared gigot d'agneau aux flageolets, beef and lamb stews. What you start off with—terrine de canard, escargots, salade de concombre, or radishes with butter—is excellent, too. Desserts are few but satisfying, with tarte aux fraises and fresh orange salad as house specialties. *First Class.*

L'Assiette au Beurre (34 Rue St.-Benoît; phone 4222-49-76) is at once atmospheric and delicious—a salute to the glory of the turn-of-the-century Art Nouveau period—with a loyal following. There's a reasonably priced menu centered on such entrées as côtes d'agneau (lamb chops) and maigret de canard (duck breasts), with profiteroles au chocolat a favored dessert. *First Class.*

Auberge Comtoise (a.k.a. Le Chevert, 34 Rue Chevert; phone 4705-51-09): Talk about silk purses from sow's ears. I was, in the course of a recent Paris visit, staying at a hotel in the École Militaire quarter, with which I was not at all happy. In the course of an evening walk, though, I came upon Auberge Comtoise, unpretentious and unassuming, but heartily welcoming—and with utterly delicious specialties from the Jura mountains of the Franche-Comté region of the northeast. Madame Laroche, who served as hostess and sole waitress of this small establishment, insisted that she would soon retire. I hope she has been dissuaded by her partners (her husband and son), but even if she kept to her promise, you want to have a meal, selecting from the well-priced menu. Open with either the day's soup (hope that it will be puréed vegetable served with grated cheese) or a platter of sausages. The chicken casserole, or gratin volaille, served with rice—is tasty, but so are the grilled sausages, presented in tandem with lentils. Conclude with either cheese or one of the made-on-premises desserts, gâteau Comtois or apple charlotte buried under apricot sauce. And if it's not too late, stay on for a digestif of marc de Jura—clear-as-crystal firewater imported from the mountains. *Moderate.*

Au Gourmet de l'Île (42 Rue St.-Louis-en-l'Île; phone 4326-79-27) occupies ancient quarters on the pretty island to the rear of Notre-Dame and operates a first-rate kitchen. Pâté or stuffed mussels are ideal starters. Entrées are specialties of the Auvergne region—chicken with lentils, for example. You may order à la carte, but the menu is a better bet. *Moderate.*

Au Monde des Chimères (69 Rue St.-Louis-en-l'Île, Île St.-Louis; phone 4354-45-27): There are, to be sure, better-value, lower-priced, albeit satisfactory restaurants on this Restaurant Row of a thoroughfare. But Madame Ibane runs her restaurant well. There's good modern art on the stone and brick walls and service is cordial. Go at dinner and you order from the à la carte, starting perhaps with oeufs meurette, wine-sauced as you remember them with pleasure from Burgundy, or leeks vinaigrette. Garlicky chicken and braised veal are entrée specialties—and tasty. Warm apple tarte is indicated as a sweet. And you do well with a carafe of the house red. *First Class.*

Au Quai d'Orsay (49 Quai-d'Orsay; phone 4551-58-58) is convenient to Les Invalides and Tour Eiffel, not to mention the Foreign Ministry. Snag a window table and you've views—through starched lace curtains—of Pont Alexandre and the Grand Palais across the Seine. Quai-d'Orsay—with green-and-gold-patterned drapes framing the curtains and matching the wallpaper—is a compact maze of shiny black banquettes that complement tables so tightly packed that you are very close to being in your neighbor's lap. The resulting discomfort is of the kind you put up with in a budget eatery with good grub. But here, hoity-toity serving staff notwithstanding, the seafood soup and capon galantine are okay, if unexceptional, and the cassoulet aux trois viandes, while adequate, does not do justice to this southwest specialty. All told, in my view, overpriced. *Luxury.*

La Belle France (first floor, Tour Eiffel, Champs-de-Mars; phone 4555-20-04): I like the name—France is indeed beautiful. I like the Eiffel Tower. And I like the Jules Verne Restaurant, up a level, and evaluated in a later paragraph. But this place, in my experience at least, is disappointing, with neither the traditional fare nor the service commendable, certainly in my experience. I can't recommend it. *Moderate/First Class.*

Bistrot de Paris (33 Rue de Lille; phone 4261-16-83) is the bourgeois bistro at its smartest, most convivial, and most delicious, with such stick-to-the-ribs dishes as coarse and tasty house pâtés, among starters; entrées like sauté de veau à l'estragon and boeuf Bourguignon. Desserts run to favorites like apple tart and chocolate mousse. *First Class.*

Blanc (26 Avenue de Tourville; phone 4421-38-82) is a sensible choice for a sensibly priced lunch when you're in the neighborhood of the Eiffel Tower; there's a wide variety of set menus, both midday and at dinner. Plain in look, but welcoming. *Moderate.*

Les Bouquinistes (53 Quai des Grands Augustins; phone 4325-45-91) takes its name from the book-, print-, and old-postcard-sellers' stalls across the road, flanking the Seine. This is a smallish restaurant, with a light, bright look, paper cloths on its tables, and two good-value menus, the least costly of which might open with the house's terrine or avocado salad, to be followed by gigot d'agneau, or roast lamb, served with the super potato casserole, gratin Dauphinois. Nice. *First Class.*

Brasserie Lipp (151 Boulevard St.-Germain; phone 4548-53-91) has been a Quartier Latin institution these many years. The fin-de-siècle interior, with superb stained and cut glass and dark woods, is among the more engaging in Paris. Fare is Alsatian. Not surprisingly, choucroute garnie is No. 1 entrée. But consider also the specially prepared Baltic herring, pigs' feet, and sweetbreads, ending with tarte maison. No credit cards. *First Class.*

Brasserie Lutétia (Lutétia Hôtel, 45 Boulevard Raspail; phone 4544-38-10): I don't know of a hotel restaurant in town with a larger proportion of neighborhood regulars among its clientele. Big and bright and humming, it works like a charm. By that, I mean the food is as satisfying as the service is kindly and swift. The menu, or *formule,* embraces thyme-scented gigot (roast lamb) garnished and served with a salad, wine or beer, and coffee. But the à la carte is extensive—omelets and terrines, snails and soups, with such entrées as coq au vin, châteaubriand, and steak tartare. And the chocolate mousse is justifiably celebrated. *First Class.*

Cafés: The Left Bank's best-known are *Café des Deux Magots* (170 Boulevard St.-Germain) and *Café de Flore* (172 Boulevard St.-Germain): They're always packed with visitors as well as Quartier Latin types, but they are considerably costlier than nearby but less-celebrated spots, as for example *Café Rouquet* (Boulevard St.-Germain at Rue des Sts.-Pères)—where a coffee is less than half the price of that at the Big Two, a few blocks distant on the same boulevard. *Café-Select-Latin* (Boulevard St.-Michel at Rue des Écoles) is ideal for observation of the Sorbonne student populace, while *Café Quartier Latin* (6 Place Edmond Rostand) offers a fine view of the Jardins de Luxembourg. *Café Notre Dame* (Rue la Grange at Parc la Grange) affords breathtaking views of Notre-Dame Cathedral from its outdoor tables. Beyond, in Montparnasse, position yourself at *Café la Coupole* (Boulevard Montparnasse at Boulevard Raspail). All are *Moderate*.

La Cagouille (10 Place Constantin Brancusi; phone 4322-09-01)—a near neighbor of Tour Montparnasse, just up Avenue de Maine—makes a specialty of seafood: tuna salad (not often encountered in France and not at all like U.S. counterparts) and assorted mollusk openers, premium-species fish as entrées, including red mullet, sole, and turbot, as well as less well known types that may be unfamiliar to you and that are grilled, sautéed, poached, or otherwise prepared. Not surprisingly, there's a copious selection of well-chosen white wines. *First Class*.

Chez Dumonet (117 Rue du Cherche-Midi; phone 4222-81-19) is unpretentiously traditional, with a menu to match. This is a honey of a Montparnasse dinner spot. Consider a meal that might consist of salade paysanne; entrecôte grilled on an open wood fire and served with the potato masterwork, gratin Dauphinois; and crème caramel or poire belle Hélène to conclude. *First Class*.

Chez Maître Paul (12 Rue Monsieur le Prince; phone 4354-74-59) is located on a not-necessarily-easy-to-find little street near Place de l'Odéon and the theater taking its name. It's a tiny, neat-as-a-pin place, with Monsieur Gaugain the expert chef, Madame Gaugain the charming hostess, service expert, and fare perfectly delicious. I counsel starting with snails, opting for one of several chicken entrées, entrecôte, or veal chop. They come with tasty pommes Pont-Neuf and a well-dressed salad. *First Class.*

Chez Toutoune (5 Rue de Pointoise; phone 4326-56-81) is an ever-reliable bistro on a street near the Seine, with a popular three-course menu that might open with the day's soup or salad, preserved (confit) goose or duck, or a roast, with the fruit flans the favored sweets. Friendly. *Moderate.*

Christian Constant (26 Rue du Bac) is an inviting salon de thé, white-walled with brocaded chairs, that is indicated for a midafternoon break of, say a pot of tea (you choose the type of leaf) with delicious pastry in tandem. Near the Seine. *Moderate.*

La Coupole (102 Boulevard Montparnasse; phone 4320-14-20)—closed for several years after it was purchased by the man who might well be termed Roi des Brasseries, Jean-Paul Bucher, a onetime Maxim's chef—reemerged as the most spectacular of its genre in town. As well it might; M. Bucher is reported to have spent $10 million to buy the place and $3 million to refurbish it, carefully preserving the Art Deco ambience of its 600-seat, 60-year-old interior, whose chefs-d'œuvre are 32 pillars painted by a clutch of artist-customers—as payment for meals—in the early years. Named for its great beige dome, La Coupole has again become the Montparnasse landmark it was in its initial heyday. Go for a mug of beer (à la pression), a sausage and potato-topped plate of sauerkraut (choucroute garnie), oysters, onion soup, or for that matter, a prix-fixe meal (there's a whopping six-course menu) with wines from an extensive list and lighter modern dishes to complement

the classics. M. Bucher's other brasseries include Vaudeville and Flo (Right Bank, above) but La Coupole is one of a
kind. *First Class.*

Le Divellec (107 Rue de l'Université; phone 4551-91-96)—
named for its congenial and talented chef-propriétaire—
looks as good as it tastes. On a street running parallel with
the Seine, near the Assemblée Nationale at Pont Alexandre
III, it embraces a stylish mix of blue-upholstered Louis XV
chairs set against walls of the same hue, with tables set in
pink linen complemented by bowls of red roses. A native
of Brittany, M. Divellec is as expert at preparing fish and
shellfish as at creating sauces to accompany his fruits de
mer. Time to go is midday, when there are a pair of set
menus. Pricier of the two might open with an amusing-
tasting platter of half a dozen house specialties, continue
with saffron-sauced mussels or cassolette of oysters, basil-
flavored, with a choice of the day's fish specials—again,
superbly sauced—as entrées, and pastries from a *chariot*
wheeled to table. The à la carte represents seafood in Paris
at its most sublime—half a dozen kinds of oysters, lobster
salad, and caviar among openers; fish soup à la rouille as
you remember it from the Midi, but Spain's chilled gazpacho as well; and such fish as St. Pierre, salmon, and sole
prepared as you direct. The cellar is first-rate and so are the
waiters. Member, Relais et Châteaux. *Luxury.*

Dodin Bouffant (25 Rue Frédéric Sauton; phone 4325-25-
14) is here accorded precious space only because its name
is known to transatlantic visitors. Alas, success seems to
have had a not very pleasant effect. A recent lunch was a
disappointment—grim service throughout, a hot soup
served cold; flat, overchilled rillettes, bland poularde de
Bresse, the lot served in the company of an oddly unprepossessing clientele. *First Class.*

La Ferme St.-Germain (5 Rue du Dragon; phone 4548-94-40)—on a restaurant-dotted street leading from Boulevard St.-Germain—has an agreeable bistro look, and offers an agreeably priced menu with a choice of openers (salads are good here) and such entrées as poulet sauté, a tasty chicken dish. Wines are reasonable. *Moderate.*

Les Fous de l'Île (39 Rue des Deux Ponts, Île St.-Louis; phone 4325-76-67): Brunch is a transatlantic creation that still has not found substantial favor in France, but Les Fous is an exception. Go Sunday morning for a menu that opens with nothing less than a Yank-style Bloody Mary and features scrambled eggs among entrées. Of course, you may opt for more conventional lunches and dinners as well. *Moderate.*

La Grosse Horloge (22 Rue St.-Benoît; phone 4548-28-12) comes close to being the prototypical Rive Gauche bistro. By that I mean you go for a convivial dinner with good friends, sticking to hearty standbys. If it's the season, begin with asperges sauce mousseline (I have had neither the vegetables nor the sauce any better prepared) and continue with steak-frites accompanied by a big *pichet* of the house red; fruit tarts are indicated for dessert. *First Class.*

L'Îlot Vaché (35 Rue St.-Louis-en-l'Île, Île St.-Louis; phone 4633-55-16) is atmospherically stone-walled, with tables nicely set off in white linen and a tasty menu that might commence with the house's own crêpes or a chicken terrine, preparatory to châteaubriand accompanied by sauce Béarnaise (my favorite) or grilled shoulder of lamb, with cheese or sweets as finales. *Moderate.*

Jardin de la Mouff (75 Rue Mouffetard, near the Panthéon; phone 4326-56-31) offers lunchers or diners a picture-window view of its neat rear garden and a value-packed set menu, with a choice of seven hors-d'œuvre and the same number of entrées. And everything that I've tried tastes good. *Moderate.*

Les Jardins de St.-Germain (14 Rue du Dragon; phone 4544-72-82) is a reliable budget eatery. The lower-priced of two menus starts you off with a salad or duck mousse, preparatory to an entrée of sole meunière, sautéed chicken, or entrecôte. Busy at dinner. *Moderate.*

Jules Verne (Tour Eiffel, second level; phone 4555-20-04): You want to book in advance for this one, and, when you approach the tower, look for signs that will direct you to its Pilier Sud, or South Column. There you'll find the restaurant's private elevator. Its attendant phones up to confirm your reservation and then whisks you to a sleek, gray, black, and white environment, picture-windowed, which is, in my view, the single best-looking example of modern interior design that I have come upon in France. It carries through to the glassware (black-stemmed), porcelain (black and white), soap in the washrooms (in black plastic boxes), and silk flowers on the tables (black-stemmed in black vases). Not surprisingly, staff is in tuxedos. The meal you'll be served from an extensive à la carte is contemporary-accented, but hearty and tasty. Start with mussel soup, puff-pastry topped (considering also smoked salmon, lobster salad, duck terrine, or half a dozen oysters). Entrées run a wide gamut—filet of salmon, filet of beef, a chicken-crayfish stew, and a delicious veal specialty, tomato- and basil-flavored. Desserts are spectacular to look upon—and taste. I counsel accurately named Le Grand Dessert Jules Verne. Lovely service. (And with a bonus: If your meal has been lunch, walk down a flight to the bottom observation deck; you won't be charged the usual admission.) *Luxury.*

Lapérouse (51 Quai des Grands Augustins; phone 4326-68-04) is an old-timer occupying a handsome house of considerable vintage on a Seine-view street. It has had ups and downs over the years that I have known it. The same people who operate Bofinger (above) with style and skill are now its proprietors, and they do it proud. Smartly refurbished, this is among the city's better-looking restaurants. Up you go from the street-floor bar to a table on either of two upper levels, preferably one at a window allowing for a vista of the river. Fare is not without contemporary touches, but remains essentially traditional. The three-course menu includes such luxurious first courses as foie gras de canard naturel or an herb-accented smoked salmon. Entrées run to inventively prepared fish or the duck-breast favorite, magret de canard. You skip profiteroles au chocolat for dessert at your peril. Wines are first-rate, service professional and polite. *First Class.*

Lous Landès (157 Avenue de Maine, Montparnasse; phone 4543-08-04) makes a specialty of southwest cuisine. Open your meal with coupe de garbure, which could be an entire meal, if you let it. The cassoulet is one of the best in Paris. For dessert: tourtière—a meld of puff pastry, prunes, and armagnac. Gracious service. *Luxury.*

Les Ministères (30 Rue du Bac; phone 4261-22-37) sports a delightful turn-of-century ambience on a street close to Boulevard St.-Germain, core of Quartier Latin. Best buy is the lower-priced of two lunchtime menus, with œuf en gelée or the house's own terrine as appetizers, and brochette of lamb as entrée. But the à la carte is extensive, with côte de bœuf and escalope de veau—Normandy-style veal—among specialties. The menu is *Moderate;* otherwise, *First Class.*

Musée d'Orsay Restaurant (Rue de Lille; phone 4549-42-33) opened as a dining room of the hotel that had for long been an appendage of the old Gare d'Orsay before it became one of Paris's most popular museums. Be grateful to the museum's architects for leaving this spectacular Belle Époque interior intact. Gilded and sculpted and frescoed and high-ceilinged, this is one of Paris's memorable interiors. Best buy is the utterly delicious buffet, when you help yourself to assorted cold comestibles, salads, and sliced meats that will tide you through the afternoon, especially when taken in tandem with a glass of house wine and the good bread that accompanies. Caveat: only one trip to the buffet is allowed; pile your plate high. The restaurant is on the museum's middle level and is *First Class*. (Note, too, that there's a smartly styled, less pricey café on the upper level, with views memorable and tabs *Moderate*.)

Le Petit Boulé (16 Avenue de la Motte-Piquet; phone 4551-77-48) is an especially appealing salon de thé. You're served on any number of patterns of antique porcelain, the cakes are delicious, the neighborhood regulars at surrounding tables loquacious (the quartier is that surrounding École Militaire), and there are a few outdoor tables. *Moderate*.

Le Petite Chaise (36 Rue de Grenelle; phone 4222-33-84; near Boulevard St.-Germain) occupies two floors of a seventeenth-century house. Look is brocaded walls, brass chandeliers, paintings in original frames. Lure is one of the best set menus in town, both as regards taste and price. Entrecôte aux frites, for example, is first rate. *Moderate*.

Le Petit Zinc (25 Rue de Buci; phone 4354-79-34) is a good bet for a mid-category seafood repast, opening with oysters on the half-shell or deliciously stuffed mussels, with any of a number of fish entrées, simply grilled or prepared house-style. This is a busy spot, but for that reason can be amusing. Near Boulevard St.-Germain. *First Class.*

Le Port Saint-Germain (155 Boulevard St.-Germain; phone 4548-22-66)—stucco-walled, with a beamed ceiling—is indicated for a reasonably priced seafood repast, with assorted mollusks served on stilted platters. But there are meat dishes as well. Not a few of your fellow diners will be tucking into lamb or beef accompanied by mounds of crispy frites. Solid value. *First Class.*

Le Procope (13 Rue de l'Ancienne Comédie; phone 4326-99-20) made a comeback during the 1989 celebration of the two-hundredth anniversary of the French Revolution. It was during the Revolution that it knew such Americans as Benjamin Franklin, Thomas Jefferson, and John Paul Jones, not to mention such Frenchmen as Pierre Beaumarchais, Georges Danton, and Jean-Paul Marat. Relatively recently restored in period style—it's good-looking—Le Procope occupies two floors, both invariably humming. Go at lunch for the well-priced menu, which gives you a choice of sweet or salad, with hearty beef (tartare de boeuf/pommes allumettes) and other entrées. Between courses have a look around, not missing the portraits and other paintings punctuating the wine, gold, and ivory decor. Celebrity notwithstanding, service is cordial. And location is on a street just off Boulevard St.-Germain. *First Class.*

Le Récamier (4 Rue Récamier; phone 4548-86-58): You're welcomed with a smile in this good-looking restaurant (tables spill into Rue Récamier in warm weather). And, if you're attached to the rich cuisine of Burgundy, this is the place—oeufs meurettes (poached and served in a wine sauce) and boeuf Bourguignon are but two stellar specialties. With a wide choice of Burgundy wines to accompany. Very pleasant. *First Class.*

Le Relais de l'Isle (37 Rue St.-Louis-en-l'Île, Île St.-Louis; phone 4634-72-34) is a case of many good things in a small package. There are just ten tables by my count, but the menu is memorable, opening perhaps with hot sausages in a pastry crust or tomato soup, following with côte de bœuf or confit de canard as entrées, with warm tarte Tatin served with cream or floating island as desserts. *Moderate.*

La Taverne du Sergent Recruteur (41 Rue St.-Louis-en-l'Île, Île St.-Louis; phone 4354-75-42): I have not come across a restaurant operated by an ex–recruiting sergeant in the United States, but this one packs them in, thanks to a romantic environment of stone walls and candlelit tables, and a tasty, well-priced menu including wine, along with openers like house terrine or sliced sausages, entrées including bœuf bourguignon and steak-frites, and a choice of cheese, chocolate mousse, or ice cream for dessert. *Moderate.*

Tea Caddy (7 Rue St.-Julien-le-Pauvre) is the perfect respite spot when sightseeing Quartier Latin, Notre-Dame, or the neighboring church of St.-Julien-le-Pauvre. Stop in, midmorning or midafternoon, for coffee or tea served with a slice of the Caddy's own cake or pastry. Setting is a *very* old house, all beamed ceilings and paneled walls. *Moderate.*

Le Télégraphe (44 Rue de Lille; phone 4011-06-65) is at once convenient to Musée d'Orsay (and for that matter the just-across-the-bridge Right Bank) and big, seating a couple of hundred usually satisfied lunchers or diners. You go for the three-course menus and the sprightly service, starting, perhaps, with leeks vinaigrette or smoked salmon interestingly garnished, selecting an entrée no doubt based on poultry or fish, and concluding with a rich dessert, ideally one of those that glorifies chocolate. Well-priced wines. *First Class.*

Tour d'Argent (15 Quai de la Tournelle; phone 4354-23-31):
If you're on an initial Paris foray, nothing is going to stop
you from booking eons in advance for a meal in this Paris
institution, which appears quite as tourist-populated as
the Beaubourg, though it's considerably pricier. You enter
a venerable riverfront structure and, reservation or not, are
led into a ground-floor bar to while away time (awaiting
your table upstairs) over a costly drink. A lift operated by a
very small boy with a very big smile (which must net him
an enormous nightly take-home in *pour-boires*) then trans-
ports you to the rooftop dining room, whose picture windows, with vistas of the river and Notre-Dame, are used to
good advantage. Serving staff, because moneybags Americans constitute a heavy proportion of its stock in trade, is
English-speaking and—especially if they sense this is your
first experience in a snazzy Paris eatery—patronizing. Order the satisfactory pressed duck, making sure that souf-
fléed potatoes accompany it. Insist on seeing the wine list
so that you may, if you like, select a relatively reasonably
priced bottle (rather than simply following the unpriced
verbal suggestion that may be proferred by the *sommelier*).
Chocolate cake is a sensible dessert choice. And if you depart wondering what all the fuss was about, you will not
have been the first. *Luxury.*

La Truffière (4 Rue Blainville; phone 4633-29-82), as its
name suggests, specializes in truffled dishes from Périgord. Escargots stuffed with truffles and ham are a fine
opener, as is the more traditional Périgordine specialty,
foie d'oie frais à la gelée—fresh goose liver in aspic. Brochette de truffes or cassoulet are counseled for entrées.
First Class.

Vagenende (142 Boulevard St.-Germain; phone 4548-44-96)
is absolutely super-looking Belle Époque. But dark paneling, intricate mirrors, and brass fixtures are only a part of

its appeal. Prime lure is sound-value prix-fixe lunches and dinners, steak grillé, liver and bacon, stuffed eggplant, coquilles St.-Jacques, for example, are one day's entrées. Although Vagenende is invariably packed, service is invariably swift and polite. *Moderate.*

La Vigneraie (14 Rue du Dragon; phone 4548-57-04) offers menus at both lunch (lower-priced) and dinner. You are seated either at a ground-floor table in front of the open kitchen or on the balcony. The chef is skilled, but an evening meal can be curious in that the appetizers—chicken liver and spinach salad as well as salade Niçoise—are so large as to constitute entrées, so that you have relatively little appetite remaining for main courses like gigot d'agneau or an excellent tuna preparation. Both midday and evening menus include a glass of Bordeaux on the house, and service is pleasant. *Moderate.*

6

Paris to Buy

SETTING THE SHOPPING SCENE

Parisians are the world's most glamorous shopkeepers. In no city are merchants—large or small, expensive or modest—able to display wares more alluringly or make them appear more desirable. The French know how to market, how to display, and how to sell, and the visitor to Paris, no matter how parsimonious, does well to savor the mercantile scene, if only as a looker or window-shopper.

Perfumes, colognes, and soaps remain the best Paris bargains and, for that matter, are as typically French as any gift can be. Women's accessories—scarves, bags, gloves, lingerie, shoes, blouses, hats, costume jewelry, compacts—can be very smart. Men's clothes, in better places, are attractive and smartly cut, but not inexpensive and often without the style of clothes from Rome, London, or the principal American cities. Neckties can be good-looking, but they are at least as pricey as those in the United States and England and often do not tie as well. Housewares—the inimitable Limoges porcelain, the matchless Baccarat crystal and Christofle silver, kitchen equipment, and gadgets—are sensible buys in this most gastronomic of capitals. Antiques can be superb, for Paris remains one of the leading international markets for them. And last, food and wines; in no city are they more temptingly presented or of better quality.

SHOPPING AREAS: RIGHT AND LEFT BANKS

On *Rive Droite/Right Bank*, my candidate for the all-around smartest street is *Rue du Faubourg St.-Honoré*, with its extension, *Rue St.-Honoré* (somewhat less fashionable); ever-so-posh *Rue Royale* is the dividing line between these two. Also browseworthy are certain streets leading from the Champs-Élysées, such as *Avenue Montaigne, Rue François 1er*, and *Avenue George V*. Avenues proceeding from the Étoile—*Wagram, Friedland, Kléber, Marceau, Iéna*—cater mainly to affluent Parisians and are not without interest. Relatively short *Rue de la Paix* has noteworthy shops, as do *Place Vendôme* (where the emphasis is on precious jewelry) and *Rue de Passy* (near Palais de Chaillot). *Place de la Madeleine's* forte is food emporiums and flower stalls, and *Boulevard de la Madeleine* is middle category. *Boulevard Haussmann*, behind the Opéra/Garnier, is the site of two leading department stores. *Rue de Rivoli* is smartest at *Place de la Concorde* and becomes more popular as it extends east, becoming a center of low-priced schlock after it passes the Louvre and extends to the Marais—a venerable quarter centered by *Place des Vosges*, now filled with trendy clothes, in both men's and women's shops. *Place des Victoires*, a long-neglected Baroque beauty, a bit northeast of Palais-Royal, has in recent seasons become a center of avant-garde fashions. Streets in the area of *Place de la Bastille*, site of the new Opéra/Bastille, have become trendy, with not a few galleries of contemporary art on *Rue de Lappe, Rue de Charonne*, and *Rue de la Roquette*. Streets in the vicinity of the Beaubourg are dotted with art galleries, too. *Le Louvre des Antiquaires*, just east of Palais-Royal, is a multilevel mall with some 250 high-quality antique dealers. *Galeries Vivienne,* also near Palais-Royal, embraces a mix of fashion and gift boutiques. *Galerie du Claridge* is a onetime Champs-Élysées hotel transformed into a 36-shop emporium, with blue-chip names—*Cacheral* through *Xavier Danaud.* *Forum des Halles,* near the Beaubourg, massive, monolithic—anything but inviting—shelters some 250 shops. *Tour Montparnasse's* lower level shelters 80 shops anchored on a department store. There's an additional mass of shops in *Palais des Congrès* (Porte Maillot); and some 260 shops, cafés, fast-food joints, and even a branch of New York–based Citibank at *Les Quatres Temps* in the futuristic La Défense complex.

On *Rive Gauche/Left Bank, Boulevard St.-Germain* is Main Street—with wares ranging from old books to *haute* clothes and superb antiques. Equally significant is *Rue de Rennes,* running south from St.-Germain and with fine shops, at least until it reaches *Boulevard Raspail. Boulevard St.-Michel* is another major Left Bank artery, with popular-priced shops, many dealing in books and shoes. A number of other Left Bank streets constitute a major antique area— quality is invariably superb—including *Rue des Sts.-Pères, Rue Jacob, Rue du Bac,* and river-front *Quai Voltaire.*

PROFILING THE DEPARTMENT STORES

Department stores are a glory of Paris, quite on a par with those of big American cities, London, Copenhagen, and Tokyo and—given a pricing policy geared to a French clientele—constitute ideal shopping territory for the visitor, in contrast to pricey boutiques catering heavily to foreigners. The Big Two are both on Boulevard Haussmann, just behind the Opéra/Garnier. Of these, *Galeries Lafayette,* perhaps the better known, is a three-building complex: the center building is the main one, with multilingual interpreters, money exchange, travel agency, men's and women's hairdressers, watch repair; two of four restaurants, as well as several upper floors of women's and children's clothes, housewares, and kitchen equipment on five; and on main an immense perfume section, souvenirs, gifts, and leather goods. Men's clothes and accessories have a building of their own, with Galfa Club (the store's house-label) and wares of ranking designers, as well, occupying three floors. A final building contains additional depart-ments. *Printemps*, directly west, is another three-building complex, with its Welcome Service, hostesses, and wom-en's and children's clothing and accessories in the building labeled Nouveau Magasin; home furnishings and kitchen-ware in Magasin Havre; and men's duds in a building to the rear of the Havre pavilion, called Brummel. Printemps is known for its fashion shows, traditionally Tuesdays and Fridays, March through October, at 10 A.M. And there are three restaurants. (Branches of both Printemps and Gale-ries Lafayette—whose second Paris location is at Tour Montparnasse on the Left Bank—can be found in cities throughout France.) Another chain—this one low-budget—called *Prisunic,* has an outlet on Rue Caumartin to the rear of Printemps and still another branch on the Champs-Élysées; both have supermarkets. Still another France-wide budget chain, *Monoprix,* has two central out-lets; one (with a giant supermarket) is a part of the Gale-ries Lafayette complex (above); another is on Avenue de l'Opéra, several blocks below Opéra/Garnier. *Aux Trois Quartiers* (Boulevard de la Madeleine) is a thoroughly re-furbished old-timer, central as can be, with all depart-ments in its main building except men's clothing and accessories—in a detached building with its own name, *Madelios.* Across the river, again in a two-building complex, is the Left Bank's principal department store, *Au Bon Marché,* with the main entrance on Rue de Sèvres; don't miss the mouthwatering food department in Building No. 2. It is worth noting that Galeries Lafayette, Printemps, and Au Bon Marché—the first two of these especially—

feature merchandise (men's and women's fashions, accessories, cosmetics, perfume, jewelry, china, crystal) by top designers and manufacturers, often in shoplike areas or counters of their own; diversity is extraordinary. *La Samaritaine* (75 Rue de Rivoli) occupies no less than a quartet of buildings in a cluster east of the Louvre, with emphasis on lower-cost goods (have a look around for bargains); and, a chief lure for visitors, an on-high restaurant called to your attention in Chapter 5.

SELECTED SHOPS

Antiques: You are in a world-class antique city. Ranking dealers—often with museum-caliber French seventeenth-, eighteenth-, and nineteenth-century furniture, accessories, and paintings—include *Didier Aaron* (31 Avenue Raymond Poincaré), *Aveline* (20 Rue du Faubourg St.-Honoré), *Étienne Levy* (178 Rue du Faubourg St.-Honoré), *Jacques Pérrin* (3 Quai Voltaire), and *Bernard Steinmitz* (4 Rue Drouot). Consider also such dealers in the 250-shop *Louvre des Antiquaires* (2 Place du Palais-Royal) as *Aubinière* (seventeenth-through nineteenth-century furniture), *Colanne* (Art Nouveau), *Avedis* (antique carpets), *Appollon* (bronzes), and *Martin de Bazine* (eighteenth-century furniture). And browse in shops like these as you amble about town: *J. Armengaud* (19 Rue du Bac), seventeenth- and eighteenth-century furniture and paintings; *Annamel* (26 Place des Vosges), African masks; *Bresset* (196 Boulevard St.-Germain), seventeenth- and eighteenth-century French furniture; *Nina Borowski* (40 Rue du Bac)—ancient Greek, Roman, and Etruscan terra cotta figurines, reliefs, and gold work, including gem-studded jewelry; *Camoin* (9 Quai Voltaire), fine Louis XV and Louis XVI furniture; *Compagnie Parisienne d'Antiquités* (22 Rue de Bellechasse)—antique porcelain, small objects, porcelain; *Philippe Delpierre* (3 Rue du Bac)—seventeenth-, eighteenth-, and early nineteenth-century (Directoire, Consulat, early Empire) furniture, mirrors, and other objects; *Emery* (157 Rue St.-Honoré)—Asian antiques; *Jacques Kugel* (135 Rue St.-Honoré)—Louis XV and XVI; *André Mancel* (42 Rue du Bac)—Directoire, Consulat, Empire furniture and accessories; *Michel Mathounet* (17 Rue du Bac)—Oriental antiques; *Mythes et Légendes* (16 Place des Vosges)—tapestries and baroque furnishings; *Ors et Arts* (44 Rue des Sts.-Pères)—antique silver; *Janette Ostier* (26 Place des Vosges)—antique Japanese screens and scrolls; *Pinault* (27 and 36 Rue Bonaparte)—antique autographs and books; *Antoine Perpitch* (240 Boulevard St.-Germain)—Gothic, Renaissance, Louis XIII, and Louis XIV tapestries, sculptures, furniture, and other objects; *Jean Sarfati* (220 Boulevard St.-Germain)—Italian and German antiques, mostly eighteenth-century; *Saurine* (23 Rue du Bac)—antique paneling as well as furniture and paintings; *Lucien Vigneau* (5 Rue des Sts.-Pères)—antique porcelain.

Antique Auctions: Drouot Richelieu (9 Rue Drouot) is the city's best-known auction house; it's enormous, and excellent buys are possible, what with a thousand sales each year, in which some 400,000 objects are sold. *Drouot Montaigne,* a branch, specializes in blockbuster sales, taking place in Théâtre des Champs-Élysées (Avenue Montaigne). Sales take place Monday through Friday between 2:00 P.M. and 6:00 P.M., but you may inspect the merchandise in advance daily from 11:00 A.M. to 6:00 P.M. About half the auctions are cataloged (including all the big-money sales at Drouot-Montaigne) and the 100 auctioneers are accorded the title maître.

Art Galleries: With New York, London, and Rome, Paris is a world leader in the complex business of vending works of art. General rule of thumb had for long been the Right Bank's Rue du Faubourg St.-Honoré, Avenue Matignon, and Boulevard Haussmann, along with the Left Bank's Boulevard St.-Germain and streets leading from it, as principal art-gallery areas. To these must be added streets in the shadow of the Beaubourg in Les Halles, the Marais/ Place des Vosges quarter, and thoroughfares leading from Place de la Bastille, site of Opéra/Bastille. Pop into any gallery with works that appeal, considering also this relative handful of specifics: *Jacques Barrère* (13 and 36 Rue Mazine)—ancient works, Chinese and Greek especially; *Claire Burrus* (3 Rue de Lappe)—moderns in a socko setting; *Révillon d'Apreval* (23 Quai Voltaire)—baroque and rococo paintings and with furniture of those periods; *Michèle Chomette* (24 Rue Beaubourg)—photography a specialty; *Crousel-Robelin-Bama* (40 Rue Quincampoix)—worthy group shows; *Delaville* (15 Rue de Beaune)—eighteenth-century paintings, with furniture of that era; *Galerie K* (19 Rue Guenégaud)—Miró and Picasso; *Keller* (15 Rue Keller)—contemporary, of-this-moment output; *Gismondi* (20 Rue Royale)—old Dutch, French, and Italian paintings as well as eighteenth-century furniture; *Lavignes-Bastille* (27 Rue de Charonne)—stellar moderns; *Boudoin Lebon* (34 Rue des Archives)—Americans like Rauschenberg and Mapplethorpe, but French and other works, too, including sculpture; *J. O. Leegenhoek* (23 Quai Voltaire)—old masters; *Marcus* (20 Rue Chauchat)—seventeenth- and eighteenth-century paintings; *Maeght* (42 Rue du Bac)—big-bucks works, with branches in Barcelona, Milan, and Tokyo; *Bruno Meissner* (23 Quai Voltaire)—top-rankers; *Mermoz* (9 Rue du Cirque)—pre-Columbian art; *Melki* (55 Rue de Seine)—name moderns like Gris and Miró; *Nane Stern* (26 Rue de Charonne)—a leader of the Bastille-area group for contemporary works; *Enrico Navarra* (75 Rue du Faubourg St.-Honoré)—works by such stars as Roy Lichtenstein; *Gilbert et Paul Petrides* (63 Rue du Faubourg St.-Honoré)— Impressionists and onward, including Chagall, Dufy, Léger, Albert Marquet, Renoir, Utrillo, and Van Dongen;

Claude Samuel (18 Place des Vosges)—interesting new names; *Urban* (22 Avenue Matignon)—aspiring painters and sculptors; *Natalie Seroussi* (34 Rue de Seine)—Cristo, Dubuffet, and Soulages are in its stable; *Wigersma Fine Art* (75 Rue du Faubourg St.-Honoré)—leading masters of this century.

Barbers and Hairdressers: *Galeries Lafayette* (Boulevard Haussmann) has a staff of half a hundred, so that chances are you won't have to wait; no need to book ahead. Next-door *Printemps* is similarly good. If you're up to shooting the works, consider such glitter spots as *Alexandre* (3 Avenue Matignon)—on scene a quarter century-plus; *Carita* (1 Rue du Faubourg St.-Honoré); and *Jacques Dessange* (37 Avenue Franklin-Roosevelt). *Henri Courant* (61 Avenue Franklin-Roosevelt; phone 4359-14-40) is reliable for men. *Julie* (180 Boulevard St.-Germain; phone 4548-98-37) is unisex.

Books: *Brentano's* (37 Avenue de l'Opéra), *W. H. Smith* (248 Rue de Rivoli), and *Galignani* (224 Rue de Rivoli)—which bills itself as the "oldest English bookshop established on the Continent"—all have English-language books—huge stocks—as specialties. *Librairie Hachette* (20 Boulevard St.-Michel) has enormous stocks of French books on all subjects. *Opéra Hachette* (Place de l'Opéra at Boulevard des Capucines) is heavy on imported newspapers and magazines, including American. *Librairie Gourmande* (4 Rue Dante) deals in cookbooks, contemporary and aged—and mostly in French. Bear in mind books on the fine arts in the *Librairies* of the *Musée du Louvre* (Tuileries) and the *Musée d'Orsay* and on the decorative arts in the *Librairie* of the *Musée des Arts Décoratifs* (107 Rue de Rivoli).

Children's Clothes: Biggest selections are in department stores (above); also consider *Jones* (Avenue Victor Hugo) and—for marvelous toys, as well—*Au Nain Bleu* (406 Rue St.-Honoré).

Chocolates: Godiva (11 Rue de Castiglione), *Marquise de Sévigné* (32 Place de la Madeleine), *Maison du Chocolat* (225 Rue du Faubourg St.-Honoré), *Au Duc de Praslin* (44 Avenue Montaigne), *Jadis et Gourmand* (27 Rue Boissy d'Anglas), and *Lenôtre* (44 Rue du Bac, 49 Avenue Victor Hugo, and additional branches) are tempting chocolate sources.

Cooking Lessons: You will have heard of *Le Cordon Bleu* (8-bis Rue Léon Delhomme; phone 4555-02-77), easily booked on relatively short notice for a sample lesson—conducted in French; other cooking schools include *La Varenne* (34 Rue St.-Dominique; phone 4705-10-16) and *Chef Hubert* (48 Rue de Sèvres; phone 4056-91-20).

Crystal: Department stores (above), of course; *Baccarat* (30-bis Rue du Paradis) and *Lalique* (11 Rue Royale). But for choice selections of Baccarat, along with Daum and Lalique, head for *Limoges Unic* (12 Rue du Paradis); and investigate *Christofle* (24 Rue de la Paix).

Duty-Free Shopping: Allow plenty of time upon departure for duty-free shops at *Aéroport Charles de Gaulle*. Besides a supermarket-type store with a big selection of French wines in varying categories and price ranges—as well as liqueurs, eaux-de-vie, liquor, chocolates, and tobacco—there are other shops selling French foodstuffs (remember that, if you're bound for the United States, meat products—even canned—are *interdits,* more's the pity), silk scarves and neckties, perfumes and colognes, jewelry, leather, and other gifts.

Food and Wine: They're everywhere: *boulangeries* (bread bakeries), *charcuteries* (French counterpart of our delicatessen, with cold meats, sausages, pâtés, terrines, salads), *pâtisseries* (wherein pastries are baked; when they have tables at which you may order, they double as *salons de thé*), *épiceries* (groceries), *fromageries* (cheese stores), and *supermarchés* (supermarkets, at which wines—nice for hotel-room aperitifs—are also sold). Have a look at the fabulous concentration of food shops on *Rue Lépic* (Montmartre) and *Rue de Seine* (Quartier Latin), also taking in the old-style open-air market—*Marché de la Mouffe* on Rue Mouffetard, near the Panthéon, on the Left Bank. And note these shops: *Fauchon* (26 Place de la Madeleine), the greatest retail food show in town, with a café (above) that's fun for lunch; *Hédiard* (21 Place de la Madeleine), a smaller-scale Fauchon, with vast varieties of tea, an excellent wine department, and a reliable restaurant; *Caviar Kaspia* (17 Place de la Madeleine, with its own restaurant, where you might enjoy caviar served with blinis); *Pétrossian* (18 Boulevard La Tour-Maubourg), celebrated for caviar and with its own pricey caviar restaurant in New York; *La Maison de Truffe* (19 Place de la Madeleine), for truffle addicts, but a full-fledged *charcuterie* as well; *Androuet* (41 Rue d'Amsterdam) is at once a restaurant (evaluated above) and cheese shop—with 150 species. *Chedeville* (12 Rue du Marché St.-Honoré), perhaps the prototypical Parisian *charcuterie*—old-fashioned and mouth-watering; *Poilane* (8 Rue du Cherche-Midi)—arguably the quintessential *boulangerie*, or bread bakery; *Berthillon* (31 Rue St.-Louis-en-l'Île, Île St.-Louis)—celebrated for its ice cream; *Lenôtre*, called to your attention above for its chocolates, but equally skilled at pastries and charcuterie, with shops at 44 Rue du Bac on the Left Bank, 49 Avenue Victor Hugo, and other locations; *A. Lerch* (4 Rue Cardinal-Lemoine on the Left Bank)—masterful fruit tarts in near-limitless variety, along with so many other scrumptious pastries that you end wanting to sample the lot; and, to conclude this paragraph, a trio of retail wine specialists. You no doubt know *Georges DuBœuf* (9 Rue Marbeuf) for exported Beaujolais bottled with his label; he sells them here, with wines from adjacent Burgundy as well. Both *Caves de la Madeleine* (25 Rue Royale) and *Galerie des Vins* (201 Rue St.-Honoré) sell wines from throughout France.

French Lessons: Long-established *Alliance Française* (101 Boulevard Raspail) teaches privately and in classes.

Jewelry: Paris is one of the world's great jewelry cities, and it doesn't cost a sou to look at, for example *Cartier* (12 Rue de la Paix)—with *Le Must de Cartier* on Place Vendôme; *Fred* (6 Rue Royale); *H. Stern* (17 Rue de la Paix); *Jean Dinh Van* (24 Rue de la Paix); and the fabulous shops on Place Vendóme—*Aldebert, Boucheron, Gianmaria Buccellati, Chaumet, Van Cleef & Arpels,* and *J.A.R.'s* (in the arcade at No. 7).

Kitchenware and Tableware: Déhillerin (18 Rue Coquillière) is the great kitchen-equipment shop, an old-timer with copper pots (which they will ship) a specialty, and a great deal else to tempt serious cooks. Also visit *Au Bain Marie* (20 Rue Hérold)—tableware, table linens, cooking equipment; *Christofle* (24 Rue de la Paix) with its own celebrated silver flatware, plus crystal and Limoges porcelain; *Culinarion* (99 Rue de Rennes), a link of a mod-look chain—clean-lined accessories for cooking, serving, dining; *Haviland et Parlon* (47 Rue du Paradis), for big stocks of Limoges china; *P. Nicholas* (27 Rue Marbeuf), with lovely patterns of fine china and crystal; *Porcelaine Blanche* (108 Rue St.-Honoré; 112-bis Rue de Rennes, and other locations) with well-priced white china the name of its game. (See also Crystal above, and inspect housewares floors of such department stores as Galeries Lafayette, Printemps, and Au Bon Marché.)

Linen: Porthault (48 Avenue Montaigne)—for table, bed, and bath, with a branch in New York.

Luggage and Women's Handbags: I've had good luck at the big luggage department in *Printemps; Galeries Lafayette's* good, too. Consider also *Aux Etats-Unis* (229 Rue St.-Honoré) with dog collars and dog bowls with French legends for your Fido—*mais seulement s'il comprend le français; Morabito* (1 Place Vendôme)—very posh, indeed; and *Schilz* (30 Rue Caumartin), from which I purchased a handsome leather carry-on bag that wears and wears and wears. For pricey women's handbags, consider *Étienne Aigner* (3 Rue du Faubourg St.-Honoré; *Hermès* (24 Rue du Faubourg St.-Honoré); *Lancel* (8 Place de l'Opéra)—with U.S. branches; *Peau de Porc* (240 Boulevard St.-Germain)—pigskin specialists; and *Shizuka* (49 Avenue de l'Opéra)—elegant and expensive Japanese leather and other accessories.

Markets: Marché aux Puces is the French for *flea market*. It's open Saturday, Sunday, and Monday each week from 7:30 A.M. to 7 P.M.; and it's a *long* Metro ride. Get off at Porte de Clignancourt and allow yourself a good half-day, as the market sprawls, there being some 2,000 dealers in seven individually named sections. Much of the stuff is new or elderly rather than antique. You must search diligently, and if your time is limited, you do well to appreciate that you're dealing with a 75-acre area patronized each week by close to 200,000 shoppers. Consider shopping in just a few of the big market areas; *Marché Bert* and *Marché Serpette* are two such. And mind, you are expected to bargain over prices. *Marché aux Timbres* is French for *stamp market*, but note that old postcards are also on sale at this one. Location could not be more fashionable—corner of Avenue

Marigny and Avenue Gabriel, just off Champs-Élysées, Thursday, Saturday, and Sunday, from 10:00 A.M. *Marché aux Fleurs* is the flower market lining the curbs of Place de la Madeleine on Tuesday, Wednesday, Thursday, Saturday, and holidays. And, on any day, take a walk on *Quai de la Mégisserie*, fronting the Seine just east of the Louvre, for a remarkable sidewalk market embracing birds, tropical fish, monkeys, and heaven knows what other lower-order representation.

Men's Clothing: I check out *Brummel*, the big, multifloor men's store at Printemps, and the also capacious *Galfa Club* at Galeries Lafayette on each Paris visit; each stocks wares of a generous variety of name couturiers, but best buys are their house-label merchandise. *Alain Figaret* is a smart France-wide chain, in Paris at 32 Rue de la Paix; *Daniel Crémieux*, a nationwide chain, is strongly influenced by classic American clothes and accessories; its Paris outlets are at 6 Boulevard Malesherbes, 24 Rue Marbeuf, and 2 Place St.-Sulpice. *Façonnable* (whose principal Paris shop is at 1 Rue Royale) has stores France-wide, as well. *Cerruti* (3 Place de la Madeleine and 27 Rue Royale) sells its own-design clothes—smart, conservative, costly. *Arnys* (14 Rue de Sèvres) is known for custom-made suits. *Emilio Batchi* (115 Boulevard St.-Germain) is, in a word, elegant; *Celio* (79 Champs-Élysées, 122 Boulevard St.-Germain, and in the big shopping malls) is a national chain, with nice, well-priced clothes, women's as well as men's; *Comme Ça* (127 Boulevard St.-Germain) is pricey but stylish; *Cravatterie Nazionali* (249 Rue St.-Honoré)—neckties; and *Hartwood* (123 Rue du Faubourg St.-Honoré and 40 Rue du Bac) is conveniently located on both banks and serves women as well as gents—and very smartly. *Marks & Spencer* (45 Boulevard Haussmann) is the very same you know from Britain—its sweaters and accessories can be good value (and there's an on-premises supermarket). *Hilditch & Key*

(252 Rue de Rivoli) is from across the Channel, too—
London's Jermyn Street—and sells costly haberdashery; so
is *Burberry* (8 Boulevard des Malesherbes); *Old England* (12
Boulevard des Capucines) seems English—but was Paris-
founded a century ago. *Lacoste* (8 Boulevard des Malesherbes) features the Lacoste line—sportshirts through
jogging gear. *Charvet* (28 Place Vendôme) is very conservative and very costly, with custom-made shirts and pricey
neckties its specialties; sold by stores like New York's
Bergdorf Goodman in the United States. *Lanvin 2* (244 Rue
de Rivoli) is quite possibly the smartest of the French-
origin men's shops. *Charles Jourdan Monsieur* (12 Rue du
Faubourg St.-Honoré) sells clothes, as well as shoes. *Yves
St.-Laurent Homme* (38 Rue du Faubourg St.-Honoré) offers
fashions not unlike those in foreign branches. *Hermès* (24
Rue du Faubourg St.-Honoré) has the most beautiful—and
expensive—ties in town; other menswear, too. *Courrèges*
(49 Rue de Rennes) is very trendy and pricey. *Givenchy
Gentlemen* (3 Avenue George V) is smart and stylish, year
in, year out. *Rodier Monsieur* (8 Rue Babylone and other locations) has sensibly priced shirts and sweaters. *J. C. d'A-
hetze* (250 Rue de Rivoli) has sold good-value neckties for
as many years as I can remember.

Which leaves men's discount clothing stores. Prestigious
French and Italian labels (more of the former than of the
latter) go at usually substantial reductions at *Club des Dix*
(58 Rue du Faubourg St.-Honoré), *David Shiff* (4 Rue Marbeuf), *Frank Beral* (7 Rue de la Boëtie and 141 Avenue de
Wagram), and *Depôt des Grandes Marques* (DGM—on the
second floor at 15 Rue de la Banque).

Perfume and Cologne: At every turn in this, the planetary
perfume capital. Department stores and certain shops sell
at list prices, albeit offering exemption from the government's 15 percent VAT tax if your purchases meet the legal
minimum of the moment. At *de Gaulle Airport*'s duty-free

shop, you pay list, but obtain VAT exemption regardless of the amount you buy—although variety of labels and bottle sizes can be limited. Trick, if your order will be at all substantial, is to buy at an in-town *discount* shop, offering diverse stocks, 20 percent to 25 percent discounts from list prices, *and*—if you purchase the legal minimum amount— VAT exemption, as well, in which case savings are around 40 percent. *Michel Swiss* (16 Rue de la Paix, up a flight) fills this bill, with huge selections; smiling, bilingual staff with time to take; mail-order service (they publish a catalog); flight-type canvas bags gratis with bulky orders; and a manager—loquacious and omnipresent Max Cohen—who knows the scent scene, Balenciaga and Balmain through Weil and Worth. (If you want any of the Guerlain scents, you may buy them in Paris only at *Guerlain's* own retail shops; those at 2 Place Vendôme and 68 Avenue des Champs-Élysées are the most central.)

Shoes: Among the leading outlets are *Carel* (22 Rue Royale and other locations); *Céline* (24 Rue François 1er, other locations), unisex; *John Lobb* (at Hermès, 24 Rue du Faubourg St.-Honoré), custom-made, as in the same firm's London store; *Alain Harel* (64 Rue François 1er), lizard, ostrich, and crocodile specialties; *Walter Steiger* (49 Rue du Faubourg St.-Honoré), very smart, and with a New York branch; and the ubiquitous *Charles Jourdan* (5 Boulevard de la Madeleine is its main address). But if you're *really* into shoes, stroll the Left Bank's Rue de Sèvres; it's Paris's Shoe Street—with *Ellen*, *Valmont*, and *Jet Set* among numerous shops.

Silver: *Christofle* (31 Boulevard des Italiens, 12 Rue Royale) is the most esteemed; beautiful and expensive. *Puiforcat* (134 Boulevard Haussmann) is justifiably noted for its own designs in sterling. (Both have New York branches).

Stationery: Armorial (98 Rue du Faubourg St.-Honoré) sells engraved note paper, personal and business cards, and invitations to your wedding.

Tuxedo Rental: Au Cor de Chasse (40 Rue de Buci) also rents top hats, tails, and morning suits. Rental fitting hours, traditionally, are 9 to 11 A.M. and 1:30 to 5 P.M. This firm, dating to 1875, asks that you phone in advance (4326-51-89) for a fitting appointment.

Women's Clothing: Women's clothes in the couture capital of the world? Where begin? Where stop? Department stores devote by far the greater part of their selling space to female fashions; you want to check out *Galeries Lafayette, Printemps,* and London-origin, good-value, unisex *Marks & Spencer*—just opposite the Big Two on Boulevard Haussmann. But, to give you an idea of how easy it is to pop into the outlets of celebrated designers, I walked down Rue du Faubourg St.-Honoré with a notebook, and these are the shop names I noted: *Pierre Cardin, Louis Férraud, Karl Lagerfeld, Chloë, Courrèges, Yves St.-Laurent, Ungaro, Léonard, Hermès, Christian la Croix,* and *Lanvin.* To these, add *Christian Dior, Nina Ricci, Chanel, Jean-Louis Scherrer, Guy Laroche,* and *Valentino* on Avenue Montaigne; the original *Chanel* shop on Rue Cambon; *Balenciaga, Givenchy,* and *Per Spook* on Avenue George V, *Ted Lapidus* on Avenue François 1er; *Maud Frizon* (shoes) on Rue des Sts.-Pères; *Lancel* and *Samantha* on Rue de Rennes; and *Daniel Hechter* on Boulevard St.-Germain (and at other locations). *Kenzo, Thierry Mugler, Stéphane Kelian, Victoire,* and *France Andrevie* are among the avant-garde unisex fashion and shoe shops on Place des Victoires. *Au Bon Marché* (with its main entrance on Rue de Sèvres) is the Left Bank's No. 1 department store and features a number of haute-couture designers' clothes as well as less costly labels. In and around Boulevard St.-Germain are many more fine shops than many transatlantic newcomers appreciate. For example: *Agnès B.* (13 Rue Michelet)—youthful designs—has New York branches; *Biba* (18 Rue de Sèvres)—noted sportswear; *Iris 4* (4 Rue de Babylone)—with a mix of trendy labels; and *Emmanuelle Khanh* (10 Rue de Grenelle).

Women's Clothing at a Discount? Paris has a number of cut-rate outlets, including *Courrèges* (7 Rue de Turbigo), *Mendès* (65 Rue de Montmartre)—for Yves St.-Laurent discounts; *Nina Ricci* (39 Avenue Montaigne)—with reduced garments in the *sous-sol*, or basement; *Cacherel Stock* (114 Rue d'Alésia), with men's as well as women's bargains; *Dorothée Bis Stock* (79 Rue d'Alésia); *Emmanuelle Khanh* (6 Rue Pierre-Lescot), on the second floor; *Stock Austerlitz* (16 Boulevard de l'Hôpital), with Daniel Hechter duds for gents as well as the ladies; and *Mic-Mac* (13 Rue Laugier), with buys for both women and men.

7

Paris to Note

ADDRESSES

French Government Tourist Office has its American headquarters at 610 Fifth Avenue, New York, NY 10020, with
branches at 645 North Michigan Avenue, Chicago, IL
60611; 9454 Wilshire Boulevard, Beverly Hills, CA 90212;
2305 Cedar Springs Road, Dallas, TX 75201. There are
FGTO offices, as well, at 1 Dundas Street, Toronto, On-
tario; and 1981 Avenue McGill College, Montreal, Quebec,
in Canada; and at 178 Piccadilly, London. These offices—
among whose functions is to provide the prospective traveler in France with gratis information and literature—are
part of a worldwide network (close to 40 cities in more than
30 countries), whose headquarters, *Maison de la France,* is located at 8 Avenue de l'Opéra in Paris. Head office of *Office de
Tourisme de Paris* is at 127 Avenue des Champs-Élysées; it is
open daily and maintains branches at Gare d'Austerlitz,
Gare du Nord, Gare de l'Est, Gare de Lyon, and (in summer) Tour Eiffel.

AIR FRANCE

France's global carrier—one of the world's largest—has
linked Paris with the United States since as long ago as

1946, although it goes back to 1933, when it was created by the merger of four smaller French-flag carriers that dated to the post–World War I period of France's great aviation pioneers.

With the advent of the jet age, Air France embraced the Caravelle in 1959, the Boeing 747 in 1970, the Concorde (heralding the supersonic era) in 1976, and the Airbuses— 310 and A310—in the eighties and nineties.

Contemporarily, the airline's routes—on which celebrated French cuisine, fine French wines, convivial French bonhomie brighten global skies—span more than half a million miles, linking some 200 destinations in 80 countries on the five continents. Nine of those cities—New York, Los Angeles, Houston, Chicago, Washington, Newark, Philadelphia, San Francisco, and Miami—are U.S. passenger gateways; there is an additional pair—Toronto and Montreal—in Canada; and Mexico City is served via Houston. Besides Paris, Air France links Nice, Lyon, Strasbourg, Lille, and Mulhouse—all in France—with the U.S.

What I especially like about Air France is that regardless of whether you fly Concorde, Première (First) Class, Le Club (Business) Class, or popular Economy, you experience the ambience of France from the moment you step aboard. A recent Air France Le Club flight Paris–Kennedy was the occasion of one of the best meals I've had aloft. It opened with a special treat—individual jars of fresh caviar—which was followed by a choice of entrées: navarin de lotte, a monkfish casserole accompanied by buttered carrots and deliciously prepared endive; or noisettes of lamb, mustard-sauced, in tandem with braised lettuce and sautéed mushrooms. A mix of greens tossed as a salad, vinaigrette-dressed, was next, in preparation for cheese from a platter, and an utterly delicious bavarian cream on raspberry-surfaced pastry, with coffee to conclude and perhaps a digestif of port. Vintage Bordeaux and Burgundies accompanied the meal, and cocktails preceded it.

(American, Delta, Pakistan International, and PanAm are among other carriers linking the United States and France.)

AIR INTER

France's principal domestic airline, Air Inter, crisscrosses France with service to 31 destinations, carrying more than 15 million passengers annually. (Inter, incidentally, is pronounced *Ann-tair.*) Air Inter uses both de Gaulle and Orly airports; in the case of departures, be sure to ascertain from which airport you'll be taking off. And arrive in plenty of time to be among the first boarders; seats are not assigned.

AIRPORTS/AIR TERMINALS

Air France and other transatlantic carriers use *Aéroport Charles de Gaulle,* at Roissy, 15 miles north of Paris. (Air France has its own terminal—No. 2—at de Gaulle.) Efficiently operated buses that depart approximately quarter-hourly connect de Gaulle with *Porte Maillot Air Terminal* in the basement of the Palais des Congrès (Paris Convention Center), not far northwest of Arc de Triomphe. From there, you may take a taxi to your hotel, or vice versa. Certain domestic flights take off from and land at *Aéroport d'Orly,* connected with bus service to *Invalides Air Terminal* on the Left Bank. Additionally, there is bus service between de Gaulle and Orly airports for passengers with connections, one to the other.

BOAT TOURS

Bateaux Mouches are the Seine River sightseeing vessels that first-timers often enjoy; they depart approximately half-hourly from Pont de l'Alma, at the foot of Avenue

George V; they have both open and glass-roofed decks. Departures at 1:00 P.M. and 8:30 P.M. are restaurant-equipped. Competition includes *Vedettes du Pont Neuf*, departing from its pier on Pont Neuf, at Île de la Cité; and *Vedettes Paris-Tour Eiffel*, which departs from Pont d'Iéna on the Left Bank, just below the Eiffel Tower.

BUSES AND BUS TOURS

Métro tickets are valid on buses, but it is worth noting that bus routes are divided into fare stages, or *sections*. One ticket covers up to two sections; two tickets are valid for three or more sections. *Buses* take a lot more getting used to than the Métro. Worth-knowing-about routes include No. 21, which takes you from Gare St.-Lazare, on the northern fringe of the Right Bank, through cores of both Right and Left banks, to Cité Universitaire, on the Left Bank's southern edge; No. 73, connecting Place de la Concorde with the futuristic suburb of La Défense; and No. 82, which begins at Jardin du Luxembourg, passing one notable monument after another on both Left and Right banks, terminating at the American Hospital in the suburb of Neuilly. *Bus tours* with varying itineraries are operated by such firms as *American Express* (11 Rue Scribe; phone 4266-09-99), *Cityrama* (4 Place des Pyramides; phone 4260-30-14), and *Paris-Vision* (214 Rue de Rivoli; phone 4260-31-25). An introductory half-day or day-long jaunt is never a bad idea, but before going off on longer, pricier tours, consider on-your-own excursions by train or rented car—of the kind I outline earlier in this book.

CAR HIRE

Many firms provide sightseeing by guide-driven car. *Car rental:* There are many options, among them *Avis* (phone

4609-92-12), *Hertz* (phone 4788-51-51), *Citer* (phone 4341-45-45), and *Serval* (phone 4504-22-13).

CHANGING MONEY

Hotels will, of course, but banks give better rates and are open from 9:00 A.M. straight through 4:30 P.M. on weekdays, bless them. There are change offices at the airports, in-town air terminals, and all six railway stations; those at Gare de l'Est and Gare St.-Lazare traditionally remain open until 8:00 P.M. weekdays. It is perhaps worth noting that even though bank change counters are open the week long (6 A.M. to 11:30 P.M. daily and Sunday) at de Gaulle Airport—a convenience should you arrive without francs—I have found that exchange rates can be better in town, even on Sunday, when many change offices are open, a number of them on Rue de Rivoli in the area between the Louvre and Rue de Castiglione. If you are changing appreciable amounts, it is worth comparing the varying rates at these offices and, as well, at banks during their open-hours. There *are* variations.

CHIENS

Although they do not vote (at least, to my knowledge), dogs have come close to being full-fledged French citizens. I have no figures, but there simply has to be a higher proportion of dogs—vis-à-vis the human population—in France than in any other country. Certain restaurants deny them entry, but they go shopping with masters and mistresses, and rare is the hotel in France that does not have special rates *pour les animaux.* I have yet to meet a French dog that I did not like (they are invariably friendly and quite prepared to charm the pants off you). Which is not to say they all have been properly trained. *Caveat:* Watch where you walk.

CLIMATE

You are, of course, in a temperate-zone country, but a relatively erratic—albeit mild—temperate-zone country. By that, I mean Paris summers may be gray, nasty-rainy, and Paris winters may be glorious and crystal-clear, with spring and autumn delightful, if you're lucky with respect to rain clouds. Winter (late November through March) averages in the high thirties and forties, with January and February the coldest months. Spring (April and May) is likely to be in the fifties. Summer (June through early September) averages in the sixties, with July and August the hottest months, averaging in the mid-seventies, but capable of being much hotter. Autumn (late September through October) is apt to be fiftyish. Rain can fall at any time of the year; do not travel without a raincoat and collapsible umbrella.

CLOTHES

Although it is *couture* capital of the world, Paris—taken as a whole—is neither as well dressed as Rome nor as clothes-conscious as London, which is hardly to imply, however, that you want to pack only jeans. Paris makes a point of looking extremely good on business and more festive social occasions, by which I mean opera, ballet, concerts, and theater, as well as both lunches and dinners in better-category restaurants. The best and simplest rule is to clothe yourself informally in the course of daytime explorations, less so in the evenings.

CREDIT CARDS

Credit cards are accepted in many—but by no means all—restaurants, hotels, chain department stores, and shops. They are not yet as widely accepted as in the United States.

Most popular are Visa, American Express, Diners Club, and MasterCard—in that order.

CURRENCY

The franc is subdivided into 100 centimes, with coins in 10-franc and lower denominations (always keep a supply of ever-so-handy one-franc coins) and notes in higher denominations. Inquire about rates from banks and currency-exchange firms before departure for France; you may want to buy some in advance. In Paris, best rates are obtained at banks and *bureaux de change*—change offices (you absolutely *must* have your passport with you)—but hotel cashiers also change money. Take the bulk of your funds in traveler's checks—they're the safest—with plenty in $20 denominations; they're the most convenient.

CUSTOMS

Entering France: Coming from non-Common Market countries such as the United States, you're allowed a carton of cigarettes and a couple of bottles of alcohol, as well as your own personal effects, including, of course, cameras and a reasonable amount of film. Coming from Common Market countries, the ante is raised by a third in the case of cigarettes and doubled in the case of alcohol. French immigration officers tend not to stamp passports, indicating dates of entry into and exit from France, unless you so request.

Returning to the United States: Each individual may bring back $400 worth of purchases duty free. That is allowable once every 30 days, provided you've been out of the country at least 48 hours. If you've spent more than $400, you'll be charged a flat 10 percent duty on the next $1,000 worth of purchases. Remember, too, that antiques, duly certified to be at least 100 years old, are admitted duty free and do not count as part of your $400 quota; neither do paintings, sculptures, and other works of art, of any date, if certified as original; it's advisable that certification, from the seller or other authority, on their authenticity accompany them. Also exempt from duty, but as a part of the $400 quota: one quart of liquor. And—this is important—there is no restriction on how much one may bring in beyond the $400 limit, as long as the duty is paid.

ELECTRIC CURRENT

The standard in France is 220 volts AC. Take along a transformer for your shaver or hair dryer and an adapter-plug to be attached to the prongs of your appliance, so that it will fit into the holes of the French outlet. American department stores sell kits containing a transformer and a variety of variously shaped adapters. Alternatively, you may buy a French-made appliance, for use during your journey, upon arrival in Paris (department stores stock them)—recommended if your stay will be lengthy.

FRENCHRAIL'S FRANCESHRINKERS

If you've a yen for beyond-the-capital exploration in the course of a Paris stay affording you limited time, consider a day-long Franceshrinker excursion; these are escorted tours with English-speaking guides that include lunch and are essentially by rail but make use of buses, as well, in the course of visits to Versailles, the Loire Valley, and other destinations. Mind, you hit only certain highlights, adhering to a rigid schedule. But if you're a believer in the maxim that half a loaf is better than none, then a Franceshrinker is bookable through travel agents or *FrenchRail, Inc.*—France's national railroad, which translates into French as *Société Nationale de Chemins de Fer Français*, or SNCF, as you will see it abbreviated—at 610 Fifth Avenue, New York, NY 10020; 360 Post Street, San Francisco, CA

94102; 100 Wilshire Boulevard, Santa Monica, CA 90401; 11 East Adams Street, Chicago, IL 60603; 2121 Ponce de Leon Boulevard, Coral Gables, FL 33134; 1500 Rue Stanley, Montreal, Quebec; 409 Granville Street, Vancouver, British Columbia; and 179 Piccadilly, London W1.

Besides the popular Franceshrinker tours, FrenchRail sells economical Rail and Drive and Fly passes, Rail and Drive passes, and BritFrance Railpasses for travel in Britain (in conjunction with BritRail) as well as France, and including trans-English Channel passage via Hovercraft. FrenchRail's supreme achievement is the development and operation of a continually expanding network, throughout France, of the high-speed (as much as 186 mph) TGV (Très Grande Vitesse) trains—extra-fare but, most important, extra-speed, cutting train-travel time by as much as a third, utilizing new tracks and innovatively designed, convenience-packed coaches, which depart from and arrive at newly refurbished terminals, Paris's pink-granite-and-glass Gare Montparnasse the most spectacular of the lot. France's TGV trains are not only all-Europe pioneers, but world-class; only Japan's high-speed trains rank with them.

HOLIDAYS

As in every country, they're a pleasure for residents, but major ones can be a bother for visitors, who do well to plan around them, noting the likelihood of closed museums and other places of interest, certain shops, and some restaurants. Besides Christmas and New Year's, take note of Easter Sunday and Monday, Ascension, Whit Monday, Labor Day (May 1, with big parades), Bastille Day (July 14, joyous celebrations France-wide), Assumption Day (August 15), All Saints' Day (November 1), and Pentecost Sunday and Monday.

LANGUAGE

It's true that many Franchmen are impatient with the less-than-perfect French spoken by foreign visitors and that, indeed—more in Paris and on the Riviera than elsewhere—they'll often rudely reply in English (if they speak it) to your French. But it is increasingly true that these same Frenchmen—themselves studying foreign languages more than has been the case and traveling increasingly abroad—realize that speaking a strange tongue is no easy matter. There is, as a consequence, more tolerance with foreigners' pronunciations than was the case a decade or so back. What is important in Franco-foreign relationships are the polite niceties of conversation. To say simply, "Thank you," to a woman is enough in English; in French it is not. One says, "Merci, madame" or "Merci, mademoiselle," and, with a man, "Merci, monsieur." It is the same with a *bonjour,* or an *au revoir;* you tack on *madame, mademoiselle,* or *monsieur*—no matter how impersonal or brief the exchange has been, and no matter the occupation or station in life of the person with whom you are speaking. It helps, believe me. And one more point: By no means everyone speaks even *un petit peu d'anglais.* Your French will be very useful with this vast majority; don't be bashful about using it. Conversely, don't hesitate about venturing forth without French. After all, English is France's most popular language, after the native tongue; 80 percent of the country's secondary and college language students are studying it. *Tip:* Before you go, pick up a copy of *Just Enough French,* one of Passport Books' excellent *Just Enough* phrasebooks; or study the language in advance of departure, with Passport's *Just Listen 'n Learn French*—a three-cassette and textbook kit.

LOCAL LITERATURE

The skillfully edited English-language *International Herald Tribune* is published as a joint venture of *The Washington*

Post and *The New York Times;* its news content is more international than Parisian, except in weekend editions. Whether you are fluent in French or not, consult the leading dailies, *Le Monde* and *Le Figaro.* And pick up the inexpensive—but amazingly comprehensive—what's-on weekly, *L'Officiel des Spectacles* at news kiosks.

LE MÉTRO

Le Métro—Paris's subway system—ranks with London's Underground, in my view, at least, as the world's best. I use taxis in Paris only for arrival to and departure from the air terminal, with baggage; otherwise, when not walking, I travel the Métro. Pick up a map of the system, gratis, at any station. There are some 15 routes, each with terminus stations at their extremities. If you want to go from Place de la Concorde to Place Charles de Gaulle/Étoile, enter the Concorde station, buy a ticket specifying the class—first or second (difference in cost is minimal and facilities identical, but at rush hour first class—identified by yellow horizontal stripes atop each car—is less crowded). Having studied your pocket map or wall maps, you know that you are to proceed to the platform of Neuilly–Vincennes line; you'll have noted on the map that your stop—De Gaulle/Étoile— is en route to the Neuilly end of the line, so you look for the track marked "Direction Neuilly," board the appropriate train, and exit at your station. Métro cars are equipped with maps of the route they travel, and sign-posting throughout the system is superb. Note, too, that some trips may involve a change of trains, or transfer. Key French word in this case is *correspondance;* by plotting out your route on a map in advance, you easily determine where to transfer.

Automatic machines at each station admit you to the Métro by ticket—but neither by token nor coin. You may buy single tickets or packs of ten tickets (the term for the packet is *carnet*) at considerable savings over individual fares. Still another money-saver is the *Carte Orange* (also good on Paris buses); it's obtainable Mondays at Métro stations, for durations of a week or a month (the weekly card is popular with many visitors), for as many rides as you like, but to obtain it *you must have a passport-type photo* to present when purchasing. Convenient, too—especially so since you may purchase it before departing the United States—is *Paris Sésame*, for two-, or four-, or seven-day durations (from Marketing Challenges International, 10 East 21st Street, New York, NY 10010; phone 212-529-8484; available also in Paris at airports and railway stations). R.E.R., which stands for *Réseau Express Régional*, is a suburban/exurban extension of the Métro and ideal for trips to such points as Malmaison and St.-Germain-en-Laye.

MUSEUM PASS

It's called *La Carte* when you buy it in advance of departure from the United States, and its name in France is *Carte Musée*. A rose by any other name ...; it's a good deal, in that it not only admits you, as many times as you like during the period of validity (one, three, or five days), to sixty museums and places of interest—such as Versailles—in the Paris area, but (and this is important in the case of crowded museums like the Louvre and Beaubourg) with this card, you may bypass whatever queue there may be and go right to the admission gate of most museums for instant entry without waiting in line. And since some museums close for lunch, the card is additionally valuable as it permits unlimited visits and reentries for as long as it's valid. To buy the card in advance, contact Marketing Challenges International, 10 East 21st Street, New York, NY 10010; phone 212-529-8484. In Paris the card is available at major museums and at the Office de Tourisme de la Ville de Paris, 127 Avenue des Champs-Élysées.

OPEN-HOURS

In Paris, hours are quite sensible. *Museums* operated by the French government traditionally close on Tuesdays and major holidays; many other—*but by no means all*—museums operate similarly. For example, the considerable clutch of museums operated by the City of Paris (Carnavalet, Petit Palais, Cognacq-Jay, Art Moderne de la Ville de Paris, Cernuschi, Balzac, Victor-Hugo, De la Mode et du Costume, among them) close on Mondays. Some—again, not all—museums close for approximately two hours at midday, as do *historic houses* and *palaces* operated as museums, and certain churches. *Department stores* have the longest hours, usually Monday through Saturday from 9:00 A.M. to 6:30 P.M., with one or two late opening nights. *Other stores* generally open between 9:00 and 10:00 A.M., some shuttering between noon and 2:00 P.M., and closing at 6:30 or 7:00 P.M., Tuesday through Saturday. *Banks* are exceptionally generous with open hours: 9:00 A.M. to 4:30 P.M., Monday through Friday, closing at noon the day before a holiday. *Hairdressers and barbers* shutter on Monday.

PASSPORTS

A passport is necessary for admittance to France and must be presented to U.S. Immigration upon your return. Apply at Department of State Passport Offices in a dozen-plus cities (look under U.S. Government in the phone book) or—in smaller towns—at the office of the clerk of a federal court and at certain post offices. Allow four weeks, especially for a first passport (valid for 10 years), for which you'll need a pair of two-inch-square photos and birth certificate or other proof of citizenship. There's a $42 fee (subject to change) for first passports; renewals are cheaper. If you're in a hurry when you apply, say so; Uncle Sam will usually try to expedite if you can show documentation indicating imminent departure. Upon receipt of your passport, sign your name where indicated, fill in the address of next of kin, and keep this valuable document with you—*not packed in a suitcase*—as you travel. In case of loss, contact local police, nearest U.S. embassy or consulate, or the Passport Office of the Department of State in Washington.

RATES

Rates for selected hotels (where I've stayed or which I've inspected) and restaurants (where I've eaten) are categorized as *Luxury, First Class,* and *Moderate:* these translate pretty much into what they would mean in the United States, adjusted, of course, to the purchasing power of the dollar with respect to the French franc at the time of your visit.

RESTROOMS

There are modern, unisex public rooms, strategically situated on streets of central Paris. They're automatically cleaned upon each customer's departure, and I say customer advisedly; there is a charge. Let me point out, too, that restrooms in railway stations charge for entrance; possibly for this reason, they are generally clean and decent. Station restrooms are well signposted and generally lead from areas directly adjacent to tracks, rather than from inner waiting rooms. And don't hesitate to use off-lobby restrooms in hotels.

SALES TAXES

The sales taxes, or VAT (the French initials are TVA), of 13 or 20 percent can be refunded, if you buy a minimum of 1,200 francs worth of merchandise in any one store. Department stores are experts at explaining intricacies of an operation that involves filling out a long form at point of purchase and presenting it upon your departure from France to customs officers based at special airport counters signposted *Détaxe*. They rubber stamp it and return it to you, along with the stamped envelope the merchant has given you, so that you may drop it in a mailbox adjacent to the counter. It is thus returned to the seller, who subsequently draws a French-franc check for the amount of the tax and posts it to your home address. Upon receipt of these foreign funds, you take them to your bank, where—unless you have a very friendly banker—charges for conversion to dollars may equal (or exceed) the amount of the check. Unless—and this "unless" is important—you make your purchase with a credit card, in which case request that the refund be credited to the card, obviating the return to you, in francs. Note, too, that in certain cases—ask on the spot—refund can take place at the time of purchase. Complicated? You bet. But I've never known it not to work. *Bonne chance!*

SENIORS

There are, to be sure, conditions, limitations, and qualifications. But seniors—generally, in France that means women who are 60 or older, men who are 62 or older—do well to take passports with them to places where they might serve as money-savers. In the case of French trains, apply for the document known as Carte Vermeil 50, which allows for the purchase of half-off tickets, first or second class. Air Inter affords reductions to seniors on certain flights, and there are reductions by as much as half at certain museums, cinemas, and other attractions. The French Government Tourist Office (addresses above) can provide details.

SHAKING HANDS

Everybody does it, toddlers onward; don't hesitate—it's appreciated. Bear in mind, too, that nonromantic kissing in France—in the nature of a greeting or a farewell—is on both cheeks. Be prepared, ladies, for your hand to be kissed upon occasion; Parisian gents can be gallant. And note that the French are positively compulsive wipers of shod feet on doormats, even in fair-weather, slush-free situations; follow suit.

STEAMSHIP SERVICE

Transatlantic steamship service is almost—but not quite—ancient history. Cunard Line's luxurious flagship, *Queen Elizabeth 2*, valiantly maintains scheduled sailings (about two dozen per year) between New York and the English Channel port of Southampton (see *Britain at Its Best*), with calls, as well, at the French port of Cherbourg—across the Channel—on selected westbound sailings. For France-bound passengers, Cunard arranges charter flights Southampton–Paris; alternatively, there is the option of crossing the Channel by the ferry service linking Southampton and Le Havre, in France.

TAXIS

Taxis are very costly, and not necessarily enjoyable; drivers more often than not have become exhausted, frustrated, and often disagreeable from the overwhelming traffic (authorities are considering barring passenger cars from the city center, it's so bad). I suggest a hotel as central as possible so that you may walk to many destinations. Otherwise, do as I do and use public transportation, reserving taxis for arrival and departure (when you've baggage) and late at night. Cabs are metered, and with two lights on their roofs: if both are illuminated, the cab is free; if both are off, the cab is temporarily out of business; one on, there are passengers inside. Taxi stands are to be found at train stations (you queue) and at certain intersections. Cabs pull up regularly at big hotels. Tip 10 percent if the driver has been at all cordial, nothing if he or she has been an uncommunicative grump.

TÉLÉMATIN

If you've TV in your hotel room, tune in "Télématin," France's counterpart of "Good Morning, America," each morning at breakfast—engaging commentators, news and weather, and interesting guests, sometimes including small animals not always housebroken. It is a delightful way to improve your comprehension of the French language.

TELEPHONES

Everything's up to date at the French telephone authority. By and large, when calling from telephone booths, or kiosks, you use a *Télécarte*, which can be bought at post offices and tobacconists. The cards have a specific number of "bits," which expire as you speak, with the remaining amount of credit available indicated on the phone. Throw away used-in-full cards, but retain those that still have unused portions. If you're calling provincial France from Paris, touch 16 followed by the number. If you're calling Paris from the provinces, touch 16, then 1, and only then the actual number.

TIPPING

Tipping is relatively effortless, thanks to the French system of adding a service charge—usually 15 percent—to restaurant bills and to café tabs as well. (*Service Compris* on menus translates as service included; so does *Prix Net.*) There's no need to tip a hotel concierge unless he has performed special services, beyond handing you your key. Hotel porters who carry your bags to and from your room expect—minimally—the franc equivalent of half a dollar per bag; more if the hotel is especially grand. Tip moderately to theater ushers if they escort you to your seat; 10 percent to barbers and hairdressers; tip taxi drivers up to 10 percent of what's on the meter. In all events, tips are for cordial, efficient service. At no time are they obligatory in Paris—or anywhere.

TOURS, TOUR OPERATORS, TRAVEL AGENTS

Agents, first: Select one who is affiliated with the *American Society of Travel Agents* (ASTA) and, ideally, who knows France firsthand. For a first trip, some travelers are happy with a package; tour operators making a specialty of France—whose packages may be booked through travel agents—include (among many) *Abercrombie & Kent, American Express, Auto Venture, B & D Vogue Travel Services, Caravan Tours, Cityrama, Extra Value Vacations, France Tourisme, Inc., The French Experience, Globus-Gateway, H. S. & Associates, Jet Vacations, David B. Mitchell & Co., Olson Travelworld, Paris Vision, Solrep International, Travel Bound, Wagons-Lits International, World of Oz, XO Travel Consultants* (food, wine, garden tours), as well as tours operated by *Air France* and other transatlantic carriers.

TRAIN STATIONS

There are half a dozen, and it's important to ascertain the correct one, especially for departures. Four are on the Right Bank—*Gare du Nord, Gare de l'Est, Gare St.-Lazare,* and *Gare de Lyon;* while *Gare d'Austerlitz* and *Gare Montparnasse* are on the Left Bank. Note—especially if you're traveling first class—that first class coaches—or sections of coaches—are indicated not only by the numeral 1 on their sides, but by horizontal yellow stripes edging their roofs.

VISITES-CONFÉRENCES

Visites-Conférences translates as guided walking tours conducted by extraordinarily well-educated specialists called *conférenciers* (who are not ordinary guides) to areas where they are experts, coordinated by the government's Caisse Nationale des Monuments Historiques; for information: *Hôtel de Sully,* 62 Rue St.-Antoine (in the Marais quarter); phone 4887-24-14. Tours are listed in issues of the what's-on weekly, *L'Officiel des Spectacles,* and in the newspaper *Le Figaro.*

INCIDENTAL INTELLIGENCE

Police emergency phone is 17; police headquarters is at 9 Boulevard du Palais. Paris *Lost and Found* is at 32 Rue Morillons; phone 4531-14-80. *Main Post Office* (52 Rue du Louvre) is open 24 hours for postage, phone calls, telegrams, . . . Other post offices are open 8 A.M. to 7 P.M. daily and 8 A.M. to noon Saturdays. Remember, too, that you may purchase stamps at tobacconists; the word *Tabac* will be above the door. *To obtain a physician at night,* phone 4578-15-00; *day or night physicians: phone* 4542-37-00. *Pharmacie Dhéry* (84 Champs-Élysées; phone 4256-02-41) is open 24 hours. . . . For an *ambulance,* phone 4887-27-50. . . . *United States Em-*

bassy is at 2 Avenue Gabriel (phone 4296-12-02); *British Embassy:* 35 Rue du Faubourg St.-Honoré (phone 4266-91-42). *American Hospital* is at 63 Boulevard Victor Hugo, in the suburb of Neuilly (phone 4747-53-00). . . . *British Hospital* is at 48 Rue de Villiers, in the suburb of Le Valois (phone 4758-13-12). *Agence Vendôme* (Rue de Castiglione at Place Vendôme) is a long-established ticket agency—worth knowing about for opera, ballet, concert, and theater seats that even hotel concierges might not be able to obtain.

8

The France beyond Paris

Even a great country like France pays a price—with respect to tourism, that is—for the celebrity of its capital. As the continent's ranking metropolis—whose very name has been synonymous over long centuries with the glamour of Europe—Paris is not only a veritable magnet in luring visitors, but often unwittingly retains them overlong, to the point where not enough time remains for provincial exploration.

Surely it is worth keeping in mind that some 53 million of the French Republic's total population of around 56 million live in what the non-Parisian French call "The Other France"—the France beyond the capital. Two areas of the country are, to be sure, not unfamiliar to foreigners. But provincial France is considerably more diverse than these regions—the Côte d'Azur and the Loire Valley. The time has come for the curious Francophile to branch out—to, say, Alsace in the northeast next door to Germany, where locals speak German about as fluently as they do French, and sauerkraut is the basis of the most famous food specialty; or to the Basque country of the southwest, adjacent to Spain, with the Spanish language widely understood, and the bullfight a spectator sport.

The France to which I devote 36 tightly packed chapters in this book's companion volume, *France at Its Best*, is presented herewith, albeit with its attributes capsulized, from Caen to Chamonix, and St.-Malo to St.-Tropez. My plea is that you consider extending your Paris stay into a Beyond-the-Capital journey, or failing that, plan a return France engagement.

EDGING THE CHANNEL

NORMANDY

Ancient Rouen, Normandy's most celebrated city, is close enough to Paris for me to outline a day-long excursion to it, in an earlier chapter; still another excursion is counseled to impressionist artist Claude Monet's home at Giverny. But the rest of Normandy—not far northwest of Rouen—awaits.

Caen, the city of William the Conqueror—who departed his castle there in 1066 to cross the Channel, vanquish the English, and become their sovereign—is among the more attractively reconstructed of the European cities heavily damaged during World War II. You go primarily to pay your respects to the long-ago Duke of Normandy who became King William the Conqueror—as did Queen Elizabeth II in a 1984 Caen visit. William's once-glorious château—elevated and enclosed by eleventh-century ramparts—is today a mix of manicured lawns, museums, and monuments, with its Big Two lures the Musée de Normandie—for regional and historic lore—and the Musée des Beaux-Arts, than which no French provincial repository has a higher proportion of beautiful paintings, with Rogier van der Weyden's *Virgin and Child* its trademark work. You want to see, as well, Abbaye aux Hommes, erected by William, containing his tomb, and with one of its buildings—a former monastery—now seeing service as Caen's City Hall.

Bayeux has, happily, remained small, charming, and visit-worthy—for its globally renowned tapestry—housed in modern quarters and actually a massive embroidery 230 feet long (and but 20 inches high) that delineates, in 58 panels, the Battle of Hastings. Nearby, Bayeux's cathedral—less well-known than it should be, thanks to the more famous tapestry—is a Gothic treasure. Neighboring Musée Baron-Gérard surprises with paintings by the likes of Clouet, Boucher, and Boudin. And Musée Memorial de la Bataille de Normandie is good preparation for a trip to the landing beaches: a graphic presentation of 1944's Battle of Normandy, with dioramas, weapons, and uniforms of both Allied and German troops.

The nearby *Plages de Débarquement*, or landing beaches, gained a place in history on D-Day—June 6, 1944—the start of the World War II campaign by Allied forces that liberated France and the rest of occupied Europe from the Nazis. There are 9,387 American war-dead buried in the Normandy American Cemetery and Memorial, atop a cliff overlooking Omaha Beach. Nearby, at Arromanches, is Musée de Débarquement; its exhibits tell the D-Day story.

Deauville represents Normandy at its most elegant; it is quite the smartest of the English Channel beach resorts and is based on Boulevard de la Mer, which flanks Les Planches, arguably the best-known of the beach-boardwalks in the republic. In summer, the wide, white-sand beach is massed with umbrellas and changing *cabines* and edged by cafés and restaurants. Just inland is a giant covered swimming pool complex, tennis courts in abundance, and the casino—immense, high-ceilinged and crystal-chandeliered, with game rooms, theater, restaurant, and bars. Deauville's next-door neighbor, *Trouville*, though older—it first gained cachet when Empress Eugénie made frequent visits with courtiers in the 1860s—is no longer as tony. Which is hardly to say you want to miss visiting its once-grand casino, local-history museum, or first-rate aquarium.

Honfleur is Normandy's enchanted village. Explorers sailed from it to the New World half a millennium back. But it was nineteenth-century artists—Britain's Bonnington and Turner; France's Corot, Daubigny, Boudin, and Monet—whose paintings of its harbor aroused international curiosity. The art museum named for Boudin exhibits paintings by that artist and other impressionists. The Church of Ste.-Catherine is a one-of-a-kind wooden structure dating to the Renaissance. There are maritime and history museums. Mostly, though, Honfleur is for strolls along the quays that line its quartet of inner harbors, pauses in its cafés, and hearty meals featuring the rich Norman cuisine built upon local apples, cream, and seafood.

Mont St.-Michel, surely the most painted and photographed monument in this region of northern France, is the celebrated Gothic abbey constructed on a fortified rock of an island that was accessible only at low tide, until as recently as a century back, when a causeway was built, joining it to the mainland. The Benedictine abbey rises more than 450 feet and is gained by a 90-step ascent, with the effort worthwhile: sublime Romanesque nave, late Gothic altar, colonnaded cloister, a maze of auxiliary chapels.

BRITTANY

St.-Malo is familiar to Canadians because it was from this Breton port that Jacques Cartier sailed, in 1534, to discover their country. Englishmen know St.-Malo because they can sail to it from their shores, the summer long. The Welsh feel a bond with St.-Malo because it is named for a wandering seventh-century Welshman, sainted for miracles performed in its vicinity. Which leaves Americans, surely the last of the English-speakers to appreciate one of the most sparkling of France's resort cities.

Walk along the venerable ramparts enclosing Intra-Muros, the part of town within the walls. Take in the pair of museums of local lore within the still-splendid town château. Pay your respects at Cartier's tomb in the Gothic cathedral. Relax on the beaches. And make excursions to fishing villages like Cancale (dotted with seafood restaurants), to the Romanesque cathedral in tiny but well-preserved Dol de Bretagne, and to the nearby Château de Combourg.

Rennes—because of its razor's edge location on the border with France—in the centuries when Brittany was a separately governed duchy—is at once history-rich and agreeably contemporary. The building that served as Brittany's Parliament from the early seventeenth century through to the Revolution is today the Palais de Justice, or law courts. No matter. Go right in, to inspect the onetime Parliament chamber, one of France's more dazzling interiors, with coffered and frescoed ceilings, Gobelin tapestries taking the place of wallpaper, and little balconies, or loggias, on three of four walls, for the benefit of baroque-era VIPs intent on watching debates from on high. A splendid Renaissance altarpiece highlights Rennes's cathedral. There are a pair of museums—fine arts and Musée de Bretagne—sharing a single building. And a pair of not-far-distant medieval castles—Fougères and Virtré, in towns whose names they take—that make for colorful excursions.

Quimper is middle-sized, small, friendly, and just inland from the Atlantic. Its big surprise is a Musée des Beaux-Arts brimming with Italian, Flemish, Dutch, and French Old Masters, with a bonus of impressionists. Twin steeples of the part Gothic, part baroque cathedral are a Quimper trademark, and nearby towns—Locronan (virtually unchanged since the sixteenth century), Pont-l'Abbé (tradition-bound and on the sea), Pointe du Raz (near

Audierne, and France's westernmost point, with a light-house on a rocky eminence just off shore)—make for pleas-ant excursions.

Nantes, largest and most important urban center in west-ern France, abounds in cultural treasures—an extraordi-narily rich Musée des Beaux-Arts, a trio of museums in the Château des Ducs de Bretagne, dating to the Middle Ages; even a museum celebrating the talents of locally born Jules Verne; and a still-classy shopping arcade, Passage Pomme-raye, that opened as long ago as 1843.

Angers—at Brittany's eastern edge and directly west of the matchless Loire Valley châteaux to which I direct you, by means of an excursion, in an earlier chapter—is itself dominated by an absolutely fabulous thirteenth-century château whose walls are punctuated by 17 towers, some nearly 200 feet high and surrounded by moats, partially surfaced as formal gardens, partially the venue for a herd of deer, and with treasure-filled interiors. A hilltop cathe-dral is nearby, along with a fine-arts museum occupying a five-centuries-old turreted palace. Beyond town, beeline for Château le Saumur, in the pretty town taking its name, with a profile of towers, turrets, slate roofs, and chimneys, and a decorative arts museum within.

THE NORTHEAST

ALSACE

Locate *Strasbourg* on the map—with only the Rhine to sep-arate it from Germany and Belgium, Luxembourg and Switzerland near-neighbors, and the considerable territory of France to the west—and you appreciate why its people speak German as fluently as French (along with a dialect of their own). This is one of France's most absorbing cities. Its Cathedral of Notre-Dame is an all-Europe Gothic ranker built over a span of five centuries, with a brilliant facade, massively scaled nave, reputed stained glass, exquisite decorative detailing. And the city's museums are exemplary. One, adjacent to the cathedral—Musée d'Oeuvre Notre-Dame—celebrates Alsatian art, medieval through Renaissance. The Château de Rohan shelters a fine-arts museum brilliant with Old Masters, Memling through Murillo, as well as decorative-arts and archeological museums. And you may tour Palais de l'Europe, to see the European Parliament.

Exit via the *Route du Vin*—embracing half a hundred villages, many of them picture-book and skirting the Rhine River and the Vosges Mountains—terminating in Colmar, where the special treat is Musée d'Unterlinden, whose principal masterwork is a Renaissance altarpiece known as *Le Retable d'Issenheim,* for the monastery from which it was taken at the time of the French Revolution. Château Haut Koenigsbourg, just north of town, a Prince Valiant castle atop a misty mountain, went up in the twelfth century and was restored at the turn of the present century by Kaiser Wilhelm II, while Alsace was part of Germany. And *Mulhouse,* not far south of Colmar, draws car buffs to its Musée National de l'Automobile—its 465 cars represent 90 makes—and rail buffs to its Musée Français du Chemin de Fer, with a car created for Napoleon III's aides-de-camp among its prime exhibits.

LORRAINE

Think Lorraine and you think *Nancy,* its principal city and for centuries seat of the Dukes of Lorraine, to which fame came in the eighteenth century when a deposed Polish king—Stanislaus by name—became duke and commissioned the architect Héré and the ironwork designer Lamour to create a monumental square. Their masterwork—Place Stanislaus—remains to this day Nancy's symbol and its soul. Its gilded wrought-iron gates and pair of fountains are complemented by flanking palaces. One houses the city hall with very grand state rooms and a monumental stairway leading to them; another is the landmark Grand Hôtel Concorde, a third is the Grand Théâtre, and the fourth houses the Musée des Beaux-Arts, one of whose Old Masters is a landscape by the Lorraine-born Renaissance painter, Claude Lorrain. The medieval Ducal Palace now houses treasure-filled Musée de Lorraine. And a third museum—Musée de l'École de Nancy—is one of the world's great repositories of Art Nouveau furniture, stained glass, woodwork, and accessories.

EASTERN FRANCE

BURGUNDY

For long centuries capital of the far-flung Duchy of Burgundy—a major power feared even by France—*Dijon* amassed riches—archeological, architectural, artistic— which warrant careful inspection. The Gothic cathedral, originally a Benedictine monastery, has as its surprise a Romanesque octagon of a crypt that's a thousand years old, and the building where monks once lived—next-door—now serves admirably and atmospherically as the city's remarkable archeological museum, with superb Roman exhibits stars of its show. The massive onetime Ducal Palace shelters an extraordinary treasure-trove of a fine arts museum, its range Rogier van der Weyden through Claude Monet. Townhouses of yore see service as mini-museums, and the city is dotted with exemplary churches. A day earmarked for the *Route des Grands Vins* south of town can be time well spent. And there are a number of worthwhile destinations to the west, including *Auxerre* with its cathedral and Church of St.-Germain; *Vézelay,* with its Basilica of Ste.-Madeleine; the Renaissance-era

Château de Bussy-Rabutin; and the fairytale village of *Semur-en-Auxois,* a veritable medieval movie set.

Beaune, smaller than Dijon, is Burgundy's principal wine center (you may taste and buy at its well-operated Marché aux Vins—one of the best such in France) and has a pair of aged attractions. Hôtel-Dieu is a fifteenth-century paupers' hospital that is at once a major mix of Renaissance architecture and Renaissance art (its ace-in-the-hole is van der Weyden's *The Last Judgment*) while the Basilique de Notre-Dame stands out for its tapestries—a series lining walls behind the choir that date to the fifteenth century and recount the life of the Virgin Mary. The *Côte de Beaune*—southern tier of Burgundy's Côte d'Or wine region—makes for an agreeable excursion, extending south through Pommard, and Meursault to Mâcon and Beaujolais.

SAVOIE

Chamonix is the best known of France's alpine resorts, with good reason. It is linked with the Italian resort town of Courmayeur (see *Italy at Its Best*) by means of an extraordinary tunnel cut through 15,781-foot Mont Blanc—the Alps' highest peak. It is framed by snow-surfaced mountains that began luring visitors—intrepid English adventurers—three and a half centuries back, not long before a trio of Frenchmen reached the Mont Blanc summit, pioneering French mountaineering and paving the way for development of what has become France's best-equipped and most scenically situated mountain town, hosting a million visitors each year. Chamonix was the site of the first Winter Olympics in 1924, has the highest cable car in the world, abounds in facilities for skiers, and offers a bonus of easily reached destinations of visual splendor (even including a half-day mountain journey to Italy) for nonskiing sightseers. There's a fabulous sports complex: Musée Alpin (with exhibits that tell the area's story as a winter-sports center) and even an 18-hole Robert Trent Jones–designed course for golf buffs.

Annecy, not far distant, is surely Savoie's best-kept secret: with a castle out of the Brothers Grimm, canals overhung with flowers and swan-populated, a lake that's a shimmering jewel. Dukes of Savoie lived in the Château d'Annecy—now a charmer of a museum of local lore—into the eighteenth century. Annecy-born St.-François de Sales preached in the cathedral. A cable car will take you to the summit of Mont Veyrier, 4,000 feet over town. And excursion boats ply Lac d'Annecy, whose most significant destination is the village of Talloires, with exceptional hotels and restaurants.

Aix-les-Bains, though but a shadow of the thermal spa it must have been a century or so back when it attracted the likes of Queen Victoria and J. Pierpont Morgan, remains an agreeable thermal center, spectacularly situated alongside Lac de Bourget, beneath a peak—Mont Revard— ascendable by cable car.

Chambéry knew wealth during the medieval centuries when it was the seat of Savoy dukes. Their castle remains a principal visitor destination, as does the adjacent cathedral and Ste.-Chapelle. And there are a pair of art museums— Beaux-Arts and Savoisien—with creditable collections.

Évian is an unassuming little spa town on the south shore of the Lake of Geneva (a.k.a. Lac Léman) just opposite the Swiss city of Lausanne (with which it is linked by fast ferries). You go to relax—drinking water at the spa, dining and perhaps gambling in the little casino, ascending by cable car to the summit of Plâteau des Mémises (4,800 feet)—and enjoying the excellent hotels.

LYON

Lyon, France's second city, was the Romans' *Lugdunum*, capital of all Gaul, site of the first meeting of Gallic chiefs at a kind of Parliament whose delegates discussed—for the first time—the idea of the confederation that would become France. Later, it pioneered with the cultivation of silkworms, becoming the silk center of Europe with a merchant class that opened France's first stock exchange. World War II saw Lyon capital of the French Resistance movement. Contemporarily, it is a world-class innovator in scientific research, and with a cuisine tradition so developed that it's known to have visitors who come only to eat.

Roman-era Lyon comes to life at Musée de la Civilisation Gallo-Romaine, built on a hillside adjacent to a still-used pair of Roman amphitheaters and a still-impressive temple. Medieval and Renaissance Lyon centers on the Old Town, or Vieux-Lyon, dominated by a magnificient Romanesque/ Gothic cathedral, with Musée Historique de Lyon occupying a nearby town house, and streets all about cut through by centuries-old, still-used passages called *traboules*.

Lyon museums are special. Musée des Beaux-Arts is housed in an enormous onetime convent, and not only brims with paintings—Flemish Primitives like Quentin Matsys through postimpressionists like Bonnard—but exhibits fine sculpture as well, including Greek, Roman, baroque, and on into the last century. The decorative-arts and silk museums that occupy neighboring Rue de la Charité mansions are of a special style. Musée des Hospices Civils, in a working hospital, portrays hospital life over the centuries, with its most popular exhibit a bed shared by five patients until 1787—which was by no means atypical. Musée de la Résistance pays tribute to the anti-Nazi underground during World War II. And the reception rooms of Hôtel de Ville, the city hall, are among the most opulent such in the republic.

Excursions from Lyon are in order to two nearby towns— *Vienne,* for its wealth of Roman art, artifacts, and architecture; and *Pérouges,* a medieval fortified village that is a protected national monument, for which praise be.

GRENOBLE

Surely the most dramatically situated of the larger French cities, Grenoble—at the foot of the Belledone massif—flanks an ever-snowy backdrop of Alpine peaks, and is cut through by the Isère River. Early Romans called it *Gratianapolis*, and it thrived over the centuries, eventually passing to control of the medieval Dauphins of Viennois (whose title eventually came into use as the name of the Dauphiné region, remaining so to this day).

This is a city that makes its money on industry generated by hydroelectric resources and on nuclear research, the while drawing more foreign students to its university—founded in the fourteenth century—than any other in France. It is as well to start at the top—boarding a cable car at Quai Stephane-Jay to the summit of the mountain on which La Bastille, a onetime fortress, is situated. Get the flavor of the city, then, by a stroll through Vieux-Grenoble—to the multi-epoch cathedral, Gothic-era Church of St.-André, the elaborate Palais de Justice (for long the Dauphins' Parliament), and to Musée Stendhal, with mementos of the Grenoble-born author in an eighteenth-century setting.

Proceed, then, to Musée Dauphinois, on the north bank of the Isère in an ex-monastery of the baroque period, and with regional lore, pottery through prints. End in Grenoble's Musée de Peinture et de Sculpture, unsurpassed in provincial France, thanks to a collection strong in European Old Masters (Rubens and Jordaens, Veronese and Tintoretto), artists of the French seventeenth century (Lorrain, Largillière), impressionists (Sisley, Renoir), and post-impressionists (Gris and Braque).

The Dauphiné countryside is woefully underappreciated by foreign visitors. Requisite destinations are *La Grande Chartreuse*, or, at least, the open-to-visitors museum of the resident Carthusian monks, which interprets their way of

life, near Voiron; a trio of superlative châteaux—*Berenger,*
Vizille, and *Touvet;* a superbly intact medieval village called
Crémieu; and *Chemin de Fer Touristique de la Mure*—a made-
for-tourists mountain railway—that runs from St.-
Georges-de-Commiers through a roller coaster–like maze
of passes, tunnels, and bridges to La Mure, and makes for
a spectacular day in the mountains.

CÔTE D'AZUR

NICE

The point about the Riviera's premier city is that it is a
city—an ancient and substantial city, in addition to being a
world-class resort. It was the Romans who named it—
Nicaea—and Greeks who followed them, to be succeeded
by barbarians, rulers of Provence and Savoy, troops of
France's François I, and—as relatively early as the eighteenth century—wandering Britons partial to the mild cli-
mate and idyllic location, with snowy mountains in the
rear and the blue Mediterranean out front.

Today's Nice is an amalgam of these disparate influences. Elegance came with Parisians who followed the first
Britons, these last bringing with them the tradition of the
grand hotel. Nice's lusty cuisine is Italian in origin. And
much of the art in its museums is a consequence of its having lured such masters as Chagall, Matisse, and Picasso,
their curiosity piqued by nineteenth-century enthusiasts
like the painter Delacroix, the writer Maupassant, and the
composer Berlioz.

Of course, you want to walk ocean-front Promenade des
Anglais and test the waters, narrow pebbly beaches notwithstanding. But inland Nice is eminently explorable,
too. Start with remains of the ancient Roman *Cimenelum,*
including a still lovely amphitheater and baths. Take in the

adjacent Musée Matisse, with works of that modern master, and, in the same building, exhibits of the Musée Archéologique.

Move along, then, to Vieux-Nice, nerve center of the city from the Middle Ages well into the eighteenth century and still vibrant and engaging. Take in the cathedral—among the relatively few in France of the baroque era—and handsome; Musée du Palais Lascaria, a sumptuously furnished baroque palace; and Cours Saleya, dotted with good-value seafood restaurants.

Belle Époque Nice is best exemplified by Musée Massena, a turn-of-century mansion whose exhibits evoke the city a hundred or so years back, in contrast to Musée Chagall—ultra-mod and rich with paintings of the artist whose name it takes. The city's fine arts museum, Jules-Cheret, is strongest in eighteenth-century work, English as well as French. Not far away, in *Biot*, is Musée National Fernand Léger—celebrating the work of the modern painter. Nearby, too, in little *Vence* is Chapelle du Rosaire, its interiors designed and decorated by Matisse just a few years before he died in 1954.

At *St.-Paul-de-Vence*, an extraordinary hotel restaurant—Colombe d'Or—has walls hung with works of such patrons as Braque, Calder, Dufy, Léger, and Picasso; and that village's Fondation Maeght exhibits modern sculpture by the likes of Arp, Giacometti, and Miró, with equally stellar contemporary paintings. At *St.-Jean-Cap-Ferrat*, the lure is Fondation Ephrussi de Rothschild-Musée Île de France—a onetime Riviera home of a Rothschild baroness filled with rococo furniture and paintings by such masters as Hubert Robert, Fragonard, and Boucher—with impressionists as an added attraction. *Cagnes-sur-Mer's* draw is Maison de Renoir—home of the great impressionist painter for his last twelve years, with a clutch of his paintings, drawings, and sculpture.

CANNES, ANTIBES, AND JUAN-LES-PINS

Unlike Nice—a substantial city before its beaches were dis-
covered by holidaymakers—Cannes, though ancient, was
but a small fishing port named for a reed called *cannae* that
grew in nearby marshes. But like Nice, Cannes can thank
the British for providing it with its true vocation: tourism.
The seafront promenade, La Croisette, is Cannes's counterpart of Nice's Promenade des Anglais. You want to take
in Old Cannes, too, by means of a stroll through the elevated Le Suquet quarter, from whose Place de la Castre
there are breathtaking views of the city below and the sea,
and with mixed-bag exhibits of Musée de la Castre as a
bonus.

It's a good idea to embark on a day-long cruise to
Canne's offshore Îles de Lérin, two in number. Ste.-
Marguerite's draw is Fort Vauban and its seventeenth-
century prison, while on the island of St.-Honorat, there's
a fortified monastery with Romanesque origins and a sublime cloister.

Antibes and Juan-les-Pins—a pair of disparate towns
east of Cannes—may be regarded as vacation destinations
in and of themselves or taken in, via excursion, from
Cannes. Juan-les-Pins is modern and composed essentially of hotels, restaurants, cafés, and discos revolving
around a summer-only casino on Square Gould. Antibes—
the ancient Greeks' *Antipolis*, then a Roman colony, and
later a seat both of bishops and of rulers related to the Gri-
maldis of Monaco—is more substantial and with a charming, centuries-old core that warrants on-foot exploration.

It's fun to walk its animated streets, take in produce at
the Marché Provençal, or pause in a café. Not to be missed,
either, are the so-called cathedral (actually a parish
church)—a mix of many architectural epochs; Musée
Picasso—an aged seafront château where Picasso lived and
which exhibits a substantial selection of his paintings and

sculpture; and Musée Archéologique, whose galleries display bits and pieces of ancient Antibes.

Grasse, in the hills beyond Cannes, is France's Perfumeville: center of the country's scent industry for three centuries, surrounded by fields of lavender, roses, and jasmine, with a number of perfume factories open to visitors, a handsome church called a cathedral (that is no longer the seat of a bishop, however), and a pair of fine museums. Musée Fragonard, in a rococo mansion, with a number of Grasse-born painter Fragonard's eighteenth-century works; and Musée d'Art et d'Histoire de Provence, occupying another fine old house, with an unusual display of antique perfume bottles.

Valauris is still another destination for Picasso buffs; the late great painter was a resident for ten years. At Musée National Picasso, in the chapel of the village's château, hangs *La Guerre et la Paix,* the master's enormous and highly charged mural on the theme of war and peace.

PRINCIPALITY OF MONACO

Monaco, a centuries-old principality independent of France—but surrounded by it on three sides—is an intrinsic Riviera community, with its Monte Carlo quarter the center of visitor life—dotted with grand hotels, pricey shops, restaurants and cafés, and—of special interest—the Casino de Monte Carlo, mock-baroque in the best tradition of the last century's Second Empire (it opened in 1863), retaining original frescoes, sculptures, stained glass, gilded woodwork, and silk-shaded lamps hung from high ceilings over the game tables. Traditionally open as early as 10 A.M., the casino has made modern concessions; there are now slot machines and a U.S.-style American Room, with Yank roulette, blackjack, craps, and Las Vegas–trained croupiers. But it's the opulent European Rooms—Salle Touzet, Salon Privé, and, if you please, Salon *Super*-Privé (where stakes are *very* high)—that you want not to miss, taking in, as well, a performance of opera, ballet, or a concert in the casino building's Salle Garnier, a jewel of a theater designed by the same Charles Garnier responsible for the Paris Opéra.

If it's summer, the art-filled state rooms of Palais Princier—Throne Room, Galerie d'Hercule, Galerie des Glaces, Chambre d'York—will be open for tours. And it's fun, while you're in Monaco, to make an excursion to the venerable French village of *Éze*, perched high atop a mountain and affording splendid vistas of the Riviera coast.

ST.-TROPEZ

St.-Tropez—Roman-founded and, indeed, named for a Roman Christian martyr called *Tropes*—gained celebrity only in the early years of this century after Maupassant exclaimed over its beauties in print. Matisse followed, pioneering among the painters, to be succeeded by a star-studded cache of colleagues: Signac, Bonnard, Henry Cross, and Marquet, to name a handful. Colette joined this pre–World War I artistic contingent. Pre–World War II St.-Tropez had become fashionable enough to attract the fashion and film worlds, innovating a casual, barefoot resort life-style on the French Mediterranean, nothing at all like more conventional fleshspots such as Cannes, Nice, or Monte Carlo.

It took only a handful of talented publicists, after World War II, to chronicle St.-Tropez's hedonism as manifested by such visitors as actress Brigitte Bardot and novelist Françoise Sagan and to place St.-Tropez on the resort map. And with reason. It is one of a kind—straddling the inner shore of an enormous sheltered gulf; climbing a château-topped hill and backed by formidable mountains; lacking grand hotels in the traditional sense, with nary a sightseers' tour bus on its streets; shopping in way-out boutiques rather than department stores; very late dining; very, *very* late disco-dancing; and the hotel social director an unknown species.

There are two requisite visitor destinations: Musée de l'Annonciade—an all-France sleeper—is a desanctified chapel exhibiting works by postimpressionist painters who worked in the neighborhood—Signac and Marquet, Matisse and Seurat, Dufy and Vlaminck, Van Dongen and Derain, Bonnard, and Vuillard, to name some. And Musée de la Marine is a hilltop citadel of yore whose exhibits tell the story—going back many centuries—of St.-Tropez and its neighborhood.

PROVENCE

AIX-EN-PROVENCE

It may, perhaps, be exaggerating to term Aix the quintessential Provence, but not by much. It evokes the beauty of this Mediterranean region in a fountain-centered, boulevardlike main street and the Romanesque cloister of its cathedral, than which there is no lovelier in France. As seat of the Courts of Provence, it was the Provençal capital for much of the period embracing the formative twelfth through fifteenth centuries; toward the end of that period, the multititle René—variously King of Naples, Duke of Anjou, *Bon Roi* René de Provence—passed his final years in Aix, where his courtiers were writers and musicians; his pastimes, painting and poetry.

Your first priority should be the dozen-century-old cathedral, noting its Gothic portal, octagon of a tower, triptych painting, *The Burning Bush,* and Romanesque cloister, each of its arches supported by a pair of pillars, no two of whose exquisite carvings are alike.

Aix's Musée des Tapisseries is the cathedral's next-door neighbor (it had been the archbishops' residence) and its collection of immense tapestries is an all-France ranker. Pay your respects to Atelier de Cézanne—the house in which Aix-born impressionist painter Paul Cézanne was born, and whip along, then, to Musée Granet, where five Cézannes highlight a distinguished collection, strong on Italian Old Masters and French masters of several epochs.

ARLES

The irony of this small city is that despite early eminence as a Roman colony founded by no less an emperor than Julius Caesar—with still-standing Caesar-commissioned constructions—it was not until after a prolific Dutch-born artist came for a 15-month sojourn some 900 years later that it achieved a measure of global repute. And the irony is compounded when one considers that even though Vincent Van Gogh created some 300 paintings, drawings, and watercolors during his Arles stay, not a single one of his works hangs in its art museum. The point of Arles today is not associations with Van Gogh, but rather, the extraordinary heritage of the Romans.

Zero in on Les Arènes, some 1,900 years young, still in use (hope that you may witness a Provençal bullfight), embracing 60 arches in its two remaining levels; Théâtre Antique—employed for summer theater; and Musée Lapidaire—an ex-church displaying mint-condition Roman-era mosaics, busts, and statues. End at St.-Trophime, a splendidly embellished twelfth-century church-cum-cloister that is Arles's major non-Roman monument.

AVIGNON

It was a fluke of history that propelled medieval Avignon into the limelight. The Italian political scene of the moment was prickly and interrelated with the coincidence of there being a bit of papal-owned territory in southern France. As a consequence, His Holiness, Clement V, a Frenchman who had been Archbishop of Bordeaux, betook himself and the papal entourage to his homeland, establishing his seat at Avignon in 1309. Half a dozen Avignon-based popes followed, remaining through most of the fourteenth century, the while Avignon became a city of consequence. Their handiwork remains. The Palais des Papes—embracing a series of massive state rooms and a trio of chapels—is somberly grand and is one of France's most visited interiors.

A onetime palace that the popes used, originally, to house official guests, is now Musée du Petit Palais; it houses a collection of Italian medieval masterworks—some 300 all told, the range Botticelli, Perugino, and Carpaccio. Musée Calvet, in an enchanting rococo palace, is one of the most beautiful in the republic. Villeneuve-les-Avignon, the town across the Rhône, is monument-filled, and an excursion to nearby Orange—to see its Roman-origin Théâtre Antique, the best preserved such extant—is in order.

NÎMES

The Romans were drawn to Nîmes by its location—convenient as a stopping-off point between colonies in Spain and home base, to the east, in Italy. Emperor Augustus lavished it with construction, to the point where it became a showplace of the far-flung Roman Empire. Its most painted—and contemporarily, photographed—Roman souvenir is Maison Carrée, seeing service, despite its 1,900-year lineage, as a museum of the choicest art treasures from the Roman period, the superb Venus de Milo being star of the show.

Les Arènes—the amphitheater—is well preserved, too, and still seeing service; it was built to seat 20,000 spectators, come to marvel at feats of gladiators or charioteers.

But this is a museum town of note: Archéologique, with Roman treasures; Beaux-Arts, with French and Italian masterworks; Vieux-Nîmes, in a baroque-era bishops' mansion and with exemplary furniture and paintings. And not far from town is Pont du Gard, a Roman-built aqueduct built 2,000 years ago—900 feet long by 160 feet high—that represents both engineering and architectural skills of the ancient empire at their most brilliant.

MARSEILLE

France's Mediterranean metropolis dates back to ancient Greeks who came upon a massive crescent of a beach—backed by high hills—some 2,600 years ago, and in establishing their colony of *Massilia*, created what has come to be the nation's oldest city. Today's Marseille is a fascinating fusion of cultures and peoples and ideas—good-looking, good fun, and a distinctive dimension of the French experience.

Its boulevard-like main street, La Canabière, extends inland and uphill from the aptly named old, or Vieux Port, quarter—where Marseille had its beginnings, and where a twelfth-century cathedral—no longer used as such—is next door to a newer successor.

There are no less than a trio of museums portraying ancient Marseille: Jardin des Vestiges—an area uncovered in the course of constructing a shopping complex in 1967; Musée Histoire de Marseille—sheltering treasures from the adjacent *jardin;* and Musée des Docks Romains—on the actual site of piers dating to the early Roman trader-settlers, with displays ranging from ancient oil jars to boat fragments.

And there are a pair of additional museums deserving of visits: Grobet-Labadie, a sumptuously furnished town house—mostly eighteenth-century—that is one of France's foremost repositories of the decorative arts; and Musée des Beaux-Arts, whose substantial range of paintings extends from Rubens through Corot.

THE SOUTHWEST

BORDEAUX

It's the core of the most prestigious wine-producing region of the world, with the magically named quartet of principal vineyard districts—Graves, Médoc, Pomerol, and St.-Émilion—encircling it. Each year, ships bearing five million bottles sail from its Gironde River docks into the nearby Atlantic, the better to please palates of discerning drinkers planetwide.

But what of the city behind the labels on the bottles? Long centuries—since Romans settled the ancient town they dubbed *Burdigala*—have seen Bordeaux evolve into one of the most elegant cities in Europe, a celebration, in large part, of its Golden Age: the eighteenth century.

Its Grand Théâtre—without peer in France (Paris's Théâtre de l'Opéra excepted)—is ringed by a magnificent colonnade, and its interior is no less dazzling. Musée des Arts Décoratifs—in an eighteenth-century mansion—ranks with counterparts in Paris, Lyon, and Marseille, and is essentially Louis XV and Louix XVI. Musée des Beaux-Arts, in still another atmospheric and aged structure—impresses with its paintings, a giant Veronese through to small-scale impressionists of uncommon charm. And its Romanesque-Gothic cathedral is among the more handsome of those in France's major cities.

TOULOUSE

Though one of France's largest metropolitan centers, Toulouse remains underappreciated. Still, ever since the Romans named it *Tolosa*, it has been busy at one sort of activity or another. Makers and doers have long dominated the Toulouse scene.

The single most significant of its interiors is that of Basilica of St.-Sernin, a nine-century-old beauty that is one of the most brilliantly designed churches in France—with a 350-foot-long nave beneath a sublime, 60-foot-high barrel-vaulted ceiling. Church of the Jacobins is a veritable Gothic tour-de-force, splendidly restored in the 1970s and not unlike St.-Sernin, an all-France ecclesiastical ranker. Toulouse's cathedral, were it not for the competition of St.-Sernin and the Jacobins, would be a stellar Gothic standout.

Le Capitole—the City Hall—is eighteenth-century, with a dazzling classic-style facade extending some 400 feet and a showplace reception room, Galerie des Illustres. Which leaves Musée des Augustins—a desanctified Augustinian monastery dating back seven centuries and only recently restored and refurbished, to emerge as a world-class repository not only of Old Master paintings but—quite special, this—of Gothic sculpture.

ALBI

A not-far-distant neighbor of Toulouse, much smaller Albi is surely the only city in France with a cathedral built to double as a fortress. Yet its look is pleasing and its interior distinctive, given the decoration—covering every bit of surface—by imported Bolognese artists. But there's another reason for an Albi visit: Musée d'Albi. Few small towns do as well by native-son artists of stature as does Albi, in the case of Toulouse-Lautrec, in this attractive setting. The Lautrec collection is not a token grouping, but extensive—and excellent. And French masters from other eras are represented, as well.

CARCASSONNE

Though extensively restored, Carcassonne remains an originally thirteenth-century walled city that could be out of a fairy tale. There is a pair of concentric walls punctuated by towers and turrets, with entrance gained by a drawbridge over a moat. An overall view—in the course of your approach—is reason enough for a visit. But you want to take time for the local treasures in Musée Archéologique, and the stunning interior of the Basilica of St.-Nazaire, noting especially capitals of columns flanking its Romanesque nave.

AUCH

A tranquil cathedral town in the gently hilly heartland of ancient Gascony, Auch is celebrated as the legendary home of D'Artagnan, leader of Dumas's *Three Musketeers*. Take time for its Musée des Jacobins—named for the long-disused monastery it occupies, displaying paintings, prints, and local furniture. And inspect the Gothic-vaulted cathedral, noting the massive Renaissance choir stalls that are masterworks of the woodcarver's art; and just under a score of 400-year-old stained-glass windows that rank among the finest such in France.

MONTPELLIER

Although it passed medieval centuries as the property of the Spanish kingdoms of Aragón and Majorca, Montpellier has been quite French ever since—the kingpin city of Languedoc, as proud of a university that dates to the thirteenth century as of its contemporary flair for industry, and an appreciation of its heritage that extends even to street signs; they are bilingual, in both the Languedoc language and French.

This is a city as rich culturally as it is economically. It impresses with its architecture—an Arc de Triomphe leads to Promenade du Peyrou, an eighteenth-century mix of paths and pools—and with its museums. Musée Fabre is one of the surprise-package provincial art museums of the republic, brimming with fine works, the range Italian (Guido Reni) and Spanish (Zurbarán) through Flemish (Rubens) and Dutch (Van Ruysdael). With a slew of impressionists, too. Musée Atger is an unusual repository of priceless prints and drawings—by the likes of Tiepolo and Fragonard—in the medical school of the university. Musée Sabatier d'Espeyran is a town mansion now seeing service as a decorative arts museum.

And châteaux: Montpellier's countryside abounds in castles, the range classic-style Mogère through history-rich Castries.

LA CÔTE BASQUE

BIARRITZ

Made fashionable—not unlike Trouville, on the English Channel—by Napoleon III's consort, Empress Eugénie, nineteenth-century Biarritz drew holidaymakers like Queen Victoria and her son, Edward VII—both of whom have streets named in their honor. Today, this onetime fishing village fronted by a still-magnificent beach— Grande Plage—draws mostly French and Spanish visitors. (Indeed, Spanish replaces English—the No. 2 language in most of the rest of France—as the second tongue.) You visit Biarritz not so much for the sights—there is a distinctly minor maritime museum and but a solitary church of importance—as to soak in the sun, populate the cafés on Place Clemenceau, and shop along Avenue Edouard VII. It can be very pleasant.

BAYONNE

Biarritz's next-door neighbor to the east is a substantial small city with a landmark castle, Château Vieux, whose inhabitants—now army officers—have included kings Louis XI, François I, and Louis XIV. The cathedral is a Gothic structure of no little beauty, and twin-steepled. There are a pair of museums; one, Musée Basque, is devoted to the culture of the region; the other, Musée Bonnat, has a positively smashing art collection—including a roomful of Rubenses, with Leonardo, Michelangelo, Rembrandt, and Dürer on scene, as well.

ST.-JEAN-DE-LUZ

Nature ordained that this little town—flanking the wide, white sands of a perfectly crescent-shaped bay—would be a beach resort. But history has made an impact on St.-Jean-de-Luz, too. Maison Louis XIV is the charming baroque mansion where Louis XIV and his Spanish bride, Infanta María Teresa, spent their wedding night in 1660 after the knot was tied in the nearby Church of St.-Jean-Baptiste; a plaque affixed to the church's facade provides details of the wedding, and it's worth noting that the door through which the royal couple passed was walled after the ceremony—and is still.

PÉRIGORD

Though lacking in a single whizbang of a metropolis, the southwest region of Périgord compensates with a plethora of pretty towns where an overnight visitor is, to this day, an honored guest. Périgord is a concentration of fortified castles on dramatic bluffs, elaborately facaded Renaissance mansions, and churches—more of them early, severe

Romanesque than later Gothic—worshiped in over long centuries. And there is a pair of even more distinctive lures: caves in which prehistoric man lived and painted, and an irresistibly rich cuisine—based on the truffle and the goose— that will never, *ever* come to terms with cholesterol.

Sarlat, arguably the most picturesque of the principal Périgord towns, boasts a core largely untouched over a period of centuries. It's fun simply to stroll about, but you want to go inside such monuments as the cathedral, tucked into its own hillside, and a Gothic-Renaissance-baroque mix; Musée de la Chapelle des Penitents Blancs— sacred art in a Gothic church long desanctified; and the just-out-of-town Château de Puymartin, with a knock-'em-dead Grande Salle.

Périgueux, ranking with Sarlat in the Périgord urban sweepstakes, is centered on Place Daumesnil, dominated by a cathedral that is among the more curious in France, looking for all the world like a southwest counterpart of Sacré-Cœur, in Paris—chock-filled with cupolas, and with a lovely cloister. Musée du Périgord exhibits neighborhood prehistoric finds (including a 35-million-year-old skeleton of a local gent)—the better to set you up for Les Éyzies, nearby, with its own Musée National de la Préhistoire, whose eight galleries delineate the significance of the adjacent caves inhabited by Cro-Magnon man. Not-far-distant Lascaux II is a remarkably precise reproduction of the neighboring Lascaux Cave, with reproductions of the wall murals painted by prehistoric man in the original Lascaux, closed for some years as a protective measure.

Other Périgord points can charm. *Bergerac,* the town of Cyrano and Roxanne as portrayed in the Rostand classic, *Cyrano de Bergerac,* is a regional wine center. *Domme* is typical of the *bastides,* or fortified villages of the region. And there are any number of visitable châteaux, *Beynac, Bourdeilles,* and *Hautefort* among them.

MID-ATLANTIC

POITIERS

Just far enough south of the Loire Valley châteaux and far enough north of Périgord to be overlooked more often than not, Poitiers has been a town of consequence ever since Eleanor of Aquitaine, the consort first of a French king (Louis VII) and then of an English one (Henry II) established a court there, in the twelfth century. Two centuries later, during the Hundred Years' War, Poitiers knew both English rule, for a period, *and* Jeanne d'Arc, as well; she was interrogated about the divine "voices" exhorting her to aid the Crown at a still-visitable building—the Palais de Justice, in the massive, and still used, Grande Salle. But Poitiers *chef-d'œuvre* is the Church of Notre-Dame-la-Grande—one of the reigning French Romanesque beauties, whose facade is an uninterrupted mass of exquisite carving. St.-Jean Baptistry is noteworthy, too—a massive space, dating to the fourth century, that is among the oldest Christian monuments in the country.

LA ROCHELLE

The most significant port of France's long stretch of Atlantic coast between Brittany and Biarritz, La Rochelle—*terra incognita* to most transatlantic travelers—revolves around its atmospheric Vieux-Port, these many centuries guarded by a pair of battlements—Tour St. Nicholas and Tour de la Chaîne, so called because a chain was extended from it to its counterpart as a way of closing the harbor. It's fun to pass an hour or two at one of the cafés lining Vieux-Port. But not at the expense of a trek through Musée du Nouveau Monde, opened in 1982 in an elegant town house—the French government was involved in its creation—as the venue for a collection of objects—paintings, of French

Canada and Louisiana, a sculpted Mohawk brave, moccasins and snowshoes, sleighs and jewelry, wampum and hatchets—that bring to life France's early connections with the New World. Take in, too, the Hôtel de Ville—a Renaissance palace now the Town Hall—and both history and fine-arts museums, each in a handsome town house of yore.

BOURGES

Close to being smack in the center of France, this ancient heartland city is, like Poitiers, too often neglected by visitors. Principal lure is a Gothic cathedral that is one of the finest in Europe, in and of itself good reason for a Bourges visit. Flying buttresses support a pyramidal-shaped apse and, around the side, each buttress is pinnacle-topped, the while serving as a divider, enclosing windows whose stained glass ranks with that of the cathedral at Chartres. The nave extends 350 feet from portals—exquisitely carved—to the high altar. And there are a pair of nearby attractions: Palais Jacques-Cœur was home to Charles VII's finance minister and represents Gothic civil architecture at its finest. Musée de l'Hôtel Lallemant is still another venerable mansion—a Renaissance cloth merchant built it— that is furnished in a range of periods and emerges as quite the handsomest museum of decorative arts in the smaller French cities.

Acknowledgments

The pleasure of researching a considerably enlarged and revised edition of a book with a subject such as this—Paris and its increasingly contemporary facade, in the era of the builder-president, François Mitterrand—has been considerably enhanced by the cooperation and friendship extended by George L. Hern, Jr., public relations director of the French Government Tourist Office in the United States, with whom I also have been privileged to work in connection with this book's earlier editions and its companion volume, *France at Its Best*, not to mention magazine and newspaper articles and columns over a sustained period. As I have said in this space on earlier occasions: It's always a pleasure. As indeed it is to work with other stars of the French travel and transportation galaxy based in New York, Air France's Jim Ferri and Bruce Haxthausen and FrenchRail's Dagobert Scher, especially; they're never too busy to answer questions and offer counsel.

I am grateful, too, to George Hern's associates at the French Government Tourist Office, Marion Fourestier, and my longtime friend, Jacqueline Moinot-Schaff, as well as the crack press team at Maison de la France in Paris, with whom I worked over the years: Nicole Garnier and Marie-

Paule Bournonville. My research editor for the *World at Its Best* series, Max Drechsler, has been of inestimable help in on-scene exploration for this new edition of this book. And, as always, I appreciate the hard work on this book (as, indeed on all volumes of this series, both new and revised—a score, all told) of my editor, Michael Ross; and my agent, Anita Diamant.

I want also to extend, alphabetically, mes amitiés et mes remerciements, to the following friends and colleagues in Paris and on this side of the Atlantic for their personal kindness and professional cooperation: Antonio Alsonso, Catherine Audin, Susan Bang, Deborah Bernstein, Florence Ceneda, Enza Cirrincione, Michèle de la Clergerie, Michel Couturier, Frederick J. De Roode, Franco Gentileschi, Suzanne Gryner, Linda C. Gwinn, Lou Rena Hammond, Nicolle Roques-Lagier, Gilles Lesguer, David B. Mitchell, Franco Mora, Sylvie Picard, Carol D. Poister, and Philippe Ruetsch.

R.S.K.

Index

About the Author

Robert S. Kane's initial writing stint came about when, as an Eagle Scout, he was editor of the [Boy Scout] *Troop Two Bugle* in his native Albany, New York. After graduation from Syracuse University's noted journalism school, he did graduate work at England's Southampton University, first making notes as he explored in the course of class field trips through the Hampshire countryside. Back in the United States, he worked, successively, for the *Great Bend* (Kansas) *Daily Tribune, Staten Island Advance, New York Herald Tribune,* and *New York World-Telegram & Sun* before becoming travel editor of, first, *Playbill,* and later *Cue* and *50 Plus.* His byline has appeared in such leading magazines as *Travel & Leisure, Vogue, House & Garden, Atlantic, Harper's Bazaar, Family Circle, New York, Saturday Review,* and *Modern Bride;* and such newspapers as the *Newark Star-Ledger, New York Post, New York Daily News, New York Times, Los Angeles Times, Chicago Sun-Times, Boston Globe, San Diego Union, Dallas Morning News, San Francisco Examiner,* and *Toronto Globe & Mail.* And he guests frequently, with the subject travel, on TV and radio talk shows.

Africa A to Z, the first U.S.-published guide to largely independent, post–World War II Africa, was the progenitor of his acclaimed 14-book *A to Z* series, other pioneering volumes of which were *Eastern Europe A to Z,* the first guide to the USSR and the Soviet Bloc countries as seen through the eyes of a candid American author, and *Canada A to Z,* the first modern-day, province-by-province guide to the world's second-largest country. His current *World at Its Best* series includes two volumes (*Britain at Its Best* and *France at Its Best*) tapped by a pair of major book clubs, and a third (*Germany at Its Best*) that's a prize-winner.

Kane, the only American authoring an entire multivolume travel series, has the distinction of having served as president of both the Society of American Travel Writers and the New York Travel Writers' Association, and is a member, as well, of the National Press Club (Washington), P.E.N., Authors Guild, Society of Professional Journalists/Sigma Delta Chi, and American Society of Journalists and Authors. He makes his home on the Upper East Side of Manhattan.